Using Technology to Improve Counseling Practice

A Primer for the 21st Century

J. Michael Tyler

•

Russell A. Sabella

American Counseling Association
5999 Stevenson Avenue
Alexandria, VA 22304
www.counseling.org

Using Technology to Improve Counseling Practice

A Primer for the 21st Century

10   9   8   7   6   5   4   3   2   1

American Counseling Association
  5999 Stevenson Avenue
  Alexandria, VA 22304

Director of Publications
  Carolyn C. Baker

Production Manager
  Bonny E. Gaston

Copy Editor
  Shawn Simmons

Cover Design
  Martha Woolsey

Library of Congress Cataloging-in-Publication Data
    Tyler, J. Michael.
    Using technology to improve counseling practice: A primer for the 21st century/J. Michael Tyler, Russell A. Sabella.
    p. cm.
Includes bibliographical references.
    ISBN 1-55620-227-X (alk. paper)
    1. Counseling—Computer network resources. 2. Counselors—Computer programs. 3. Psychotherapy—Computer network resources. 4. Psycotherapy—Computer programs. I. Sabella, Russell, A., 1965– II. Title.

  BF637.C6T89   2003
  158′ .3′ 0285—dc22   20030014835

Dedication

To my wife Catherine, and children Alison and Andrew. You inspire me to seek more, accomplish more, and love more.

—Mike

To the many enthusiastic, innovative, and forward-thinking counselors who have engaged me in my technology workshops. Their hunger to practice more effectively and efficiently and to use the most modern tools available makes my job fun and exciting. My FGCU counseling students deserve a hearty thank you for helping me experiment with new technological procedures; you have journeyed with me through some exciting and unknown terrain. Most importantly, I could not serve in my profession without the loving and caring support of my family—Betty, Matthew, and Joseph—you encourage me every day in words, deed, and action.

—Russ

Table of Contents

Foreword

Technology is having a profound impact on nearly every aspect of life, including education, business, religion, government, medicine, and science. We now use e-mail instead of the regular mail, thus saving untold time—and trees. We used to lug overheads and handouts to meetings and classes, whereas we now walk into meetings with a small disk in hand to make PowerPoint presentations with technological features that were unimagined only a few years ago. We used to think that counseling could only occur with a counselor and client in the same room, whereas now we think nothing of counseling with clients thousands of miles away that we have never seen, nor probably ever will. We used to believe that counselor education could only be provided within the hallowed walls of a university, but now Internet-based (fully accredited) counseling courses are being provided throughout the world—and without walls.

The introduction of technology into counseling and counselor education is an evolutionary process that is happening quickly, if not always easily. Those who grew up at a time when there were no computers or Internet have struggled to gain the skills necessary to function in a rapidly changing, technologically literate society, whereas those of younger generations use technology almost effortlessly, as they were introduced to it at a very early age. It is no longer possible to be an effective counselor and not be technologically literate. The most recent advances in assessment and diagnosis, counseling techniques, and career development use technology in one fashion or another. From Internet-based counseling to telecounseling, the range of human services provided in schools, agencies, and private practice is changing and advancing (Hohenshil, 2000).

This is what makes this timely book by J. Michael Tyler and Russell Sabella such a valuable addition to the counseling literature. They have taken the technical competencies the Association for Counselor Education and Supervision (ACES Technology Interest Network, 1999) has deemed necessary for practicing counselors and constructed the book around them. The book is a valuable addition to counselors in a variety of settings and who have various levels of technological expertise. For those who are relatively inexperienced with technology, the book uses the ACES competencies as a framework and provides extensive examples and resources for use in each competency area. The authors make a special effort to provide a user-friendly book by avoiding the overuse of technical jargon. For counselors who already have considerable technical expertise, the book provides a virtual wealth of ideas and suggestions for the effective use of technology in counseling and counselor education. This is a book counselors and counselor educators will consult frequently as they continue to infuse technology into their work in the years ahead.

—Thomas H. Hohenshil, PhD
Virginia Polytechnic Institute and State University

References

Association for Counselor Education and Supervision. (1999). *Technical competencies for counselor education students: Recommended guidelines for program development.* Retrieved January 6, 2003, from http://filebox.vt.edu/users/thohen/competencies.htm

Hohenshil, T. H. (2000) High tech counseling. *Journal of Counseling & Development, 78,* 365–368.

Preface

With every major project there is a vision and intent. Our vision is to provide counselors, all types of counselors, a unique resource that will assist them in advancing their own levels of technological literacy and implementation. Our intent is to provide, in a limited space, a balance of knowledge and techniques for successfully understanding and using technology in your work and in your life. Along the way, we also hope to encourage and inspire the integration of technology through practical and meaningful examples and anecdotes. Our examples are designed to demonstrate how off-the-shelf software that is reasonably priced (sometimes free) can be customized to accomplish many tasks of the professional counselor. As well, we look at specialized software products that are especially conducive to helping us in what we do. Another focus is to make this resource user-friendly. We paid careful attention to the words and language we used so that you would not get lost in a maze of technological jargon. We tried as best as possible to be sensitive in addressing the wide range of types of computers, operating systems (e.g., Macintosh vs. Windows), and other setups among readers. Finally, our aim is not to present all that we have come to know over more than a decade of study in this area. To capture all of the current issues of technology and how they apply to counseling was not practical nor necessarily desirable. Instead, we want you to better understand and use the parts of technology that you might find most compelling in your work—a mixture of both longer-standing and cutting-edge technologies.

We wrote this book primarily around the 12 technical competencies for counselors (see http://www.acesonline.net/competencies.htm) established by the Association for Counselor Education and Supervision (ACES) Technology Interest Network and later endorsed by the ACES executive committee. Starting with this work as a base, we expanded key areas to address additional technological concerns that were not considered, as well as others that were not widely recognized just 3 short years ago. Also, we paid particular attention to the most pervasive and what we believe to be the most robust applications, those that will be available and will continue to develop in the coming years.

From our experiences as counselor educators, we recognize that many current counseling students do not have the technological skills necessary to fully engage the high-tech tools available to them. On the basis of our work as trainers in other settings, we believe that the level of technological literacy is even lower among the general population of practicing counselors in school, mental health, and similar human service settings. This book is intended to meet the needs of both preservice and in-service counseling and human service professionals. As a foundational text book, it can be used in counselor education, human services, psychology, social work, and other similar arenas. This book will help students understand the skills they will need to develop, compete, and practice effectively and efficiently in the future. It will serve well as a primary text in an individual class, but we also recommend the book be used as a supplement that a student refer to at varying times during training. Used in this manner, the technology competencies discussed can be readily infused across a curriculum to help professors in many areas increase student knowledge and skills.

Also, we believe that the book will meet the needs of the professional counselor already in the field who is in need of updating his or her skills, better understanding possibilities, and achieving currency in this changing arena. For instance, two primary issues confront the practicing counselor. The first is a lack of time. This book will provide basic information necessary to help practitioners in the field immediately begin to reap benefits from increasing their use of technology. Tips to save time, automate processes, maintain contacts, and find and deliver information will help practitioners as soon as they read the material. Focusing on basic issues, the text works to ensure that the ideas and skills are readily accessible to everyone. The second problem confronting many professionals in the field is a lack of knowledge of the possibilities presented by emerging technology. Many individuals already have basic computer skills, but they have not thought through the possible applications and integration of those skills in their specific work settings. As a result, they do not understand that they do not require special software or dedicated systems. Again, the book focuses on presenting practical, immediately useable information that can be implemented in a wide variety of settings.

We are confident that you—much like our reviewers—will find the contents of this book to be enlightening, helpful, and resourceful. As summarized below, each chapter is carefully crafted to provide you with a solid foundation and launching pad for advancing your level of technological literacy and implementation:

Chapter 1, Counseling and Technology: An Overview, provides the reader with an introduction to the evolution of computers, the nature of technological literacy and its importance for counselors, a review of the ACES technical competencies, and the case for how counselors can use technology in various areas of their work.

Chapter 2, Recording Technologies, takes the reader through the nature of both analog and digital audio–video recording possibilities. Included are descriptions of handheld devices as well as webcams, computer-based recordings, and streaming audio–video. Also, the appropriate (ethical) use of recording technology, especially as it relates to client feedback, behavioral practice, psychoeducation, consultation, and its use in counselor training and supervision, is delineated. This chapter also informs readers of innovations and opportunities in recording technologies, such as speech-to-text conversion.

Chapter 3, Productivity Software, focuses on technological tools that have the potential to make some aspects of the counselor's role more efficient, accurate, and automated. In particular, the focus includes productivity software that promotes both the completion of tasks and collaboration among counselors within a local or global community. The aim of this chapter is to help counselors provide high quality services to a broader base of individuals more effectively and efficiently (i.e., doing more with less).

Chapter 4, Statistical Software, assists counselors to understand and use computerized statistical and data-processing packages (e.g., database and spreadsheet software) in a friendly and practical manner. In addition, other data driven decision-making tools such as treatment planners are explored as well as methods for electronically collecting data, especially online. Finally, readers will find various useful tips for working with different types of data.

Chapter 5, Technology and Assessment, discusses how to use computerized testing, diagnostic, and career decision-making programs with clients. Readers are first taken through an overview of psychometric issues of electronic assessment and then made to think about related issues such as confidentiality, security, appropriateness, interpretation, the pros and cons of computerized assessment, and a method for evaluating online assessments.

Chapter 6, Use of Database Information, focuses on helping counselors access and use counseling-related CD-ROM databases. This chapter helps counselors understand and navigate various professional databases by going "under the hood" of several popular ones. Also, readers will learn about related tools such as the most pervasive bibliographic managers.

Chapter 7, E-mail and Listservs, combines two of the ACES competencies into one chapter: Competency 5, regarding e-mail, and Competency 7, regarding listservs. These two powerful communication and collaboration tools (and others such as chat rooms, instant messaging, and videomail) are fully explored with many practical easy-to-follow examples for how they work and how counselors use them.

Chapter 8, Evaluating Information on the Internet, will help readers make important choices about material on the Internet—what information to accept, what to question, and what to reject.

Chapter 9, Helping Clients Use the Internet Effectively, endeavors to assist counselors in helping clients search for various types of counseling-related information via the Internet. Included is information about careers, employment opportunities, educational and training opportunities, financial assistance/scholarships, treatment procedures, and social and personal information. This chapter does a thorough and detailed job of covering the various parts of this hefty competency.

Chapter 10, Continuing Education Opportunities on the Internet, helps readers to use the Internet for finding and using continuing education opportunities in counseling. Indeed, among the thousands of providers that are registered with accrediting agencies and state governing boards, many are providing their services online. Specifically, this chapter helps counselors take better advantage of the promise of "any place, anytime" education.

Chapter 11, Legal and Ethical Issues, strives to advance the reader's knowledge of the legal and ethical codes that relate to counseling services provided via the Internet. The focus includes topics such as confidentiality, file security, identity verification, responding to emergencies, liability insurance, and the nature of accessibility, to name a few.

Chapter 12, Counseling Services Provided Over the Internet, details the nature of Web-based counseling, its strengths and weaknesses, current examples, and its potential future, as well as the cybercounselor's tools.

Chapter 13, New Technologies Mean New Challenges, describes several costs—financial, human, and others—for advancing technological literacy and implementation. Similarly, the "dark side" of the Internet—areas such as cyberaddictions and pornography—is explored. Most importantly, however, this chapter suggests viable solutions for minimizing the risk or overcoming each challenge to help counselors maintain focus, balance, and safety.

We would like to thank Laurence Roberts for taking the time to review this manuscript in its entirety. His suggestions have helped to ensure the accuracy of the technical information provided throughout the work. We would also like to thank the anonymous reviewers for their excellent feedback, which has contributed to the overall quality of the work. Finally, we would like to express much gratitude to Carolyn Baker, director of ACA publications. Her feedback and guidance have been invaluable in facilitating the entire process, from conception to final product.

J. Michael Tyler, PhD
Russell A. Sabella, PhD
January 2004

About the Authors

J. Michael Tyler, PhD, is the dean of research at Baker College. His research interests and publications cover a number of topics including technology; small group behavior; gay, lesbian, bisexual, and transgender issues in counselor training; and ethics. He has worked in various community mental health and human services agencies, and worked for 10 years as a counselor educator and faculty member in a department of psychology. A member of the ACES Technology Interest Network, he was instrumental in preparing the *Guidelines for Online Instruction in Counselor Education* (ACES Technology Interest Network, 1999) and contributed to the *Technical Competencies for Counselors* (see http://www.acesonline.net/competencies.htm). Correspondence may be sent via e-mail to jmiketyler@yahoo.com or via post to Baker College, Center for Graduate Studies, 1116 West Bristol Road, Flint, MI 48507.

Russell A. Sabella, PhD, is associate professor of counseling in the College of Education, Florida Gulf Coast University. His concentration of research, training, and publication includes counseling technology, comprehensive school counseling programs, peer helper programs and training, sexual harassment risk reduction, and solution-focused brief counseling. He has authored various articles in journals, magazines, and newsletters. He is coauthor of *Confronting Sexual Harassment: Learning Activities for Teens* (Educational Media Corporation, 1995) and author of the popular *SchoolCounselor.com: A Friendly and Practical Guide to the World Wide Web* (2nd edition; Educational Media Corporation, 2003). He enjoys conducting his Technology Boot Camp for Counselors workshops throughout the country as well as being president of the American School Counselor Association (2003–2004). His most important challenge and valued accomplishment, however, is being husband to his wife Betty and father to sons Joseph and Matthew. Correspondence may be sent via e-mail to sabella@ schoolcounselor.com or via post to the College of Education, 10501 FGCU Blvd. South, Fort Myers, FL 33965–6565.

Counseling and Technology: An Overview

The march of human progress has been marked by milestones in science and technology. Gutenberg's creation of moveable type in the 15th century laid the foundation for universal literacy. Watts's invention of the steam engine in the 18th century launched the Industrial Revolution. The inventiveness of Bell and Marconi in the 19th and 20th centuries—creating the telephone and radio—helped bring a global village into being. The United States and the world are now in the midst of an economic and social revolution every bit as sweeping as any that has gone before: Computers and information technologies are transforming nearly every aspect of American life. They are changing the way Americans work and play, increasing productivity, and creating entirely new ways of doing things. Every major U.S. industry has begun to rely heavily on computers and telecommunications to do its work ("Getting America's Students Ready," 1996).

The 1990s was a particularly exciting and energizing period in this realm. Technology, fueled by rapid advancements in microprocessor design as well as the development of the World Wide Web, affected every aspect of life in the United States. Virtually no industry was left untouched and no profession left unaltered by these changes. In the counseling field, practitioners were left with new ways to meet and interact with clients; changes in how we managed our offices; and alterations in how we received training, updated research, and prepared for the future. We developed new words and new concepts and began to think about what we did in new ways because of these changes. Like most people, counselors are awed by the ways that technology can assist us in achieving more than we could achieve without technology. We are surrounded by "smarter" machines, from automobiles that can anticipate and assist in preventing a crash to kitchen toasters that "know" when your pastry is hot enough. Equipment inside our homes, including computers, televisions, stereos, and other appliances, are increasingly being networked and can be operated on-site or remotely using the Internet or even a cellular phone. The 1990s witnessed the spawning of new technology-related careers and made others extinct. Some of these new careers were not even envisioned 10 years ago by most Americans.

One would be hard-pressed to find any aspect of our modern lives that is not being affected by the rapidly expanding enterprise of computer-related technology (CRT). Lindsay (1988, p. 326) wrote, "computer technology has revolutionized many aspects of our society and is without a doubt the most significant innovation of the century." It is therefore inevitable that computer technology is changing the mental health professions as well. As Sampson, Kolodinsky, and Greno (1997) pointed out,

"[D]uring the past 30 years, computer applications have become an increasingly common resource used in the delivery of counseling services" (p. 203; as cited in Cabaniss, 2002). The future holds only more changes and developments that promise to create new opportunities (and challenges) for how we work, live, and play. Whether we like it or not, information technologies are now essential tools for manipulating ideas and images and for communicating effectively with others—all central components of a counselor's job (Sabella, 1998).

With all that has changed, and the lasting impact those changes have had, some things did not change. The expectation (or perhaps hope) of a typical 40-hour work week remains. The need to focus our time and energy on meeting the social, emotional, and developmental needs of our clients has not changed. The expectation that counseling professionals remain current in the body of knowledge that comprises their field remains. The daily stresses and overcommitments that mark the identity of many professionals has been left unaltered. Add to these the need to know, understand, and interact competently with a wide range of new technologies, and the dark side of these technological changes becomes more obvious (see chapter 13).

• Technology Tip 1.1 •

This book was built around the ACES Technical Competencies for Counselors (see http://www.acesonline.net/competencies.htm). Although there may be some benefit to reading the chapters in the orders presented, they by no means must be consumed in this fashion. We encourage readers to seek out those aspects of the book that are most useful to you today, and return another day to review different aspects of the text if that best fits your needs.

However, as these technologies develop they become easier and more user-friendly. Many technologies promote time savings, and others promise greater efficiency in our efforts.

In this chapter, we will overview the nature of counseling technology, including technological literacy and implementation.

Technological Literacy

Imagine the frustration of suddenly living in a new country where you cannot effectively and efficiently communicate or interact with others—you are not able to decipher road signs or navigate basic living tasks because you are unfamiliar with the country's language and customs. Children watch you in amazement and find it difficult to believe that you live in such a place without these basic capabilities. Increasingly so, such might be the experience in any developed country, especially here in the United States, for counselors who do not have a basic level of technological literacy. For now, some people still take refuge by being able to live their lives in a relatively low-tech manner, although this lifestyle is becoming more difficult every day. Americans understand the rapid progress in the development and integration of technology through everyday experience and have thus embraced technological literacy as the "new basic" for today's world, along with reading, writing, and arithmetic.

Today's children find it difficult to imagine a life as we lived it not so long ago—without compact discs, high-powered computers, and palm-sized appliances such as cell phones and personal digital assistants. It is likely that our future counselors, now in grade school and even college, will not hesitate to integrate high-tech tools in their work. They will merely continue along an already well-established path of learning to use and apply new technologies as they become available, probably assisted by the technologies themselves. The majority of today's counselors grew up learning and practicing counseling in a very different environment. We used index cards instead of spreadsheets; typewriters instead of word processors; reference books instead of online journals and the Web; overheads in lieu of multimedia presentations; and we waited until class to communicate with the professor and our classmates instead of sending e-mails or conversing in chat rooms. Many of today's counselors acknowledge the usefulness of computers and the need for keeping up with the rapidly changing times, yet remain frozen in the fear generated by an unknown frontier. "I feel intimidated by computers," has been a common comment by counselors who, even after training, sometimes revert to more traditional procedures. The customary statements, "My kids know more about computers than I do" and "I'm not a technical person" suggest that although counselors may be interested or even intrigued, they frequently feel awkward and uneasy with computers and their operations (Myrick & Sabella, 1995). Our own experience, luckily, is that once such counselors are exposed and truly begin to learn how to use technology in their work, they quickly become excited and adept. Many of our older students who are forced to learn high-tech tools in our courses often tell us that they receive many kudos from their own children who perceive their moms or dads to be "more with it." Their more technologically literate friends and partners share in their delight and also get excited about new shared interests. And the students themselves bask in the pride they take in working with contemporary tools.

According to Sabella (1998), counselors who took an early interest and continued to gradually follow technology's progression have probably accumulated relatively high levels of technology literacy at a manageable pace. Veterans of the Internet, for instance, may find themselves only having to keep pace with incremental changes, new additions, and creative ways for harnessing the Internet's power to do their jobs more effectively and efficiently. For those who have more recently taken an interest, or force themselves to be exposed to technology because of trends or new standards, becoming technologically literate may be perceived to be a burdensome venture. The good news, however, is that you can effectively start today. The road to technology literacy does not necessarily have a beginning and an end, but like an intricate system of highways and sideroads, can be accessed from many on-ramps. Today's software is more user-friendly and more highly automated than ever before. Beginning a course of self-study and formal training will better assure more enjoyable travel for the road ahead. Before you know it, you will be traveling alongside others who have laid many more miles behind them on the information superhighway. And sooner, rather than later, you will be staking and claiming your property on this vast electronic terrain.

What Exactly Is Technological Literacy?

Many people have written on the subject of technological literacy. Hayden (1989), after a literature review, took the position that technological literacy is having knowledge and abilities to select and apply appropriate technologies in a given context. Although he did not reveal the source of his thoughts, Steffens (1986, p. 117–118) claimed that technological literacy involves knowledge and comprehension of technology and its uses; skills, including tool skills as well as evaluation skills; and attitudes about new technologies and their application. This insight is similar to that of Owen and Heywood (1988), who said there are three components to technological literacy: the technology of making things, the technology of organization, and the technology of using information. Applying a Delphi technique to opinions expressed by experts, Croft (1991) evolved the following panel of characteristics of a technologically literate student: ability to make decisions about technology; possession of basic literacy skills required to solve technology problems; ability to make wise decisions about uses of technology; ability to apply knowledge, tools, and skills for the benefit of society; and ability to describe the basic technology systems of society (Waetjen, 1993).

• Technology Tip 1.2 •

How do your answers about technological literacy compare with those surveyed by the ITEA/Gallup poll on technological literacy? Find out at http://www.nae.edu/nae/techlithome.nsf/(weblinks)/KGRG57BV8W?OpenDocument. Relatedly, download, print, and complete a technological literacy self-assessment at http://www.ola.bc.ca/tll/pdfs/tsa.pdf.

A theme among various attempts to define technological literacy is that technology has evolved to become a powerful medium, not just a set of high-tech tools. If technology functioned merely as a set of tools—as the pervasive mechanical, user-in-control view of technology holds—the problem of advancing technological literacy would not be so challenging. A few more required courses or conference training sessions, and more specialists to teach them, could simply be added. But technology has become more than a set of devices to be picked up and used when a person decides he or she needs them. It has become a required medium that mediates experience in most aspects of peoples' lives (Fanning, 1994).

Broadly speaking, then, technological literacy can be described as the intellectual processes, abilities, and dispositions needed for individuals to understand the link between technology, themselves, and society in general. Technological literacy is concerned with developing one's awareness of how technology is related to the broader social system, and how technological systems cannot be fully separated from the political, cultural, and economic frameworks that shape them (Saskatchewan Education, 2002). These definitions, together with one provided by the International Technology Education Association (2000), have provided the foundation for our definition of counselor technological literacy:

> The intellectual processes, abilities, and dispositions needed for counselors to understand the link among technology, themselves, their clients, and a diverse society so that they may extend human abilities to satisfy human needs and wants for themselves and others.

This means that counselors who have adequate levels of technological literacy are able to do the following:

- understand the nature and role of technology, in both their personal and professional lives;
- understand how technological systems are designed, used, and controlled;
- value the benefits and assess the risks associated with technology;
- respond rationally to ethical dilemmas caused by technology;
- assess the effectiveness of technological solutions;
- feel comfortable learning about and using systems and tools of technology in the home, in leisure activities, and in the workplace; and
- critically examine and question technological progress and innovation.

ACES Technical Competencies

We have said that technological literacy is more than simple computer and related skills or competencies. However, such skills are a critical part and are the primary means for demonstrating technological literacy. What are the agreed upon technological competencies in the profession and how were they created? For counselors there are two main sources of general technological competency standards: (a) The National Educational Technology Standards Project by the International Society for Technology

• Technology Tip 1.3 •

Throughout this book we have included the uniform resource locator (URL) of many Web sites that contain additional information or will otherwise enhance the information presented. In some cases these Web sites may also offer software for trial or purchase, or links to additional resources. You can visit these sites by typing in the entire URL exactly as it appears here, into your browser. In some cases, these URLs are quite lengthy and contain a variety of special characters. An alternate way to visit these sites is to start at the Web site for this book, where links exist for all pages cited in this text. We can be found online at http://www.21stcenturycounselor.com.

in Education (http://iste.org/standards), and (b) the Technological Competencies as established by the Association for Counselor Education and Supervision (ACES Technology Interest Network, 1999). The latter, developed especially for counselors, serves as the basic outline for this text and deserves a bit more attention.

In 1997, a group of counselor educators, with the support of ACES President Margaret Fong, decided to form the ACES Technology Interest Network in response to the increased use of and dependence on technology. The network identified three initiatives for itself: develop a set of technological competencies for counselors, develop a Web site for the network, and develop guidelines for Web-based counselor education. In developing the competencies, the network sought advice from literally hundreds of counselor educators from around the world. After circulating a draft of objectives throughout the network of 30 people, the network chair, Thomas Hohenshil, posted the proposed competencies on the CESNET–L listserv (http://listserv.kent.edu/archives/cesnet-l.html), soliciting comments from its 400-plus subscribers. After discussing the proposed competencies further at the American Counseling Association World Conference in Indianapolis in March of the following year and making minor modifications, Hohenshil distributed them to the entire network for a vote a few months later (Morrissey, 1998). The final approved competencies include the following (available online at http://www.acesonline.net/competencies.htm):

1. Be able to use productivity software to develop Web pages, group presentations, letters, and reports.
2. Be able to use such audiovisual equipment as video recorders, projection equipment, video conferencing equipment, and playback units.
3. Be able to use computerized statistical packages.
4. Be able to use computerized testing, diagnostic, and career decision-making programs with clients.
5. Be able to use e-mail.
6. Be able to help clients search for various types of counseling-related information via the Internet, including information about careers, employment opportunities, educational and training opportunities, financial assistance and scholarships, treatment procedures, and social and personal information.
7. Be able to subscribe, participate in, and sign off of counseling-related listservs.
8. Be able to access and use counseling-related CD-ROM databases.
9. Be knowledgeable of the legal and ethical codes that relate to counseling services via the Internet.
10. Be knowledgeable of the strengths and weaknesses of counseling services provided via the Internet.
11. Be able to use the Internet for finding and using continuing education opportunities in counseling.
12. Be able to evaluate the quality of Internet information.

New Technologies Mean New Opportunities

Indeed, new technologies can create challenges to which we must learn to appropriately respond. However, throughout these challenges exists a wave of new opportunities for the professional as well as the client. Understanding these new opportunities and exploiting them may help decrease some of the unintended and negative consequences introduced by technology. For instance, the World Wide Web—the most popular and powerful part of the Internet—is an example of technology that was once seen as only a store of information. Today, the Web is a medium for communication, collaboration, data and file warehouses, and much more. What once required different software applications or procedures for e-mail, chat rooms, sharing files, and so forth can now be done with only a browser and a connection to the Web. As you think about the potential of various technologies and the Web in particular in your work, you might use the following schema to help conceptualize the range of available technologies (Sabella, 2003).

- **Information/Resource:** In the form of words, graphics, video, and even three-dimension virtual environments, the Web remains a dynamic and rapidly growing library of information and knowledge.
- **Communication/Collaboration:** Chat rooms, bulletin boards, virtual classroom environments, video conferencing, online conferences, electronic meeting services, e-mail—the Web is now a place where people connect, exchange information, and make shared decisions.
- **Interactive tools:** The maturing of Web-based programming has launched a new and unforeseen level of available tools on the Internet. Interactive tools on the Web can help counselors build and create anything ranging from a personalized business card to a set of personalized Web site links. In addition, interactive tools help counselors to process data such as calculating a GPA or the rate of inflation, convert text to speech, create a graph, or even determine the interactive effects of popular prescription drugs.
- **Delivery of services:** Most controversial, yet growing in popularity, is how counselors use the Web to meet with clients and deliver counseling services in an online or "virtual" environment.

In fact, many technology-assisted tasks or endeavors are actually a combination of two or more of the above types of areas. Let us now turn our attention to several examples.

Information and Resources

The biggest change that the Internet and the World Wide Web has brought to the lives of most individuals directly is the ability to access previously unimagined amounts of information. It seems there is no topic that cannot be entered into a search engine that will not result in at least a few sites being found. For many topics, the number of sites runs into the thousands or tens of thousands. In the 1980s, when we (the authors) entered counseling as young professionals, clients sought information by looking through the dozens of titles on counseling, psychology, or self-help available at the local bookstore or a franchise store in the mall. By the early 1990s clients had access to hundreds of titles available in the large bookstore chains such as Barnes & Nobles or Borders, which were quickly replacing the smaller outlets such as Walden Books. Today, if clients want a book, online giant Amazon.com offers millions of titles to search. However, clients need not wait the 48 hours necessary for a book to arrive via ground shipment, because there are millions of Web sites available to search immediately and for free. And, the availability and popularity of electronic books (i.e., e-books) which can be instantly downloaded is steadily increasing.

Like so much in technology, this creates challenge as well as opportunity. The challenge lies in helping clients sort through the available information to find that which is of high quality and targets their particular needs. Many clients, while technologically capable, may not have the skills necessary to evaluate a site or the information provided. Lacking any sort of review or oversight, anyone can put any information they choose on the Web. With basic technology skills (or the money to purchase assistance) a site can be created that looks quite polished. Without adequate knowledge and skills to evaluate sites, clients may be drawn to sites that appear professional and are easy to understand rather than sites that are slightly more difficult to understand and navigate but contain more accurate and current information.

•   Technology Tip 1.4   •

One way to learn about good Web design is to look at bad Web design such as those presented by Vincent Flander at http://www.webpagesthatsuck.com.

As professionals with a particular body of expertise, we have the capacity to help clients in two ways. First, clients can be provided with information that will assist them in evaluating information they are obtaining, whether from the Internet, books, friends, or even counselors! One way to implement this intervention is to work with others within your school or agency to create a pamphlet with tips and approaches to evaluating information. Chapter 8 provides a synopsis of how to evaluate information on the Internet. These guidelines, while supplied here for professionals, can be used by clients as well. Second, a more active approach may be helpful. By knowing the particular client population, the professional counselor may be the best person to evaluate specific types of information for clients to review. By spending time evaluating sites on the Internet in collaboration with colleagues, schools, and agencies can then create lists of Web sites to provide to clients on various topics. School counselors may find it beneficial to create lists of quality Web sites on topics including parenting, homework help, discipline, developmental changes in children, handling transitions in children's lives, or other topics about which parents have expressed concern. For students, lists of topics such as career development, college applications and financial aid, handling bullies, time management, or maintaining anti-drug values may be appropriate. In clinical settings, lists of Web sites focused on a particular diagnosis or problem areas such as depression, chronic medical concerns, or surviving divorce may be helpful. In all cases, counselors should never recommend a site that they have not personally visited and thoroughly evaluated. Sites that may initially appear appropriate may have less appropriate content buried within. Never provide a recommendation to a client of which you do not have clear and current personal knowledge.

Helping clients by referral to information created and disseminated by others can be helpful, but may not be as useful as information created locally by professionals. The World Wide Web makes it easy to allow anyone to access information, and simple hypertext markup language (HTML) programming packages (as discussed in chapter 3) make it easy to create content. Rather than referring clients to other Web sites about depression, local agencies may consider setting up a team to work in conjunction with psychiatrists, psychologists, social workers, and counselors to create a rich and locally directed Web site. Such a site would include information about a variety of local resources including counseling help, support programs, financial assistance, and emergency access. Schools may choose to create a local site through a committee including teachers, counselors, social workers, and building administrators. A career development site that helps students identify vocational options within the school, summer or vacation programs, and timelines for their own career and academic planning might be quite useful. The site may be extended to help parents by providing information about postsecondary opportunities as well as providing information about what activities students will be engaged in during the normal school curriculum. These types of local sites may better support our clients and students because they allow us to reinforce the learning and growth that clients are doing in a very direct manner. This type of support allows our intervention efforts to be extended beyond the walls of our offices into other aspects of the lives of students and clients. Thus, while we see that technology may creep into our lives in unwanted ways, we can also harness technology to effect positive change.

• Technology Tip 1.5 •

Like counseling professionals, clients can also become overwhelmed by the invasion of technology in their lives. Be sensitive to how technology affects clients and work to find ways to reduce stress while also improving efficiency.

Expert Consultation, Collaboration, and Shared Decision Making

Collaboration is a process by which people work together on an intellectual, academic, or practical endeavor. In the past, this has meant in person, by letter, or on the telephone. Electronic collaboration, on the other hand, connects individuals electronically via the Internet using tools such as e-mail or through access to sites on the World Wide Web. This Internet-based work allows collaborators to communicate anytime, from anywhere to any place. People from different parts of a building, state, country, or continent can exchange information, collaborate on shared documents and ideas, study together, or reflect on their own practices.

Most counselors are accustomed to short-term professional development seminars and workshops that provide finite information. Electronic collaboration—because it can be done at any time, from anywhere—allows for a sustained effort where participants can propose, try out, refine, and shape ideas themselves. The potential to communicate with others from all over the world provides a pool of resources and professional companions that counselors might not find within their own school or agency walls. It can also provide them with a sense of belonging, a sense of identity within a larger community.

Collaborating electronically can take many different forms. Some of the more common activities include the following (Koufman-Frederick, Lillie, Pattison-Gordon, Watt, & Carter, 1999):

- Discussion groups are focused around a topic or a specific activity, goal, or project. Some groups are open-ended and unmoderated, allowing users to solicit information from each other. Other more structured groups may use a moderator to guide the discussion by filtering and posing questions or making comments, suggestions, and connections.
- Data collection and organization activities use databases and search engines to organize and retrieve data. Users contribute data individually to a shared database and retrieve data from it as needed. Data can be in the form of references (such as pointers to related work and Web sites), information (e.g., legislative or other alerts related to counseling), curriculum projects, research papers, and contact information for colleagues.
- Some projects involve sharing documents—from simply displaying them to having several people work on them simultaneously. Collaborators can display documents online and discuss the contents via e-mail, video conference, or chat. They can use annotation systems to comment on shared documents and editing tools to coedit documents online.
- Synchronous communication activities such as Internet "chatting" and videoconferencing differ from the other types of activities in that they happen in real-time, over a short period. In text-based chat environments, participants see what the other person is typing on the screen in real time. Videoconferencing is like a conference call with pictures. These technologies allow users to discuss ideas, debate problems, and share information electronically when face-to-face interaction is desired but not possible.

According to Koufman-Frederick et al. (1999), advantages of online collaboration include the following:

- Electronic collaboration brings people out of isolation and allows counselors to connect to a new set of colleagues. Participants can communicate with people who share the same interests and experience the same challenges. Because it allows for the inclusion of many people, electronic collaboration promotes the exchange of a larger range of opinions and resources.
- Electronic collaboration provides time for reflection. During the day counselors typically are pressed for time and lack opportunities to stop and reflect on their work experiences or move beyond on-the-fly brainstorming that may happen by chance in the hallway. The asynchronous nature of some types of electronic collaboration allows participants to contribute to the conversation when it's convenient and to reflect on what others have said before responding. In addition, having to articulate in writing the nature of professional struggles and suggestions requires writers to take time to be thoughtful and reflect carefully about new ideas and pathways.
- One of the most common uses of the Internet is gathering (or "surfing" for) information. Electronic collaboration adds a different dimension— participants don't just surf for resources on the Internet, but actively and interactively contribute to exploring innovative ideas. With electronic collaboration, the adage "two heads are better than one" could just as well be "two hundred heads are better than one." One person's provocative question can lead to many creative, exciting solutions. By sharing what they know with others, participants advance their own knowledge and the collaborative community's knowledge.

There now exist several free collaboration tools on the Web. Examples of these include the following:

- **NetMeeting** is a Microsoft product that provides a conferencing solution for the Internet and for corporate intranets. Powerful features let you communicate with both audio and video, collaborate on virtually any Windows-based application, exchange graphics on an electronic whiteboard, transfer files, use the text-based chat program, and share control of programs (e.g., PowerPoint). Using your personal computer and the Internet, you can now hold face-to-face conversations with colleagues from around the world, inexpensively and conveniently (see http://www.microsoft.com/windows/netmeeting/). Similar to NetMeeting is CUseeMe from White Pine software (http://www.wpine.com/).
- **Instant Messenger (IM)** programs such as those provided by America Online (AIM; www.aim.com), Yahoo! (Yahoo Instant Messenger; http://messenger.yahoo.com/), and Microsoft Network (MSN IM; http://messenger.msn.com) allow users to be alerted when a colleague logs on to the Internet. Similarly, many of the IM software programs can be set up so that users can indicate their availability and exact location to authorized buddies. Once online and

connected through this tool, colleagues may chat, exchange files, videoconference, and exchange e-mail.

• Technology Tip 1.6 •

You can now use AOL's Instant Messenger from any computer with Internet access in the world by going to http://www.aim.com.

- **Usenet newsgroups** is a free worldwide discussion system. It consists of a set of "newsgroups" with names that are classified hierarchically by subject. Articles or messages are posted to these newsgroups by people on computers with the appropriate software; these articles are then broadcast to other interconnected computer systems via a wide variety of networks. Some newsgroups are moderated, which means the articles are first sent to a moderator for approval before appearing in the newsgroup (What is Usenet?, 2002). Google Groups (groups.google.com) contains the entire archive of Usenet discussion groups dating back to 1981. These discussions cover the full range of human discourse and provide a fascinating look at evolving viewpoints, debate and advice on every subject from politics to technology. Google's search feature enables users to access this wealth of information with high speed and efficiency, providing relevant results from a database containing more than 700 million (and growing) posts.
- **Profiler** is an application that inspires cooperation and collaboration among educators to help them improve their skills around a general topic. Profiler (http://profiler.hprtec.org) can strengthen your school district's or organization's ability to share expertise. For instance, you can take a survey to assess your technology abilities and find someone who can help you strengthen these skills within your school.

The field of telemedicine has grown substantially over the past decade, in part because it allows physicians to access experts in various areas to assist in diagnosis and treatment planning. Although mental health and other counseling practitioners have been slower to adopt technology for these purposes, as providers become increasingly skilled in technology use, it is likely that they will also increase their use of technology to seek consultation. Carefully designed Web sites can provide clinicians with assessment materials and expert systems to assist in diagnosis and treatment planning. In some instances, these Web sites will allow the clinician to enter client information, whereas in other instances, the client will be able to access the site directly. Using sophisticated database-querying techniques, these sites will be able to match client information with stored data to determine diagnosis as well as appropriate treatment interventions. It is easy to imagine that experts in varying specialty areas may be contracted to work as advisors and to assist by responding to e-mail, phone calls, and other inquiries as the need arises. Carefully planned and constructed, such sites will be able to direct clinicians to the most recent research on etiology, treatment, medications, and outcome.

By automating tasks, these sites will have the power to provide expert consultation at a fraction of the cost normally associated with consulting.

Delivery of Services

Historically, counseling has been practiced primarily as an activity that occurs in a professional setting, controlled by the counselor, and visited occasionally by the client. However, there is nothing sacrosanct about the office of the counselor, and much good work can occur in other settings. Indeed, many proponents of brief counseling have argued that real change only occurs in the client's life, not in the counselor's office. Careful planning allows counselors to reach into the client's life to continue counseling interventions and growth easily.

The most obvious way to reach out to a client outside of our office is via e-mail. In cases where appropriate, an e-mail message may be sent to a client sometime after a meeting to remind the client of some particular detail or discussion, or to raise new issues. Imagine a client who demonstrates a pattern of discounting his or her own strengths, expressing feelings of low self-worth and -efficacy. Knowing that the client engages in downing self-talk particularly during the work week, a counselor may send the client an e-mail following a weekend. The e-mail may contain several quotes from the client's last session where the client expressed strong feelings of personal power. This early-week boost might help to reinforce the client's in-session work and allow the client to feel his or her own power more directly between sessions. Another example is an e-mail sent to a student-client who has agreed to complete homework midweek with his mother's help. This client might receive an e-mail message on Tuesday evening reminding him of the agreement for a particular exchange with his mother the following evening. The same client may then send an e-mail back to the counselor after the homework has been completed. This between-sessions correspondence may help the client stay focused and follow through on a difficult assignment. Similarly, with the client's permission, information may be provided to a parent or partner that may assist those around the client with providing appropriate support and assistance.

Increasingly, however, we can move beyond simple e-mail messages to more striking interventions to assist clients. Counselors who operate from a perspective that is highly educational may find that computers are a powerful tool to reinforce various concepts. One example comes from the work of a counselor using rational emotive behavior therapy (REBT). The counselor created a series of worksheets for high school students to help track their thinking, emotions, and behavior. The worksheets, stored on a computer disk, were easily taken home by clients who then created daily journals based on the provided templates. The templates helped the young clients track their irrational thoughts and their attempts to confront these thoughts in a manner that was appealing and consistent with their lifestyle. The templates were saved back to the disks as completed files and then brought to session where they could be shared with the counselor.

Another more intriguing example comes from an elementary school. Many elementary schools use Macintosh computers, and one popular educational program that is widely available is Hyperstudio. Hyperstudio is a program that is designed for children and is very simple to use. However, it is also quite powerful and capable of creating very sophisticated output. The basic premise behind Hyperstudio is that users create a "hyperstack" of cards that can be easily manipulated and seen in any order chosen. For those unfamiliar with the program, it may be helpful to think of it as creating a stack of index cards, each of which may contain a sound clip, picture, text, or any combination of the above. These index cards are then connected together in any fashion the user chooses with hyperlinks. The result is something like a book without specific page numbers or page order. Very often, the user will move from one card to another on the basis of the answer to a question or some other decision. Using Hyperstudio, an older elementary client created a hyperstack about bullies in her school. She was able to create cards based on specific instances where she felt harassed and then generate various responses she could choose to use. By clicking on a particular response, she was taken to a new card where some outcome was written. The creation of this hyperstack between counseling sessions allowed her to consider various situations where she felt attacked or harassed, consider her own behavior, and then try to predict outcomes based on the choices she made. This proved to be a wonderful opportunity for the child to fully explore her behavior and behavioral choices in a structured manner. Once created, she could share the information with her school counselor who helped her consider the reality of the scenarios, the choices, and the outcomes. Certainly the entire process could have been handled in a conversation with no technology at all. But by utilizing technology the counselor is able to capitalize on a skill the client has and is proud of, increase the client's focus on behavioral concerns between sessions, and provide a structure for the client to express her thoughts and emotions.

Increased Access

Another benefit that technology has brought is increased access to clinicians and services. Traditionally, clients have been limited to seeking services from a relatively small group of providers within their own communities. Financial considerations, stigma associated with seeking help, and other concerns at times decrease access further. A variety of technologies today allow clients access to an international array of service providers any time of the day or night. Clients do not need to miss work to seek services, and concerns about local gossip are eliminated. Clients who do not have transportation or for medical reasons have difficulty leaving home to seek treatment now can bring services into their homes on their own schedule.

Many services are available to receive counseling over the Internet. To fully understand these services, it may be beneficial to explore a few of them in more depth. One such service is TherapyOnLine.ca. This Canadian-based service attempts to provide counseling by exchanging e-mail with clients. Clients are asked to write an e-mail to their counselor about their concerns, and the counselor then responds. Because the client controls the flow of e-mail, "sessions" may occur as often or seldom as the client chooses. Another online service, ReadyMinds.com, focuses on career counseling. ReadyMinds uses a highly structured approach that begins with an online assessment including both open-ended questions and the completion of the Self-Directed Search (SDS). This is followed by 2 hours of counseling provided over the telephone and then the client receives a written report. Along the way clients also engage in other exploration activities and career research. This model, because of its focus on the specific topic of career exploration, takes a more structured approach than TherapyOnLine.ca.

While controversial (see chapter 12 about cybercounseling), these services are meeting a need and it is anticipated that Web-based counseling services will continue to grow in the coming years. As the profession of counseling better understands and learns how to use the Internet to support services, it is likely that online counseling will become increasingly routine and accepted.

Professional Development

The ACES Technology Interest Network developed technology competency 11 (Use the Internet for finding and using continuing education opportunities in counseling) because it realized the importance of such a skill as a result of the steadily increasing demand, and consequential availability, of professional development opportunities now available online (known as distance learning). According to the *Merriam-Webster Collegiate Dictionary* (Merriam-Webster Online, 2002), distance learning is learning that takes place via electronic media linking instructors and students who are not together in a classroom. In the same way, workshops and other training opportunities are available for practicing counselors as part of their own ongoing professional development and continuing education. What exactly is the appeal? Consider the following advantages of distance learning (Sabella, 2001):

1. The cost of attending traditional workshops (e.g., travel and lodging) is becoming increasingly prohibitive. Because most people already have access to the Internet, cost of a distance learning class includes only tuition and supporting materials.
2. Distance learning materials and other content are available at any time of the day or night.
3. Distance learning allows counselors to engage at their own pace, completing a course over a day, week, or month if needed.
4. Learning is portable—it moves with you at home, work, at the library, or across the country for that matter.

5. You can "earn while you learn" since distance learning's flexible schedule prevents counselors from having to be absent from work or give up income.
6. You can test and apply your new knowledge as you progress through the course, which means that stakeholders can gain immediately from your increased capabilities.
7. A well-maintained and updated online learning course or workshop gives counselors knowledge that is highly recent.
8. You can choose instructors with certain qualifications or backgrounds from among many. One way to evaluate the quality of online courses is to refer to the ACES Guidelines for Online Instruction in Counselor Education (ACES Technology Interest Network, 1999).
9. Electronic media more efficiently supports multilingual instruction.
10. Distance learning is typically supported by a rich mix of delivery methods including print, streaming video, interactive Web-based tutorials, chat rooms, e-mail correspondence, bulletin boards, audio and video cassettes, Internet teleconferencing, and CD-ROMS.
11. Some online courses or workshops include "virtual meetings" that are conducted at a scheduled time. This affords participants a rich array of perspectives from other participants who log on from all over the world.

At the same time, counselors should also be aware of some of the disadvantages of distance learning:

1. Learning at a distance requires a high level of self-discipline, study skills, and time management (especially the ability to set and meet self-imposed deadlines) for successfully completing the work. Counselors must have the ability and motivation to stay on track in an unstructured environment.
2. Distance learning limits or even eliminates face-to-face instruction that some counselors may desire or need. Many counselor educators would agree that the majority of counseling skills can only be adequately learned by supervised practice and role modeling, which is currently very difficult to do at a distance. Thus, distance learning for counselors at this time is limited to knowledge, attitudes, and less complicated skills. We expect that this may change in the near future as newer technologies will allow us to share a virtual reality space as if we were physically together.
3. Similarly, computer-mediated communication systems may increase social isolation and curb important informal interactions that contribute to overall learning.
4. Counselors must have an adequate level of technological literacy to launch Web sites, streaming video, and other software programs.
5. Not all distance learning courses or workshops may be acceptable to licensing boards, certification boards, or universities—do some research before enrolling.

6. It is yet unclear how the effects of distance learning on counselor competencies compares with that of traditional or live methods of instruction.

Counselors can become aware of distance learning opportunities by checking with counseling association Web sites, universities, and other professional development service companies by conducting an Internet search.

Research and Development

The transfer/collection of data over the Internet has made research and development in all areas a new and exciting venture. Sampson et al. (1997) wrote that "computer networks potentially reduce data collection costs and increase research participation. Online connection costs, when charged, are less expensive than equivalent postage, printing, and supply costs to mail survey instruments." The same is certainly true today except for one thing: counselors with basic technological literacy can now perform many of the research tasks that once required high levels of technological (and statistical) expertise. Software is available that can facilitate the entire research process and is quite user-friendly.

Career Development

According to Sabella and Isaacs (2002), probably the most extensive use of computers in counseling so far has been in the area of career development, where there is a need to process a great deal of information. Information includes knowledge about various careers, the career decision-making process, and an assortment of clients' personal and professional characteristics. Computers do a splendid job of compiling and sorting data to help individuals select the best fit among workplace environments, required aptitudes, interests, values, and other human qualities. The Internet in particular has made various interactive tools available that can assist counselors in obtaining up-to-date information, communicating with others, and even developing advanced competencies in areas of weakness. Interactive tools can include search engines, online databases, personal Web sites, e-mail, instant messaging, wizards, and videoconferencing. As an example, we provide the following self-guided career development Webquest for school counselors:

> Your fantasy takes place in cyberspace, where you begin by perusing the online Career Development Manual from the University of Waterloo's Career Services (http://www.adm.uwaterloo.ca/infocecs). Here, you review important information and links addressing each step of the career development process, from self-analysis to life planning.
>
> While continuing to close your eyes and taking deep breaths, you then think about the beginning questions for your career search ... Do I have what it takes to be successful and happy in school counseling or another field? What exactly are my current or renewed career goals? What kinds of tasks get me really motivated and excited? What skills do I have that will help me to effectively fulfill my various needs? To answer these **Self-Knowledge Questions**, you need to learn more

about yourself. So, you beam yourself over to the Job Hunters Bible Web site (http://www.JobHuntersBible.com). This site is developed by the author of *What Color Is Your Parachute?*, Richard Bolles (2003), and comes with a "Free Online Tests Dealing With Careers" section, a brief review of test-taking procedures called "The Seven Rules About Taking Career Tests," links to John Holland's SDS, The Career Interests Game, and The Career Key. Other sections of the site include links to help you create and post your resume, salary information for specific jobs, and a search engine for contacts. After you engage this site, you recognize that it could be the focus of an entire classroom guidance unit for your students!

Now you transport yourself to your next stop—Franklin Covey's Create a Personal Mission Statement site (http://www.franklin-covey.com/missionbuilder/). This fun and enlightening exercise helps you to create your own personal mission statement by first defining your values, principles, and what matters most to you in your life. At the speed of thought, you then go to www.keirsey.com to take the Keirsey Temperament Sorter. The results of this free online question-naire are similar to the Myers–Briggs Type Indicator (MBTI). Your results inspire you to know more and so you quickly click over to www.typelogic.com to read the details about your profile. You are intrigued by the insights you gain about yourself and notice that your curiosity only elevates. Click … Whiz … Whoosh … you're now off to Queendom (www.queendom.com), a site that offers a variety of per-sonality, intelligence, and health-related tests, trivia quizzes, and much more. Although the tests are for entertainment purposes, they provide you with much food for thought. You notice the joy and sense of peace that comes with advanced self-understanding.

Now consider the personal profile information you have just gathered as a career criteria list against which to apply **Information about the World of Work**. Your first stop is the U.S. Department of Labor's Bureau of Labor Statistics' Occupational Outlook Handbook (www.bls.gov/oco), one of the best resources of general occupational information. Its Web version, like its printed predecessor, is revised every two years and describes what workers do on the job, working conditions, the training and education needed, earnings, and expected job prospects in a wide range of occupations. You hear your mind buzzing with potential. You jump over to O*NET OnLine! (http://online.onetcenter.org/), a database that includes information on skills, abilities, knowledge, work activities, and interests associated with occupations. You realize that you've hit the jackpot with this massive supply of information which is composed largely from data supplied by occupational analysts using sources such as the Dictionary of Occupational Titles (DOT).

You are ready to continue. You open the next virtual door which takes you to ACT's World of Work Map (http://www.act.org/wwm). According to the site, the map "organizes occupations into six clusters (parallel to John Holland's six occupational types), 12 regions, and 26 career areas (groups of similar jobs). It shows you how occupations relate to each other according to primary work tasks." You take the map with you to further help you navigate the world of work. A career path that you never before imagined—theatrical design—becomes apparent as one that can potentially meet your interests and values. You need to find a search tool that can help you locate a post-baccalaureate certificate program in this area. You find just the thing at www.grad-schools.com and proceed to investigate.

Your personal mission and search has led you to the conclusion that you wish to remain a school counselor but you might consider changing school districts or geographic locations. You are now at the point of conducting a **Job Search**. To begin, you update your resume at JobStar's Resume Center (http://jobstar.org/tools/resume/) by first reviewing resume style and function tips. You check out examples of chronological and functional resumes. You also notice that this site has links to help you learn how to post your resume electronically. Before posting your resume, however, you "snap" yourself over to The CareerLab Cover Letter Library (http://www.careerlab.com/letters/) to see samples of cover letters designed to communicate different messages ranging from "Answering Want-Ads Like a Pro" to "Saying Thank You with Class." Oh, and one other thing, you will need an updated business card for interviews so you click over to VistaPrint (http://www.vistaprint.com/vp/) where, for a small shipping and handling fee, you design and order your own custom business cards.

With a quality resume ready to be printed and electronically posted, you are ready to "hit the virtual pavement." First, you head over to the American School Counselor Association (ASCA) Job Bank (http://www.schoolcounselor.org). Because you are a member, you can view available positions, submit your profile or resume, and even view information about other applicants. You are also sure to head over to Monster.com (http://www.monster.com) to search over one million posted jobs by location, job category, and/or keyword. At Monster.com you can post your resume and create/manage a personal career account. Similarly, you also venture over to http://www.hotjobs.com, http://www.careerbuilder.com, http://www.ajb.org, http://www.nationjob.com, and http://www.jobtrak.com to do the same.

As you locate potential positions, you begin to conjure up questions about each respective school district and the community in which you might relocate. And you remember that the URL or Web site address for most school districts' follow a formula, www.xxx.k12.yy.us where xxx is the name of the district and yy is the two letter acronym for the state. For example, the Lee County School Board's Web site in Florida is located at http://www.lee.k12.fl.us. And, if this happens to be unproductive, you are sure to learn more about any school and its district by consulting the American School Directory (http://greatschools.net), an extensive database of public and private schools in the United States. Once you arrive at the district's Web site, you can learn more about who to contact with any questions (e.g., certification reciprocity), download handbooks, read Board meeting minutes, and more. You also remember to visit the National Center for Educational Statistic's National School Locator (http://nces.ed.gov/ccdweb/school/school.asp) to learn about other characteristics and demographics about your schools of interest. Finally, your research would not be complete without visiting the Runzheimer International's Relocation Web site (http://www.runzheimer.com/scp/scparmy/scpstart.asp) where you create a free report that provides extensive comparisons between where you currently live and where you may move. Comparisons include community demographics, housing, crime, climate, travel to work, and more.

You continue to be relaxed and confident. You are pleased with your career journey as of yet because you have identified several new schools that could provide you with a welcomed change. Your journey continues over several days as you persistently pursue new knowledge about yourself, about the world of school counseling, and about available jobs in the field. After only three weeks, you receive a job offer from your first choice of possibilities. The job is yours if you want it, and you need to decide whether it is worth making the move. You need to evaluate **The Job Offer**. As is typical, the first question on your mind is, "Is my new salary truly better than my current salary?" Although salary is only one part of a total benefits package, it is quite an important one for many people. You decide to conduct a comparative analysis of salaries which take into consideration cost of living for given locales at http://www.salary.com and http://www.homefair.com/homefair/calc/salcalc.html. After determining that the salary is acceptable, and before accepting the job, you consult with the U.S. Department of Labor's tips for evaluating a job offer at http://www.bls.gov/oco/oco20046.htm. You also complete a worksheet at the University of Virginia's Career Center (http://www.virginia.edu/~career/handouts/evaluating.html) which is designed to help you weigh important factors of a job offer.

You accept the offer and are now ready for **The Move**. Most people would agree that relocating is difficult at best. In your imagination, you envision a wizard that can provide a financial calculator, property locator, and look up mortgage rates and property values in real-time, for instance. Poof! You are taken to www.realtor.com, www.homegain.com, and Monster.com where these services and more are available.

As you arrive to your final cyberspace career development destination, you sigh with relief as you check the remaining few items on your list of things to do. All that is left now is to download a new eBook and a few easy listening music files, both of which you will enjoy as you ride as a passenger in the moving truck—the truck that you happen to have reserved online.

Software Tools

The proliferation in the last several years of software useful for counselors is incredible. Software allows counselors to complete a vast array of tasks more effectively and efficiently, such as managing one's practice, completing reports, generating treatment plans, studying student and client data, conducting assessments, and communicating with others. Some counseling tasks are best achieved using general office suite software such as Microsoft Office or Corel Office with advanced customization, especially when using macros (see Chapter 3).

When off-the-shelf software is not enough, counselors now have a vast range of choices for evaluating and purchasing specialized software to assist them in their work. For instance, the Computers in Mental Health Web site (http://www.ex.ac.uk/cimh/swintro.htm) maintains a database of software for mental health practitioners. Here are a few examples:

- **1CarePlace.com** offers electronic solutions to service provider agencies that enhance the quality of clinical care and greatly improve the organization's ability to use the information it gathers on the services provided to clients. Referral, intake, assessment, treatment planning, progress notes, discharges, and case closure are all built into 1CarePlace.com. Available: http://www.1careplace.com/

- **Therascribe,** a software program, assists counselors in developing Individual Educational Programs (IEPs) or Therapuetic Treatment Plans and conducting functional assessments. The treatment planning program helps you choose from thousands of prewritten treatment statements to help you create comprehensive plans and detailed progress notes. The program recommends appropriate combinations of behavioral definitions, long-term goals, short-term objectives, and therapeutic interventions for all major *DSM–IV* diagnoses. It tracks client demographic data, mental status and prognosis, treatment modality, discharge criteria, and provider credentials; it also provides treatment outcome tracking with 3-D graphing. Available: http://www.wiley.com/legacy/products/subject/psychology/therascribe

- **Advocate** is a digital cumulative folder for college counselors. It is an easy-to-use, powerful tool that replaces thick paper files and dramatically reduces paper shuffling. Advocate is built using FileMakerPro and is multiuser, cross-platform, and network capable. Available: http://www.inresonance.com/iRsolutions/info_advocate.htm

- **TimeGen** is a time-tracking utility that is designed to help you keep track of the time you've spent on various tasks and projects throughout the day. You add projects or tasks to TimeGen and click between them as you work on different things. TimeGen keeps a running total of all time spent on specific projects and displays accumulated time in the format you specify. Available: http://www.brianhansen.com/timegen.

- **The Child Behavior Toolbox Professional** is a database of over 2,350 intervention strategies for professionals who work with children with behavior and learning problems. The program covers the age range from infancy to age 12. Available: http://www.childbehaviortoolbox. com/

- **Hypnosoft** creates a custom, spoken hypnosis over the Internet. You can choose from 32 self-help topics including stress management, weight loss, smoking management, or any custom topic. Available: http://www.hypnosoft.com/

- **The Self-Directed Search Form R** helps people find the occupations or programs of study that best fit their individual interests and skills. Available: http://www.parinc.com

- **The Parenting Stress Index Software System** assesses the multidimensional factors of parent–child interactions. Available: http://www.parinc.com

- **Mood Monitor** software lets the patient track mood, activity level, sleep, symptoms, major life events, medications, menstrual periods, and notes for each day. Mood Monitor can graphically show how a patient's treatment is progressing. Available: http://www.moodmonitor.net/

- **AdvisorTrac** is a management software for advisement and counseling centers. Available: http://www.advisortrac.net/

Other software products have been specifically recommended by school counselors (http://www.schoolcounselor.com/software-survey-results.asp), including the following:

- **Bridges** is an online and CD-ROM resource that allows users to explore their education and work options, make solid plans for the future, and apply those plans in meaningful ways. Available: http://www.bridges.com/
- **Coin** offers effective tools that guide students to successful career planning from elementary to middle school, high school to special needs. Available: http://www.coin3.com/products/
- **Boulden Publishing** provides interactive resources for children in distress—including books, CD-ROMS, games, and videos—to help parents and counselors guide children on issues such as abuse, anger, divorce, self-esteem, conflict, character, and death. Available: http://www.bouldenpublishing.com
- **SASI** (Schools Administrative Student Information Software) is a comprehensive student information systems. Available: http://www.pearsonedtech.com/products/studentinfo.cfm
- **PowerSchool**, a Web-based student information system from Apple, simplifies data-driven decision making by providing real-time information to all stakeholders—over the Internet. Available: http://www.apple.com/education/powerschool/
- **Sierra's Print Artist** is a publishing product which features 4000 layouts, professionally-designed clip art and premium stationery, cards, and envelopes to make 50 projects. Available: http://www.sierra-home.com/prod_pa_printkit.html
- **Intervention Pro** provides common forms and related documents to create, publish, and update Behavior Intervention Plans for any school district. Available: http://www.iepware.com/BIP.html
- **ReadPlease** is a text-to-voice converter. Available: http://www.read-please.com
- **The Achenbach System of Empirically Based Assessment (ASEBA)** makes it easier and more economical to gather assessment data from multiple informants. Available: http://www.aseba.org/.

Summary

No counseling professional is immune from the significant impact technology has made on how we practice, communicate, manage, and measure the outcomes of our work. As noted in Table 1.1, technology is changing the way we all work, regardless of our own desire to implement specific changes in our personal approach.

In addition, technology is also changing the types of counseling issues presented by our clients within the various systems in which they live and work (e.g., family, peer). This chapter overviewed the nature and importance of this impact while providing specific examples of when and how this

Table 1.1
Technological Changes That Already Affect Your Practice

1. Increasing expectations that counselors will do more of their own clerical and record-keeping work.
2. Desktop computers that alter the manner in which records are kept.
3. Electronic transfer of data via fax, direct-connect modem, e-mail, or file transfer protocol (FTP).
4. The ability of clients to readily locate information about their concerns and treatment on the Internet.
5. The use of e-mail for professional-to-professional communication and counselor–client communication.
6. The use of multimedia presentation software and hardware to present information.
7. The use of personal digital assistants (PDAs) to manage schedules, contacts, and other aspects of our lives.
8. The intrusion of technology into the lives of counselors and clients, creating increased stress and decreasing some human contact.
9. Increasing reliance on computer-based assessment and interpretation software.
10. Increased use of online services by clients, creating additional difficulties in maintaining caseloads in agency and practice settings.

may happen in our work. The message is clear: Opting out of technological literacy and implementation in today's high-tech world reduces effectiveness and efficiency while increasing the risk of unethically practicing beyond one's competence. On the other hand, counselors who march along with the progress of high-tech tools and electronic media stand to enjoy the benefits and temper the potential dangers that prevail. Technological literacy and implementation is not merely a response to a problem, but an important and lifelong part of professional development and training. For better or worse, the availability of various technologies and how we apply them will continue to change. Changes will be pleasant or unpleasant, in large part determined by our familiarity and abilities to adapt.

Internet Sites for Additional Information

- **http://careerplanning.about.com.** This site is About.com's Career Planning Center.
- **http://www.att.com/learningnetwork/virtualacademy.** AT&T Learning Network Virtual Academy is a centralized resource of online courses designed to help educators effectively integrate technology into their curriculum while updating their professional credentials on their terms—anytime, anywhere.
- **http://www.athealth.com.** Athealth.com is a provider of mental health information and services for mental health practitioners and those they serve. This online community consists of psychiatrists, pediatricians, family practitioners, psychologists, psychiatric nurses, social workers, counselors, researchers, educators, school psychologists, caregivers, and others who meet the diverse needs of those with mental health concerns.

- **http://healthlinks.washington.edu/help/navigating.** This site, from the University of Washington Health Sciences Library, is called "Navigating the Web: Using Search Tools and Evaluating Resources."
- **http://www.healthyplace.com.** HealthyPlace.com is a large consumer mental health site, providing comprehensive information on psychological disorders and psychiatric medications from both a consumer and expert point of view. Included are active chat rooms, hosted support groups, people who keep online journals/diaries, psychological tests, breaking mental health news, mental health videos, online documentary films, a mental health radio show, and more.
- **http://www.learnonline.com.** LearnOnLine, Inc., is in the business of project-based Distance Learning using the Internet and World Wide Web for both courseware content and student–teacher collaboration.
- **http://www.counseling.org/site/PageServer?pagename=resources_online.** This site provides information about online courses from the American Counseling Association.
- **http://www.onlinecommunityreport.com.** Online Community Report tracks news and best ideas in online collaboration.
- **http://www.schoolcounselor.com/newsletter.** SchoolCounselor.com newsletter is a free publication for the purpose of advancing technology literacy and application among school counselors.
- **http://www.iteawww.org.** Standards for technological literacy as presented by the International Technology Education Association (ITEA).
- **http://www.digitaldividenetwork.org.** The Digital Divide Network Web site offers a range of information, tools, and resources that help practitioners stay on top of digital divide developments. It also serves as forum where practitioners can share their experiences with colleagues around the world.
- **http://www.universityofthenet.com.** University of the Net provides online training and record keeping for businesses with government-mandated employee training obligations and for individuals with professional prelicensing and continuing education obligations.

Recording Technologies

Competency: Be able to use such audiovisual equipment as video recorders, audio recorders, projection equipment, video conferencing equipment, and playback units.

Technology associated with recording the human voice has been available to most professionals for decades. The use of Dictaphones in office settings dates to the 1930s, and reel-to-reel tape became widely available in the 1950s. By the late 1960s cassette tape recorders arrived with the widespread use of transistors, and voice recording became very easy and popular. At this same time, training programs for mental health professionals began to use audio recordings of students to aid in the education and supervision process.

As well, during the 1960s, video recording equipment and playback became increasingly accessible, particularly in institutional environments. In the same way that reel-to-reel gave way to cassettes, videotape recorders gave way to videocassette recorders, prices fell, and the technology quickly arrived in offices and living rooms around the country. Videocassettes quickly replaced film as a prime training medium, and video cameras replaced older and less versatile 8mm movie cameras.

Like many electronic devices over the past several decades, videocassettes have become a part of daily life for many people. Newer technologies, including DVD (digital virtual disc or digital video disc), CVD (computer video disc), mp3 technology (a format for condensing sound recordings) and streaming media over the Internet are poised to render audio and video cassette technology as obsolete as Dictaphones and reel-to-reel videotape recorders. However, it appears that mental health professionals, armed with an exciting new array of tools, may continue to use these new tools as they have experienced the older tools in their own past—that is, primarily for purposes of training and supervision. Although these are important processes, mental health professionals who limit their use of audio and video recording and playback to these arenas are limiting themselves and their clients in important ways. This chapter reviews a variety of technologies associated with recording and playing audio and video and considers their use throughout professional practice.

Audiocassette Recorders

Most mental health professionals become acquainted with the use of audiocassette recorders in professional practice during their training years. Audio recordings are often made early in training programs as students role-play counseling situations with other students and then use the tapes to review their practice. This work continues as students move into clinical and field settings, where audiocassettes are used to create recordings that may be turned over to or listened to with a supervisor. Being able to hear oneself outside of the actual counseling session can be quite useful. Able to focus on themselves rather than the need to respond to clients, students generally find this type of exercise very beneficial. Supervisors, often unable to observe student work live, find cassette tapes invaluable to help understand and shape trainee behavior. Because of their small size, cassette recorders are unobtrusive and clients almost always quickly learn to ignore a recorder sitting unobtrusively on a table or desk.

One of the unfortunate occurrences for most mental health professionals is that when they transition from a student role to a professional role, they leave their tape recorder behind. Anxious to shed the role of student and to wear the cloak of the competent professional, young mental health practitioners may see the discarding of the tape recorder as a step toward their own independence. However, it may more correctly be seen as the first step away from lifelong learning. Practitioners are constantly faced with new challenges and difficult opportunities. Clients with ever more convoluted issues arrive in our offices, and the changing demands of the work environment constantly require new ways of working and introduce pressure to work more quickly and more effectively. Research evolves, and through professional readings, conference attendance, and home study, well-informed practitioners are always ready to expand their skills and knowledge. Abandonment of the trainee's recorder separates the practitioner from the only objective witness available to our work. Without it, we are forced to recall through our own lenses the work we perform. Supervision becomes less multidimensional, and opportunities for professional growth are reduced. By recording at least some sessions, mental health professionals at all levels offer themselves the luxury of reviewing cases in detail, seeking opportunities to grow and prosper. When necessary, the benefit of having a tape available for consultation or supervision is of great benefit to aid in our own growth as well as that of our clients. Tapes once made can easily be destroyed, and clients are no more concerned about the experienced practitioner taping a session than the inexperienced. In fact, clients are likely to see the tape as less intrusive for the experienced practitioner because the tape is less likely to be used or reviewed in a training setting.

• Technology Tip 2.1 •

All clinicians, regardless of skill level, should make taping a routine part of their practice, at least on a limited basis, to foster opportunities for professional growth.

Understandifng the Basics

As you prepare to work with audiocassettes, a few basic concepts need to be kept in mind, both about their use and about the equipment. We start with some basic issues related to the hardware, then turn to appropriate use.

Cassette recorders come in a wide range of quality, prices, and models. Many of the differences are aesthetic and will not affect the quality of the tape produced. However, there are some differences worth noting. The first issue confronting the purchaser of equipment is price. Generally, the old adage "you get what you pay for" applies as well here as in many situations. Individuals who purchase the least expensive recorder available will often be confronted with disappointing results. Recorders made essentially as toys for children will contain components of low quality that will impede recording quality as well as decrease the longevity of the recorder itself. We recommend, in terms of price, a mid-range recorder. As of this writing, something in a $40 to $70 range is likely a recorder of reasonable quality that will provide good service.

•   Technology Tip 2.2   •

One way to save money is to look for a recorder without additional features like voice-activated start and stop (VOX), variable playback speeds, and integrated radio tuners.

Electronic specialty stores and office supply stores often carry high quality equipment made specifically for recording discussions in meetings.

Tape Size

A second issue of concern is size. Audiocassettes come in two sizes: standard (or full-size) and microcassettes. We prefer the standard cassettes because of their flexibility. Standard cassette players are more widely available, and when tapes are used as part of a supervision process or provided to clients, the standard size is likely to be easier to replay in existing equipment. As electronic components continue to become smaller, even standard cassettes now fit in quite small recorders, and the size advantage of the mini-cassette recorder has largely been lost. Of course, if the purpose of the recording is only to provide the professional clinician with the opportunity to review his or her work, then the size simply becomes a matter of personal preference.

Microphones

With either cassette tape size, we strongly recommend the use of an external microphone. Most cassette recorders come standard with a built-in condenser microphone. These microphones do an adequate job of picking up sound when they are held near the speaker, but when they are laid on a desk or table several feet distant, the amount of ambient noise picked up from the room is too great, creating a recording that will be difficult to hear. The investment in a quality microphone will make a tremendous difference, even in a low quality cassette recorder. We consider the external microphone a required accessory. Specialty electronics stores carry microphones specifically created to pick up discussions in a room. Omni directional boundary microphones are designed for purposes such as recording a conversation in a room with the microphone not directly in front of the discussants and provide an excellent recording in most settings.

Some recorders offer variable speed playback and voice-activated (VOX) on and off features. As mentioned above, we do not recommend these features. Playing back a tape at a speed other than that at which it was recorded will usually result in some distortion of the voices. We believe that this is distracting in mental health settings because it decreases the reviewer's ability to understand and interpret client voice tone, decreasing one channel of communication. As well, speed compression interrupts the natural flow and rhythm of the conversation, shortens pauses, and removes information about pacing. These valuable clues about the client and clinician during the session are one of the advantages of taping and need to be maintained.

Voice-activated equipment also tends to decrease the quality of the recording. Counseling is often composed of many brief and discrete disclosures, both from the client and the clinician. Voice-activated recorders stop recording whenever silence occurs. This is beneficial because it saves battery life and allows a single cassette to record over a longer period of time because the cassette is not turning during silence. However, the cassette always takes a brief amount of time to detect the beginning of the conversation, to start turning the tape and to begin recording. Every time the tape restarts there will be a brief pause and then some blurred dialog as the cassette returns to normal speed. These brief lapses are especially troublesome when clients speak softly or are responding with one- and two-word answers, as is often the case during particularly emotional disclosures. Therefore, we recommend that recorders not have this feature or that this feature be disabled during use in clinical settings.

Types of Tape

The next issue is the type of tape to purchase. A baffling array of cassette tape types and qualities are available. Tapes are made out of many different materials and will normally be labeled as Type I (Iron-oxide), Type II (Chromium-oxide) or Type IV (Metal). Type III is no longer in use. Each type of tape has special characteristics, and these are apparent when recording music. To take advantage of these differences, manufacturers will set up their recorders to work optimally with a particular type of tape.

• Technology Tip 2.3 •

The best tape is that recommended by the manufacturer for the particular recorder that you have purchased.

However, most people will find that these differences will have little impact on a recording of a counseling session with a client. For the type of recording that mental health clinicians will generally make in their professional setting, Type I tapes will provide adequate recording, and Type I is less expensive than Type II or Type IV. Some recorders detect the specific type of tape inserted and adjust automatically. In these cases, Type I remains adequate for most purposes. In general, any tape can be used in any recorder, so when no other tape is available, an exact match is not required, although some loss of sound quality may occur.

In addition to the specific type of tape purchased, there are many brands from which to choose. Two of the largest distributors in the United States are TDK and Maxell. Tapes from these or other major manufacturers are probably fine for the purposes discussed herein. We do not recommend the purchase of extremely inexpensive tapes as these may be of inferior quality and may break or unroll in your cassette recorder, which in addition to being annoying may even damage some equipment.

Tape Length

Cassette tapes come in a variety of lengths. The time listed on a tape will be calculated for a standard tape, at normal speeds, using both sides of the tape. Therefore, a 60-minute cassette will record for 30 minutes on each side. Since clinicians often work in 50–60 minute increments, there is a temptation to purchase 120-minute tapes that will record an entire session on one side. Cassette tapes themselves are all the same size regardless of the recording time. What varies is the amount of tape in the cassette. To allow more tape in a cassette with a longer recording time, the tape itself must be thinner. Therefore, the tape in a 120 minute cassette is much thinner than that in a 60 minute cassette. These longer recording tapes have a tendency to stretch and are more likely to become entangled in the working mechanisms of the recorder. Many manufacturers recommend against the use of any tape over 90 minutes. We support this recommendation and suggest either that the tape be turned in the middle of the session, or that a second tape be available to be started when the first has reached the end.

Sound Quality

Some recorders may include specific sound-filtering technology, including Dolby B, C, S, and DBX. These are compression schemes designed to decrease certain background noises including "hiss" from the recorder itself. If you choose equipment than contains this technology, then you must also choose tape designed to work with that same technology if it is to work properly. Thus, if you choose a recorder with Dolby B technology, you must use a tape designed for Dolby B recorders. Using a tape that does not match the Dolby technology on your recorder simply means that the Dolby enhancements will not work correctly. As a result, your tape may contain more background noise, hiss, or other unwanted elements than it would contain with the correct tape. However, this is generally less of a concern with voice recordings than with high-quality music recordings. Also, many handheld recorders do not include Dolby enhancements, rendering the issue unimportant for many people.

If your tape recorder is maintained, it will likely produce years of service. A few simple steps can increase the lifespan of the recorder and the quality of the tapes made. Tape players will become dirty over time and require some cleaning. Isopropyl alcohol and lint free swabs can be used to clean the tape heads. Simply place a drop or two of alcohol onto a swab and wipe the heads of the recorder gently. Allow the heads to air dry before use. Do not wipe the rollers in the machine as these may become damaged by the alcohol. Completed once every few months, this procedure will improve the quality of your tapes and maintain your equipment. Batteries should be maintained to ensure that the recorder does not stop during session. Many people find that the use of an AC/DC adapter is much easier than using batteries and reduces problems of not having a working recorder available at all times.

Video Recordings

The range of options to create video recordings has exploded in recent years, and is now larger than the options available for audio recording. Camcorders, the choice of most individuals who want to create video recordings, was until recently dominated by three types of machines. These included VHS tapes (which can be played in any VCR), VHS–C (which can be played in any VCR with a special converter), and Super-8 cassettes (which can only be played back in a Super-8 machine). However, a number of new options are now available, including Digital-8, mini digital videocassettes, and micro video cassettes.

Fortunately, the crowded field is not entirely distinct one from another. New technologies generally provide a better image and sound. As well, more expensive equipment, in most cases, will provide better results and have more features. However, for an individual counselor who is interested in capturing counseling sessions on tape, any of these options will provide suitable results. Higher end machines with advanced zoom technology, ability to record in near darkness, and built-in title and editing features are not necessary.

•   Technology Tip 2.4   •

In practice, a very basic machine with few extras will be easiest to use and will require the least amount of work to master.

To achieve the most flexibility, consider a standard VHS camcorder. These machines use standard size VHS videocassettes, which can be played back in any VCR. In addition, the tapes are easy to purchase, and the tapes and machine are the least expensive of the available options.

When considering tapes, fewer options are available than with audiocassettes. Almost all videocassettes are rated for 2 hours of recording at standard play (SP) speeds. This can be tripled to 6 hours if your recorder supports extended play (EP) recording. However, standard play will give the best results, and will provide enough record time to meet the needs of almost all counselors. As with audio recorders, an external microphone will greatly improve the quality of your recording. Not all camcorders will allow connection of an external microphone. If this is important to you, be sure that this feature is available prior to purchase.

The most common of the new camcorders are those featuring mini digital video (DV) cassettes. These camcorders digitally record both audio and video, resulting in a very high quality recording. Because the recording is digital, it can easily be downloaded to many multimedia computers, and the recording can then be edited. Titles can be created, soundtracks added, and separate pieces of the recording can easily be brought together to produce a finished presentation. If you need to create training materials that are video-based, a digital recorder will be a great asset. However, cassette tapes for digital recorders are quite expensive compared to standard VHS tapes, do not record as long, and in general cannot be recorded over repeatedly. A standard VHS tape can be recorded over dozens of times without significant loss of quality. Mini DV cassettes contain tape that is very thin, and, much like a 120-minute audiocassette, these tapes are quite fragile. Many users report that it is not uncommon to see significant loss in recording quality or to have a tape break after only six recordings. Unless there is a compelling reason to purchase digital equipment, most counselors will be satisfied with a standard VHS or VHS–C camcorder.

Webcams and Computer-Based Recording

A look at any advertisement for your local discount office supply or computer warehouse outlet will likely contain at least one webcam on sale. These small cameras that connect directly to your personal computer (PC) allow you to record video and store it for later use, or to broadcast across the Internet. Add a microphone, and your computer becomes a complete recording studio. On sale, these small webcams can often be purchased for under $50. For many counselors, who have a computer sitting on a desk next to where they see clients, this may seem like an alternative to a camcorder which can cost many times the price.

Webcams are fascinating pieces of technology, and because of their cost, are quite popular. However, they are designed to capture video that will be sent over the Internet as a video-stream. The quality of the picture obtained is generally quite poor and will be inadequate for professional purposes. As discussed later, these cameras have a role that can be quite useful, but should not be seen as a substitute for a quality camcorder.

Appropriate Use of Recorder Technology

One of the potential problems of using any recording device is the potential for a breach of confidentiality. As with all issues of professional and

ethical behavior, it is the responsibility of the clinician to inform and protect the client as regards these matters.

Whenever any recording is going to be used, express written consent is
required from the client. This consent should contain a statement of what is
to be recorded, how the recording is to be made (e.g., audio, video, computer-
based) and the exact purpose of the recording. Whenever possible, the
consent should also contain an explicit time frame concerning how long
the recording will be maintained and who will have access to the recording and for what purpose. These written materials should be maintained
in the client files.

To decrease the potential for a breach, written materials including consent forms should not be maintained with the actual recording. This way,
if a recording were to be lost or taken, no specific name would be attached,
decreasing the potential for damage. On the recordings themselves, labels
should not contain the names of clients. It is highly preferable to use case
numbers, record numbers, or initials on recordings. Again, this will minimize the potential breach if something happens to a recording. As with all
sensitive materials, recordings should be maintained in a secure environment, and only those who have been granted explicit access should be
allowed to handle the materials. Whenever possible, all recordings should
be maintained within the facility where they were created and not transported to a clinician's home, secondary worksite, or other setting where a
breach is more likely to occur. If tapes are to be transcribed, the transcrip-
tion should only be performed by the clinician, and not by a hired typist
or clerical worker. Once transcribed, appropriate care must be taken to
protect the computer file. Once the computer file is no longer needed,
appropriate security measures to ensure destruction of the file should be
taken. Additional discussion of this topic is in chapter 11.

Uses of Audio and Video Recording

As noted previously, the most popular use of audio and video recording in
the past has been for training and supervision purposes, primarily with
beginning clinicians. While a wonderful opportunity, this is only one way
in which recording can be incorporated into clinical work. Table 2.1 provides a summary of many opportunities that are available to counselors to
use recording technology to improve their practice. The remainder of this
chapter examines these technologies and offers suggestions for their use.

Most clinicians have some experience using tapes in training settings.
However, students often do not have the skills necessary to use their tapes to
maximum benefit. A few tips can greatly increase the effective use of tapes.

The first thing all clinicians need to remember is that a tape is of little
training value if it is not reviewed. Often people complain that they don't
like the way they sound, or they do not believe that what is captured on
the tape is representative of who they really are and how they always
behave. Tapes can only capture what exists. Unlike still photos that cap-

Table 2.1

Eight Recording Technologies to Improve Your Practice Today

1. Use an audiocassette recording to record a session weekly for your personal review or to share in supervision.
2. Keep a microcassette recorder in your car to allow you to record notes to yourself while commuting.
3. Use a camcorder to record a skills-building session with a client and provide them with the tape for review.
4. Use a webcam to create a 7-minute introduction to your theory of counseling that potential clients can access from your Web site.
5. Loan a digital voice recorder to a client for the week so they can keep track of their emotional state.
6. Download an article of interest from the Internet and use text-to-speech software to create an mp3 file that you can listen to while you exercise.
7. Allow a child to use voice-recognition software to dictate a therapeutic tale, then print it out so the child can take it home.
8. Download an audiobook from the Internet (try www.audible.com) and listen to something trashy and cheap, just for fun.

ture just a brief moment—leaving what led to the picture and what occurred in its wake up to the imagination—audio and video recordings capture entire exchanges. Although we may complain that we do not like the way we sound, the recording is a reasonably accurate reflection of how we do sound. Understanding that sound and how it is received by the client is an important component of understanding ourselves as professionals. And, across time, if one makes many recordings, the unfamiliar becomes familiar and the personal discomfort of hearing oneself will diminish. In the meantime, it is beneficial to remember that when others listen to the tape, they are only hearing what they always hear and will not think of the sound as unusual or distorted. If a tape does not capture what the clinician "usually" does, then the tape is truly an anomaly and can be discounted. However, if tape after tape is viewed as not having captured the clinician's typical behavior, then the clinician likely needs to alter his or her perception of what is typical.

The novice clinician may be thrown by the introduction of a tape recorder, but like his or her clients, the novice clinician will quickly learn to focus on the session and ignore the recorder operating silently in the background. More experienced clinicians will rarely alter their behavior when tapes are introduced because their style is more developed and their sense of comfort greater.

When reviewing a tape prior to supervision, the clinician can prepare best for reviewing the tape with specific questions in mind. Simply listening to a tape without a constructive framework from which to work will likely allow the clinician to achieve an emotional response to the session but may not lead to increased understanding. Questions focusing on what the goals of the session were, what was accomplished, what was handled skillfully, and what was not accomplished are all beneficial. Depending on the skill level of the clinician and the specific purpose of the supervision, additional questions may need to be addressed as well. In all cases, the clinician will find it beneficial to have the tape cued to a specific point to be shared with the supervisor or consultant. As well, specific questions about the session as represented at specific points in the tape will allow for a more productive exchange with the supervisor or consultant.

•   Technology Tip 2.5   •

In-session recording is a very useful way to provide feedback to clients and help them understand how they are viewed by others.

Providing Feedback to Clients

A basic assumption that many clinicians operate from is that many clients do not understand how they are viewed by others and their impact on those around them. Using audio and video recording equipment, clinicians can provide clients with an immediate look at how they are viewed by others. For instance, in a family therapy session, a father becomes argumentative with his wife and son but maintains a very engaging and constructive dialogue with his daughter. Asked about his behavior, he focuses on his even voice tone and volume and expresses a belief that he has treated everyone equally. By quickly rewinding a tape that has been recording the entire session, he can be shown that his voice tone did change between interactions and that while the volume remained steady, the emphasis placed on specific words created a demanding quality. In another situation, a young girl who was having social difficulties was allowed to view a tape of the start of a session with her school counselor where she had been bragging about the quality of her school work compared with her peers. By seeing herself from this new vantage point, she was able to understand that others saw her as someone who feels superior and interacts in a condescending manner. Neither of these situations needed to be contrived through role-plays. Both built on the natural interaction within sessions, much like how a group worker might use solicited feedback to help a member understand his or her impact on others.

•   Technology Tip 2.6   •

Clients may gain more from in-session behavioral rehearsal if they can see and hear their own behavior on videotape.

Practicing Skills Learned in Session

Often clinicians engage clients in behavioral rehearsals in session to prepare for specific events or to build a general set of skills. Following role-plays, clients are asked to reflect on their achievements and consider how well they enacted particular skills. By recording these role-plays, the client can be provided with an additional level of feedback and can be taught to act as his or her own coach to further increase skills in the future. In this manner the client is encouraged to become increasingly independent from the clinician, making his or her own decisions about the quality and efficacy of his or her own behavior rather than seeking external verification.

With clients who have some difficulty understanding and identifying their own emotional state, the use of video recording equipment can be quite beneficial. Reviewing a portion of a videotaped session can provide clients with the opportunity to look at themselves from a distance. With a little coaching, most clients are able to identify specific body language, movements, or gestures that represent or imply emotion. At times, by replaying a portion of a video recording with no sound, a focus can be maintained on nonverbal cues. Clients may begin to recognize how they display various emotions even without using words. This new understanding can then be used in the session to help clients directly identify their feelings in the future and to begin to live with more awareness of their emotional state.

Refinement of Behavior Between Sessions

Some clients may find it beneficial to review sessions between meetings. Oftentimes, this will be clients who have difficulty remembering content from sessions because the emotion was overwhelming, or clients who have some cognitive difficulties. This latter group may include those with substance abuse difficulties who have trouble recalling specific session events that they believe may be important. Such clients can be provided with a tape (audio or video) to review between sessions. In some circumstances, the clinician may choose to formalize the use of these tapes by asking the client to create a reflective journal entry following the review or to prepare specific comments about the tape to begin the next session. Note that using tapes in this manner may require the client to take the tapes away from the clinical setting to review them at home. Care must be taken to ensure that the client understands the potential for a breach of confidentiality and that the client is capable of providing adequate security for the taped materials.

Another use of taped materials from a session may be to reinforce certain behaviors between sessions. As an example, when working with a client on progressive relaxation techniques, it is quite common to provide the client with a commercially produced audiotape to use as a relaxation stimulus between sessions. However, a more effective tape may be created during a session. By taping an in-session relaxation session, a clinician can capture on tape the subtleties of the individual client's processes, as well as specific exchanges between the clinician and the client focusing on any client difficulties such as mastering a breathing technique. This custom tape then becomes a review for the client in the following days as he or she works on relaxation at home. If the problem of mastering the technique re-emerges at home and the client needs a visual reminder, he will have the tape along with the familiarity of the clinician working with him to resolve the problem. As well, the audio track from the tape provides the familiar voice of the clinician reciting a progressive relaxation script for the client rather than relying on an unfamiliar prerecorded voice. Also, because the in-session tape was created as the clinician watched and responded to the client, the pace of the tape, at least in the early learning stages, may match the pace and needs of the client better than a prerecorded tape.

Another example comes from work with a client on assertiveness training skills. Over the course of a session, a client becomes quite good at identifying appropriate assertive responses. However, several days later, as the client approaches a class project at school where she expects to use these new skills, she finds that she has forgotten what she wanted to say from an in-session role-play. By having the taped session available, the client can review not only general principles of assertiveness, but her own well-developed assertive responses designed specifically for the upcoming situation.

Self-Monitoring

In some settings, it may be beneficial to have clients create tapes outside of a session to bring in for review during a session. The creation of a tape in this fashion may replace or extend other types of between-session work in which a client may engage. An example of a tape produced between sessions comes from a man who was having difficulty at work with a supervisor. The client was becoming extremely angry and the anger led to inappropriate responses in the workplace. Using the principles of REBT, the clinician worked to help the client understand his own thought processes. However, during session, the client was unable to identify specific thoughts from these encounters at work. The clinician surmised that the client, following a heated exchange at work, talked to himself repeating in his own mind a variety of demands of his boss and work setting, as well as a series of self-downing statements. The client was encouraged to use a tape recorder to record conversations with himself following one of these angry exchanges. Following one of these situations at work where the client became angry, he was able to record pieces of his thoughts on his drive home. The tape was then brought into session and reviewed by the client and clinician. The client was able to better connect his irrational thoughts with his emotions and was then able to prepare and engage in more effective disputes.

Another way to use recording devices between sessions is to create self-monitoring logs. In the past, self-monitoring logs have generally been written accounts of behavior, emotion, or interactions. However, some clients may find it is easier to maintain an audio record rather than a written record. Using technology such as a digital recording pen, some clients may even be motivated to maintain a more accurate record just because they can use the technology. This "cool" factor may be particularly appealing to children or young teens who find carrying a digital voice recorder creates in themselves a sense of maturity or sophistication.

Confidentiality

Many options exist for incorporating recording technology into work with clients. Regardless of which one you choose, a few precautions are important. As with all records of client activity, any recording of a client creates an opportunity for a breach of confidentially. In addition, clients may inadvertently draw attention to themselves by using a recorder at inappropriate times. Clinicians can help their clients by engaging them in a discussion of the use of this technology, including a consideration of time, place, and security before it is used. Finally, caution should be taken that clients not use recording technology to record the behavior of others. Creating surreptitious tapes of an argument with a spouse or employer to prove they have been wronged is not a healthy manner in which to express oneself, and in some settings may be illegal.

Even tapes made with the consent of the other party can create difficulties. For instance, a tape of a client's spouse may provide some information that raises the clinician's concern for the welfare of a child. In this situation, the clinician's responsibility to the child may be clear, but given that the spouse is not a client and has not been provided with adequate disclosure information, it is unclear how the clinician should treat the client's spouse. As well, a tape of two people arguing may present the appearance that the client was wronged, leading to a potential collusion between the client and clinician to avoid addressing more salient issues and focus on the perceived maltreatment. However, such a focus is unfair to the third party, and may ultimately be unfair to the client who needs to continue work on his or her own specific issues. Although a tape may capture an entire exchange between a client and a clinician who meet only briefly once or twice per week, a tape cannot capture all the nuances including what leads up to an exchange between a client and a spouse or partner.

Recording Technologies as Educational Tools

Another area where video and audio recordings may play an increasing role is in the use of recordings to help educate clients during and between sessions. Education settings of all kinds are increasingly using video and audio recordings as another tool to enhance the learning process. As educators and students become increasingly comfortable with this technology as a format for learning, it is likely that additional materials will be created that can be used in clinical settings. One example of how this might be used in the future is the creation of a lending library of medication management tapes. These tapes would contain specific information about medications that are commonly prescribed in mental health settings. The tapes may include information about side effects, common dosages, usage, drug interactions, and so forth. The tapes can then be supplied to clients who have been prescribed a new medication. This will allow the clinician to reinforce teaching from the tape, rather than be the sole provider of information. As many clinicians who interact with clients have little training in psychopharmacology, such a collection of materials would help to ensure that accurate, current, and consistent information is available to clients. These would not replace the clinician as a provider of information, but would supplement the clinician's work, improving efficiency and quality through standardization.

Additional information may be provided on almost any topic for which a client may seek services. Parenting advice, relationship enhancement, medical treatment compliance, chronic pain, and the entire range of psychiatric illnesses are all potential areas where clients can benefit from increased information. Some clinicians are successful in their use of bibliotherapy, but as clients become more attuned to video-based information there will be an increased demand for information from mental health professionals provided in this same format.

Of course, the use of prerecorded materials for training purposes is not limited to client needs. Professionals have used such materials for years to update their skills, reinforce past learning, and improve their knowledge base. The American Counseling Association has been a leader in providing "masters" tapes for clinicians to view. In these tapes, clinicians can view accomplished and noted leaders in the field as they demonstrate techniques, often with real clients. While these tapes may be beyond the financial means of many individuals, most universities that have training programs for mental health practitioners will have some tapes in the library. In cases where there are not tapes available locally, they can almost always be borrowed from another lending institution through interlibrary loan agreements.

Streaming Media

A newer method of providing recorded material is through the use of streaming media over the Internet. Streaming media technology allows audio and video signals to be highly compressed and then transmitted over the Internet and received using any Internet connection, including a standard dial-up modem. The quality of streaming media can vary quite a bit depending on the speed of the Internet connection, capabilities of the computer, and the exact streaming technology used. Today, there are two primary competitors in the streaming media market: Windows Media Player and RealOne Player. To listen to or view streaming media, the user must be connected to the Internet and have one of these software products installed. In most cases, Internet sites support both of these software packages; there are differences, however, so users will need to make a choice or have both installed on their machine. Windows Media Player comes installed on most new Windows-based computers and can be obtained free of charge from Microsoft Corporation (http://www.microsoft.com/windows/windowsmedia/download/default.asp). RealOne Player can be downloaded free of charge from Real.Com (http://www.real.com). Once installed, users simply click on a streaming media link on the Internet and the file is automatically downloaded to the user's computer and the appropriate software will start. Using this technology, any information that can be provided to a client in a prerecorded fashion can be made available to clients over the Internet. Although not as flexible as using an audiocassette in a portable tape player, streaming media is about as flexible as using a videotape in a home machine. Also, streaming media over the Internet has the added advantage of allowing users to click to other Internet sites to obtain more information based on their own needs and desires.

Mental health professionals are increasingly using streaming technology to stay current in their own fields through continuing education opportunities. Streaming media allows clinicians from all over the world to join together for training without ever leaving their office or home. In some cases, training sessions are scheduled "live" with the presenter delivering information at the same time the audience is viewing the information. At other times, the presentation or material is recorded and then delivered to the user whenever the user has the time to view it. The first method has the added advantage that the presenter can be contacted, often via e-mail, so that questions can be asked or points clarified. The latter has an advantage in that it allows for greater scheduling flexibility on the part of the audience. It also allows individuals to view a portion of a training session and then return at a later time to finish the materials.

Collaboration Tools

A similar method of sharing information over the Internet includes collaboration tools like Microsoft NetMeeting, AOL Instant Messenger (AIM), and Mirabilis ICQ. These products mix recording technologies and streaming Internet technologies to achieve varying levels of interaction and communication. Like recording devices, these products use microphones or cameras attached to a computer to record, in a digital format, whatever input they receive. Then, like streaming technologies, they transmit the digitized information in a highly compressed format that allows the receiver to begin listening to or viewing the file before it has completely downloaded. The receiver, using the same software, then decodes the file allowing real-time interaction between two or more people.

AIM is perhaps the best known communication tool of this type available today. Also known as chatting, IM is the preferred method of communication (often replacing telephone calls) for millions of people, particularly teens and young adults. The advantages of using an instant messaging tool include an increased opportunity to multitask (there is always some down-time while one waits for their partner to type) and the ability to communicate with multiple individuals at the same time. Instant messaging software is a relatively secure format for communicating privately with another person. As clients become increasingly adept at communicating in this manner, clinicians may find that it is increasingly a valuable way to stay in touch with clients, particularly between sessions. As an example, a clinician can make arrangements with a group of clients to "meet" them online at 10-minute intervals on a particular evening. Then, over the course of a 1-hour period, the clinician can briefly check in with six clients who each log in, describe how their week is progressing, receive an updated homework assignment, and then return to their lives as the clinician moves on to the next client. Of course, the same task can be accomplished using a phone call. However, some people may find that they are more able to avoid being drawn in to a complete counseling session in this computer-mediated interaction than in a phone conversation. As well, many clients will be more willing to interact briefly in this manner, particularly if they are regular users of instant messaging software.

Videoconferencing

Similar to instant messaging software, but with more capabilities, are Internet-based videoconferencing products. One of the oldest and still widely used is a product called Pal Talk available from Paltalk.com. Pal Talk allows users to connect with a single user or to an entire group of users. It was among the first IM programs with the capacity for users to talk directly to one another. In most situations, a phone conversation is a more secure method of communicating, but voice chat over a computer network has advantages. For instance, in a school setting a school counselor may choose to connect with a small group of students after school to present a psychoeducational program on goal-setting. In this context, some voice communication is advantageous. By being connected over the Internet, the counselor has the added advantage of being able to show the participants various Web sites of interest such as career sites, college admissions sites, and career mentoring sites. This is an example of where Internet communications are more effective than face-to-face conversations because the Internet allows for additional levels of information to be immediately integrated.

• Technology Tip 2.7 •

Always start your use of technology with an explicit plan of what you want to accomplish. Then locate the tools necessary to achieve your goals. Never let the tools drive the goal.

Another full-featured program is Microsoft's NetMeeting. NetMeeting is installed on many new computers running Microsoft Windows, or can be obtained free of charge from http://www.microsoft.com/windows/netmeeting/default.asp. Not only does NetMeeting support chat (like AIM) and voice chat (like Pal Talk), it also allows video-conferencing. In addition, this software is specifically designed to work with Microsoft Office software. Therefore, individuals using this software can collaboratively work on any Microsoft Office document. This opens a wide range of possible applications for professionals and clients.

One innovative example of how NetMeeting can be used with clients comes from a small group of older elementary children participating in a school-based group for children whose parents were separated or divorced. After getting to know one another, the children were paired-up and given the assignment to write a fable about a child who was confronted with some difficulty in the world. The fable was to show how the children used their own wisdom and creativity to overcome the problem. After a brief introduction to NetMeeting and armed with instructions, the children set out to meet with their parents and arrange a time to work collaboratively with their partner online. Between sessions, the children met and jointly constructed a fable using Microsoft Word. The fable was created in real-time, with both children able to type to a single document, and then bring a printed version of their story to the next group session. This activity is positive on many levels. The most obvious is its ability to reinforce the idea that each child has the strength necessary to address life's difficulties. However, there are other levels as well. This exercise also teaches the children how to negotiate and collaborate. Without face-to-face interaction, it may be more difficult for one child to dominate the other, and quieter children may have more opportunity to contribute. Additionally, the children are reminded that they are not alone in the world. There are other people in similar circumstances, even if we do not see them.

Another use of Net Meeting is to allow a counselor directly into the lives of clients. In school settings, counselors can easily observe classrooms without ever leaving their office. A simple webcam placed in a classroom and connected to the school computer network allows a counselor to "sit in" and observe interactions, collecting valuable assessment information. In this manner, the school counselor can observe and provide consultation to teachers, assess student behavior between sessions, and gain information about classroom dynamics in preparation for group-guidance activities. As with all technology, care must be taken to protect everyone involved. Even when a camera is connected to an in-school network that is not accessible from outside the school, security must be provided within the building. It would be inappropriate to have an open video feed that any teacher or any administrator could tune in to at any time. As well, appropriate precautions related to informed consent must be observed.

Although a complete discussion of the topic is beyond the scope of this chapter, it should also be noted that these communication and collaboration products can be used to provide counseling, consultation, and supervision services directly over the Internet. As computers become more powerful, compression technology better, and high-bandwidth Internet access more common, the quality of video and audio signals will continue to increase. This will bring increasing pressure on mental health professionals of all types to provide their services directly over the Internet. Clients value the time savings available by not commuting to a clinician's office, and many may feel more comfortable seeking services in the more anonymous environment created by the Internet rather than visiting a mental health services agency in the community in which they live. This topic is more thoroughly discussed in chapter 12.

Voice-to-Text and Text-to-Speech Software

Two newer technologies that have yet to gain widespread acceptance are voice-to-text and text-to speech software. The promise that these technologies offer is great, and although some difficulties remain, their use is rapidly growing and the software will continue to increase both in usability and availability.

Voice-to-text software has been a dream for years not only among computer software engineers but among many special education professionals, individuals with a variety of physical limitations, and others seeking greater independence for individuals or usability for computers. With today's powerful computers, the current generation of voice-to-text software can provide many users with an acceptable alternative to the standard keyboard.

While several companies compete in the market for voice-to-text technology, the two dominant players are IBM with its product ViaVoice (http://www-3.ibm.com/software/speech/) and Dragon Systems Inc., which produces Dragon Naturally Speaking (http://www.scansoft.com/naturallyspeaking/). Both of these products are in constant development and come in several varieties, including basic limited feature packages all the way to professional versions. Among users, there is no clear favorite. Both software products have advantages, and neither is clearly superior over the other. When installed, these products allow a computer user to simply dictate into a microphone and whatever is dictated is then transcribed into text in the word processor of your choice. Upon installing each product, the number of mistakes will be very high. However, the user can "train" the product to recognize his or her own voice, and the more it is used, the better the quality of the translation. Recent reports indicate that after training, the software can be expected to correctly identify over 90% of the speaker's words. Through the creation of specialized word lists, this accuracy can climb to over 95% accuracy. In our experience, both products will require the user to edit whatever document is created, but for those who cannot type, or do not want to learn to type, voice-to-text technology is an acceptable alternative. This means that any practitioner with a computer can now create case notes, summaries, intake and termination reports, and other documents simply by dictating to their computer. As these products increase in power and flexibility, their use will become commonplace in many settings.

Voice-to-text software allows clinicians to alter their record-keeping practices. Session notes can be quickly dictated, as can intake reports and termination summaries. For many professionals, this will result in a significant time savings when compared with typed notes. In addition, these computer-generated notes and reports will allow for easier review than in the past, when handwritten notes were the norm. Session notes will be available in a professional format when needed by insurance companies, other clinicians, or for quality review purposes.

The opposite of voice-to-text is text-to-speech software. With a text-to-speech product, any electronic material such as a word processor document, a page scanned from a journal, or a Web page can be instantly translated into a .wav file which can be played over any multimedia computer. This technology allows a practitioner to create sound files from any printed material and listen to the file when reading would be difficult, such as in a car, on a train at night riding home from work, or while engaging in light exercise. Using simple software, files can easily be changed from the .wav format (a standard file type for sound files) to an mp3 format (a highly compressed file type, usually used for music) that can be played on a wide variety of portable audio players. These files can even be recorded on a CD and played in many newer CD players.

Although we have never seen it done, this technology would allow a professional association like the American Counseling Association to easily transcribe every paper presented at its annual meeting to sound files that can be included on a CD. Every attendee would then have access to every paper presented, allowing for a much greater audience for each individual paper. Also, every paper could be easily accessible well after the meeting for individuals to refer back to.

On the client side, text-to-speech holds promise for clients who cannot read because of age, cognitive impairment, lack of education, or any other reason. Suddenly, the potential opportunity to provide bibliotherapy becomes much greater. A word of caution: It is unclear what copyright laws exist that govern the individual's ability to create sound recordings of written materials for their own use. As professionals, we have a responsibility to protect the intellectual property of authors and to respect their copyrights.

If you want to learn more about voice-to-text technologies, we suggest a brief foray on the World Wide Web. Information about ViaVoice can be found at IBM (http://www-3.ibm.com/software/speech/). Additional information about Dragon Naturally Speaking can be obtained at Dragon Systems (www.dragonsys.com/products/naturallyspeaking/professional).

The market for text-to-speech software consists of a larger number of entries at the present time. In addition to information available from IBM, we recommend a product called Read Please, which is available as a demonstration product online (www.Readplease.com). Even if never used in a professional setting, the demonstration is a worthy download, installs easily, and is a fun and informative way to learn more about the capabilities of your computer. As a source of amusement, click on the picture of the person reading in ReadPlease to see the "personality" of the reader. Such small additions to software products continue to make our computers seem more lifelike all the time.

Technologies Designed for Accessibility

There are a number of technologies available to assist counselors and clients with visual impairments, some of which are an outgrowth of recording technologies or text-to-speech technology. One example of this type of technology is JAWS for Windows (http://www.freedomscientific.com/fs_products/software_jaws.asp). JAWS is a screen reader program that integrates with the Windows desktop so that users can "hear" what is on their screen. Unlike other text-to-speech products, JAWS does not require the user to open a file within the program. Rather, the program loads on startup and will automatically read anything on the computer screen. This program integrates with all Windows software, and is designed to be installed and configured by individuals who have no sight, so assistance is not required. In addition, the program comes with extensive audiocassette training. For clients as well as counselors with visual impairment, this is an important tool that can provide complete unassisted access to computers as well as the Internet. Two similar products for the Mac are outSPOKEN (http://www.floridareading.com/outspoken.shtml) and Macintosh iListen (http://guide.apple.com).

Some individuals who have limited sight are in need of programs that enlarge what they are viewing on screen so they can see and read. A number of software options are available. For the Mac, a product called inLARGE (http://www.floridareading.com/inlarge.shtml) will meet the needs of many individuals. This product will enlarge the image on a screen (or any part of the image) 1× to 16×. Options are also available to invert the screen to white on black to aid in viewing. There is a scanning mode that automatically enlarges all of a screen for easy continuous reading. A similar program for Windows, called MAGic (http://www.freedomscientific.com/fs_products/software_magic.asp) has many similar features and is available with or without built-in text-to-speech features.

Another similar group of products are optical character recognition packages for the visually impaired. These products are designed to allow individuals to scan material that can then be displayed as magnified screen images, or read with built-in text-to-speech support. For Windows, users may try a product called OpenBook (http://www.freedomscientific.com/fs_products/software_open.asp). Extensive information is available online about these and other assistive technologies. Additional resources are listed in the Internet sites list at the end of this chapter.

Summary

Audio recordings, and to a lesser degree video recordings, have a long established connection with the counseling profession. Primarily used as tools in training and supervision, recordings are an excellent way for counselors to observe their own and others' counseling technique. This is important for the ongoing development of the seasoned as well as the novice counselor.

The wide variety of recording technologies available mean that counselors today have more recording options that at any time in the past. This array of options makes it easier to use audio and video recordings in new and beneficial ways. In addition to supervision, recordings can help clients gain new insight into their behavior, help track client behavior between sessions, and help clients learn new skills. Skilled clinicians are very adept at modifying their interaction with clients in creative ways to meet immediate needs. Using these same skills, and armed with knowledge of the possibilities, you will be able to promote growth in your professional practice as well as in your clients by utilizing recording in your professional practice.

Internet Sites for Additional Information

- http://www.ecoustics.com/Home/Home_Audio/Cassette/ Cassette_Articles/. This all-in-one site covers many aspects of cassette recorders, including choosing a recorder, tape types, and cleaning.
- http://electronics.howstuffworks.com/cassette.htm. This site provides an array of information on how recorders work, differences in tape materials, and associated technologies.
- http://products.consumerguide.com/cp/electronics/background/ index.cfm/id/11121.htm. This site provides a great deal of information that will help in choosing a camcorder style and features. The included glossary will help to make sense of features that are often advertised, but frequently misunderstood.
- http://www.camerasrolling.com/systems/camcorder_reviews.html. Another camcorder review site, this one provides access to reviews on specific equipment that may be helpful to those looking to purchase particular models.
- http://shopping.msn.com/softcontent/softcontent.asp?scmId=709. This full service site covers many of the features that distinguish camcorder models from one another.
- http://www.creativepro.com/story/feature/18452.html. This introduction to streaming media describes the entire process of developing and delivering media. A good place for those who want to create streaming media for their Web site.
- http://www.nwfusion.com/research/streaming.html. An in-depth look at streaming media, this site is for those with solid tech skills.
- http://www.vaip.werro.ee/elvar/playlist/help/index.html. A good resource to help get your streaming media plug-in (Windows Media, RealPlayer, or WinAmp) working with your browser.
- http://www.bbc.co.uk/webwise/askbruce/articles/chat/instantmessage_1.shtml. A good primer for those who want to get started with instant messaging software.
- http://www.linc.org/voicerec.html. A brief look at voice recognition software, this site also provides links to some other assistive technologies of interest.

- **http://www.techworthy.com/magarchives/software/96656.html.** This site contains review of text-to-speech software products.
- **http://guide.apple.com/uscategories/assisttech.lasso.** This site, maintained by Apple computers, provides detailed lists of assistive technology products for Macintosh computers.
- **http://www.wheelchairnet.org/WCN_ProdServ/Products/ OtherATprod.html.** This list provides access to information on many types of assistive technologies and goes well beyond computer software.

3

Productivity Software

Competency: Be able to use productivity software to develop Web pages, group presentations, letters, and reports.

E conomists define productivity as the ratio of outputs to inputs, or more generally as the ratio of benefits to costs. Using this definition, productivity can be improved by the following:

- Producing significantly greater benefits, encompassing quality as well as quantity, at modestly greater unit cost ("doing more with more");
- Spending significantly less resources while limiting benefits reductions to modest levels ("doing less with less");
- Producing greater benefits while spending less money or time ("doing more with less"); or
- Improving quality at the same unit cost ("doing more with less"; Massy & Zemsky, 1995).

Most counselors would agree that they perceive themselves as having to meet increasing workloads with either the same or reduced resources— that is, they are having to "do more with less." Thus, the common cry among counselors is "How can I provide quality services and programs (i.e., continue to be effective) for my clients in a more efficient manner?"

The appropriate use of current and emerging productivity software is one viable solution for dealing with this problem. The necessity for a comprehensive and integrated approach to counseling, including accountability, has become increasingly mandated, especially as fewer counselors are working with increasing numbers of clients in all sectors. Without help, counselors may feel overwhelmed, unorganized, or lost as a result of the sheer quantity of information they need to manage. Consequently, effectiveness and motivation may suffer. Technological tools have the potential to make some aspects of the counselor's role more efficient, accurate, and automated.

A variety of basic software packages are available to assist in the timely completion of daily counseling chores. Software intended to help users increase and manage their productivity, called productivity software, include a variety of tools and utilities that promote both the completion of tasks and collaboration among counselors within a local or global community. Similarly, some productivity software is designed to help the user measure their level of productivity as well as the nature of any outcomes. Productivity, or a counselor's rate of production, can be improved on by a range of strategies from reducing the time required to locate information (e.g., a phone number) to automating more complicated tasks such as aggregating numbers or generating multiple dynamic reports. With careful planning, the high tech tools of the new millennium will assist in decreasing the time required to complete traditional counseling tasks, increase your ability to work with more clients, demonstrate your effectiveness, and decrease your overall workload. At their best, productivity software (and hardware) will help counselors provide higher quality services to a broader base of individuals more effectively and efficiently (i.e., doing more with less; Sabella & Tyler, 2001).

More than 20 years ago, Bleuer and Walz (1983) alluded to the use of productivity software when they suggested that school counselors in particular need to explore how computer applications can be used in "computer-managed counseling (CMC)." This still rings true today for all counselors. CMC can help with the clerical and administrative tasks associated with their work and tasks that frequently inhibit their ability to undertake meaningful counselor interactions. For instance, practical applications of CMC include client record keeping, counseling activity logs, student and client attendance records for both individuals and groups, scheduling of individuals and groups, resource files for the counselor's personal use, and general word processing such as writing reports and personalized letters (Bleuer & Walz, 1983).

The remainder of this chapter focuses on specific categories of productivity software that can be of particular use to counselors. These include word processing, spreadsheets and databases, multimedia, Web authoring, personal information manager, and graphics editors.

Word Processing

Perhaps the most commonly used software program (with the exception of the e-mail client) is the word processing program. Word processing programs allow the computer to be used as an electronic typewriter in which the author can compose a document and view it on the screen, make corrections, move passages around, delete and insert new passages, and in general perform all the tasks of writing and rewriting. Word processors are the primary computer solution for writing problems, whether developing ideas, writing final reports, composing letters, or recording notes (Brent & Anderson, 1990). Modern word processors are comprehensive desktop publishing solutions and can handle tables, charts, graphics, special styles, columns, and more. Today's word processing programs seamlessly integrate with other software as part of a suite of programs. As a result, word processing documents can be shared or linked to databases, spreadsheets, or multimedia programs or converted to other formats such as that needed for the Web (i.e., HTML). More elaborate word processing software can include a voice recognition utility that allows the user to dictate words and commands instead of typing them. The key to increasing one's productivity with word processing software is going beyond the basics and knowing how to use several time-saving features such as merging, macros, and table functions.

Merging

Merging capabilities allow users to create personalized copies of a document using a template and data source such as names and addresses. For instance, Sabella (1996) wrote about how a school counselor wanted to send a letter home to the parents of a group of students with whom he had been working. The purpose of the letter was to invite them to an award ceremony for celebrating the achievements of the group. He created a standard letter/template that contained a greeting and outlined all pertinent information. Throughout, he inserted special codes, called fields, which essentially ask the computer to "fill in the blank" with personal information stored in a second file. Then, with a click of the computer mouse, the computer generated a letter for each student that had the student's name, the parent's name, the address, and the date the letter was printed. Using the same procedure, he then generated envelopes with respective addresses for each student. Using the same procedure once again, the counselor created an award certificate template and merged the student's name and the name of the award, also included in the data file, resulting in a personal certificate for each student. While he was at it, he also created personalized name tags, a list of participants for the school's newsletter, and then merged the information into his semester report to administration. The first time, the entire process required 45 minutes. However, subsequent production of these documents with different groups required significantly less time because the only file that changes is the data file. The standard materials or templates such as the letter, certificate, name tags, and report stay the same or only require minor edits.

Data sources used in a merging procedure can encompass a variety of formats including word processing data files, tables, spreadsheets, databases, address books, or delimited text. When data is in the form of a table or spreadsheet, each column is considered a field (bits of information, such as a first name), and each row is considered a record (complete available information about, say, a person). A merge document is simply a template with both constant information for each personalized document and, embedded throughout, personalized data. Personalized data is included by simply inserting a code called a "field" such as first name, last name, birth date, or grade. Each field typically has a descriptive name determined by the first record (or row) in the data set. Very similar to merge documents, a delimited text file contains data in a format such that each piece of data is separated, not by a code, but more simply by a specific character such as a comma. When the data itself includes a comma (e.g., the city, state, and zip code in an address), it is surrounded by quotation marks so as not to confuse the merge process. A new record in a text-delimited data file is usually separated by a "page break," that is, the start of a new page in the file. Delimited text files are quite popular for transferring data from one application to another because most word processors and database systems are able to import and export comma-delimited data with ease.

Merging data and documents has versatile applicability in counseling. Consider the following examples:

- Susan, a community counselor, needed to provide periodic reports to a funding agency regarding the nature of clients served over several months as part of a grant. Counselors at her work used the same software over a network for record keeping so that demographic data, diagnostic information, treatment plans, and insurance information, among other types of information, were uniformly stored for each client. The system allowed Susan to first choose only data of interest by delineating a certain time span or date range before exporting it to her spreadsheet program, Microsoft Excel. After she opened the file using Excel, she then added several basic formulas to aggregate the data to display descriptive statistics (e.g., average age, percentages of clients with certain diagnoses, changes in GAF scores over time). Finally, she merged relevant information into a report template provided by the funding agency. To generate future similar reports, she would only need to repeat the procedure for exporting the data from the system and then copy and paste the existing formulas instead of re-creating them.
- A school counselor, Thomas, conducted an outdoor adventure field trip at the beginning of each semester for students who were falling behind academically. He asked the county office to e-mail to him a file with the names, race, sex, lunch numbers, last semester GPAs, and homeroom teachers for all students at his school. He also asked that the list be sorted first by GPA, then race, and then sex. On receiving the file, Thomas was able to identify a balance of boys and girls among various races with the lowest GPAs who were eligible to participate in the field trip. Using this data and his word processor, Thomas then generated certificates, permission letters, and a list of participants that would be used for gathering pre- and postintervention data. He even saved time by merging a list of names with corresponding lunch numbers to give to the cafeteria staff who provided bagged lunches for the trip (Sabella, 1996).
- For an annual eating disorder screening day, a mental health counselor maintained a spreadsheet containing information about speakers and other participants. Every year, he merged this information into standard invitations, confirmations, brochures, and thank-you letters.
- Another mental health counselor in private practice who specializes in working with children and adolescents is interested in writing letters to school counselors to introduce herself as a viable referral source for students in need of therapy. Luckily, the school district's Web site contained a list of school counselors and each of their respective addresses, which she could copy and paste into a word processing file. Once pasted, she could then "clean up" the data by putting it into a table format which could then easily be merged into

personalized letters and envelopes. Because the counselor knew how, she recorded a couple of macros (see next section) which automated much of the process and only required 12 minutes from start to finish. Eventually, she decided to go online to a mail house where she could upload the data and her favorite photo, then design a postcard on the Web site using a "wizard," and have the company conduct the mail-out for her (e.g., see http://www.amazingmail.com).

Macros

Most word-processing programs have their own macro programming languages. Essentially, macros are mini-programs that can perform frequently needed tasks or keystrokes. To create a macro, a user usually (a) enters a particular keystroke that tells the computer to "start recording what I do"; (b) enters a short name for the macro (e.g., ltrhead) or keystroke combination (e.g., Alt-L) that assigns the macro to that keystroke; (c) completes the task (e.g., calling up a frequently used file or generating a report); and (d) enters another keystroke to tell the computer to "stop recording what I just did." To invoke the macro, a user simply needs to enter the assigned name or keystroke and the computer immediately "plays" what was recorded (Sabella, 1996).

•   Technology Tip 3.1   •

When recording a macro in Microsoft Word, you can use the mouse to click commands and options, but the macro recorder doesn't record mouse movements in a document window. Learn about using shortcut keys by clicking on Help and typing "macro" in the Answer Wizard.

For example, one counselor found that she frequently needed to retrieve a file containing her personally designed letterhead. Rather than using an eight-step procedure to do this every time, she created a macro that, with one keystroke, retrieved the file, automatically inserted the current date (another feature of most word processors), and placed the cursor at the point where a letter would begin. If ever she wanted to change her letterhead, all she would have to do is edit and save the letterhead file. Counselors have found many other uses for word processing macros in their work such as in the following examples:

- Placing the directory and file name for a document in tiny letters at the bottom is called "branding." Branding makes it easy to locate files when needed.
- Every quarter a school counselor found that she needed an updated phone directory of peer mediators at her school. After updating the data file, she simply invoked the macro with the touch of a keystroke that merged the data into an indexed phonebook format and printed it out.

- One marriage and family therapist recorded a macro that allowed him to back up a set of important documents to a computer disk.
- Headers and footers that show the document title and page number on each page can automatically be placed in documents.
- The headings of a table can automatically be centered and changed to boldface.
- When a counselor needs to write a memorandum or prepare a fax cover sheet, a macro is used to "call up" the appropriate template, which can then be completed and printed.
- Some word processing software automatically completes groups of words that are commonly used, such as the name of a school or community counseling agency; the program "remembers" these names after you use them several times.
- With one keystroke combination, one counselor created a macro that would instantly save a confidential document and clear it off the screen if someone were to walk in the office.
- Another counselor found a set of free and useful macros for his word processor on the Web. One macro allowed him to create customized monthly or weekly calendars. Another macro enabled him to maintain a to-do list that automatically sorted tasks by category and priority level.

Tables

Tables give a document structure, whether used for a short multicolumn list beside standard paragraph text or for an entire document's layout, such as in a newsletter or resume. A table can let you organize data in rows and columns of cells and can contain text, graphics, and formatting such as lines and shading. You can use tables to present lists, schedules, financial data, comparisons, and accountability summaries. Most word processors let you choose from a number of preset table formats or you can create your own format. Organizing data in tables is only one of the advantages of using tables in word processors. Once data is entered it can be sorted, merged into another document, or automatically turned into charts or graphs. Charts and graphs can enhance the presentation of data in a document by displaying comparisons, trends, and statistics. Or, you can use organizational charts to display an organization's structure such as with a flow chart (Corel Corporation, 1999).

Tables can also be used as layout tools in all types of documents. A table does not have to be as strictly defined in rows and columns as you might think. Cells can be merged or divided and can even hold other tables. For instance, you can use tables to create a sophisticated form that others complete with information which can then be processed in various ways. Floating cells—which are single table cells usually placed within a sentence—can be used to link to other parts of the document or to other documents to present a snapshot of information, such as total number of clients in a given period. For instance, a sentence such as the following,

"The total number of clients with whom I have worked, [floating cell here], reflects a [another floating cell here] percent increase this quarter" will perform calculations based on other fields within other areas of the document and place the results in the floating cells.

• Technology Tip 3.2 •

You can echo a piece of dynamic data (e.g., number of clients served) throughout a report by using a floating cell. That is, the information is entered once, then it is echoed throughout a document. When the data is changed, it is changed throughout the document.

Preparing documents such as letters, reports, awards, and lists by hand can be a tedious and time-consuming task. Without the aid of a computer, these tasks might force a counselor to limit or dismiss a counseling activity because of a high work-demand-to-product ratio. The merge, macro, and table functions of computer word processors can help save time, make more complicated projects manageable, increase productivity, and contribute to counselor effectiveness.

Spreadsheets and Databases

Taking slightly more skills than a typical word processor table, spreadsheet and database programs are another essential tool for the productive counselor's desktop. According to the Webopedia (2002b), a spreadsheet is a table of values arranged in rows and columns. In a spreadsheet application, each value sits in a cell. You define what type of data is in each cell and how different cells depend on or "relate" to one another. The relationships between cells are called formulas, and the names of the cells are called labels. Once you have defined the cells and the formulas for linking them together, you can enter your data. You can then modify selected values to see how all the other values change accordingly. This enables you to study various "what if" scenarios. (Note that chapter 4 presents more information about the statistical capabilities offered by spreadsheets and databases.)

There are a number of spreadsheet applications on the market, Lotus 1-2-3, Microsoft Excel, and Corel Quattro Pro being among the most common. The more powerful spreadsheet applications support graphics features that enable you to produce charts and graphs from the data. Most spreadsheet applications are multidimensional, meaning that you can link one spreadsheet to another. A three-dimensional spreadsheet, for example, is like a stack of spreadsheets all connected by formulas. A change made in one spreadsheet automatically affects other spreadsheets.

Similar to a spreadsheet, a database is a collection of information organized in such a way (i.e., indexed) that a computer program can quickly select desired pieces of data. You can think of a database as an electronic filing system organized by fields, records, and files (similar to merge codes as used in a word processor). A special type of database is called a *relational database*. A relational database is one in which any object or record, whether it be a piece of text, a graphic, or Web link, is linked (or in some way related) to some other object. Relational databases are particularly useful for organizing large amounts of disparate information in a way that is nonrepetitive. However, they are not designed for numerical analysis such as with spreadsheets. Once a database is created, a program called a database management system (DBMS) is needed to retrieve and processes information from the database. Popular DBMSs include Microsoft Access, and Oracles's SQL (Structured Query Language).

Sabella and Tyler (2001) reported on the following examples of spreadsheet/database uses in counseling:

- One school counselor created a simple database to track types of referrals to the counselor's office. He could then call up the information in an organized manner so that all similar referrals were grouped, providing a "snapshot" of the kinds of counseling problems being presented. This information helped the counselor decide to focus more on certain skills when doing classroom guidance.
- Similarly, the same counselor accessed the school's discipline referral database to better determine the nature of discipline problems. Interestingly, he believed that more referrals were made as a result of violence than for other reasons, probably because these are the most emotionally evocative. However, by tracking the information carefully, he recognized that in fact most referrals were made as a result of off-task behavior. This information then helped to justify the development of a skills-based attention-enhancement program rather than focusing primarily on issues of violence. Unexpectedly, he also learned that a pattern in referral behavior existed with two teachers. The teachers made most referrals immediately following students' return from a "special" class. This might indicate the teacher can use assistance handling transitions. The database query turned out to be an excellent data-driven method to identify consulting opportunities for the counselor. Another teacher, for instance, might be found to make referrals primarily of female students for off-task behavior. This teacher may need assistance in developing classroom management strategies specifically for girls.
- One counselor accessed the simple database template provided in her database program for use as a Rolodex, or phone book. This system maintained important names and contacts for easy access.
- At one local school the authors found a database that—with the click of a few buttons—generated a report that identified all children who missed 10 or more days of school in a sample 4-week period. This provided an immediate list of children in need of services. A few more clicks of the mouse generated a list of all 5th grade students failing a given subject and included their 4th grade teachers for that

same subject. This report provides important information about where weaknesses may exist in the school and suggests a need for intervention or consultation.

- Using a spreadsheet program, a counselor maintained an activity log that included time spent in various categories of activities (consulting with parents, individual counseling, large group guidance, peer helper training, and professional development, to name a few). With one click of the mouse each quarter, he could print out a report which he provided to his boss with complete textual descriptions and bar graphs.

- The director of a mental health agency used a database program to keep track of how 12 different counselors used only seven available rooms to do their work. Also, she was able to quickly query the database to identify common available times for staff meetings.

- One agency used a networked database program written especially for counselors which was used to conduct intake, diagnosis, treatment planning, billing, and collections.

- Another counselor used a database to track outcomes, especially comparing clients who completed counseling versus those who dropped out or self-terminated prematurely.

Multimedia

One popular technology tool for persuasive communication is multimedia presentation (MMP) software. An MMP is created by a computer program and incorporates a series of projected images called slides. Slides may incorporate into an integrated series files such as animated text, graphics, pictures, audio and video clips, graphs, tables, and any other electronic representations (Sabella, 1998). Effective comprehensive school counseling and mental health programs and services require the support of a diverse group of stakeholders, including students, administrators, teachers, staff, families, community members, and others. Helping stakeholders advance knowledge and understanding of your work and how they may become involved can be a daunting task. A highly expedient and yet effective method is needed. Technology such as MMPs is one tool that can help you to effectively and efficiently disseminate a message about your work among many important people. Also as important, multimedia software may be a feasible answer to the question, "How can I provide others training in skills, knowledge, behaviors, and attitudes that will help them better cope and succeed with various counseling or development issues?"

Specifically, coupled with the power of the Internet, using multimedia software can help counselors:

- Communicate a message that is rich with sound, animation, clip art, photos, graphs, data, and other elements.

- Provide information that is highly up-to-date and easily accessed anytime, day or night.
- Present to others without having to be present at a conference or meeting. This has the added benefit of being quite cost and time effective.
- Tailor information to each specific audience without building a new presentation from scratch. Existing MMPs can be altered and saved under a new name.
- Collaborate with others more efficiently by enhancing the democratic process.
- Communicate to others that they are knowledgeable and capable of using desirable technology skills which can respectably be modeled for the clients they serve. In this case, the medium is the message.

Perhaps the most important use of electronic tools for communicating with others is the ability to shift time and location. No longer are counselors required to be present for collaborating and communicating with others. An MMP can be stored on various media to accommodate a wide variety of recipients' needs. Using the Internet to share presentations literally allows counselors to cultivate the message across a global (or targeted) audience within a matter of seconds. Once a presentation arrives, audience members can access and view the presentation at their own convenience, location, and pace. Because today's multimedia software allows the counselor to include narration and timed slide transitions, an audience member can listen to and learn from a presentation, almost as if the counselor were present. And, if the recipient chooses, he or she may study the information as frequently as desired, pass along the information to others, or respond to the counselor for further inquiry or feedback.

Microsoft Corporation's PowerPoint is a computer program that has become widely used throughout business, government, and schools for communicating a sundry of topics among a wide variety of audiences. One feature of the program that probably makes the software a popular choice is its presentation "wizard." The wizard is a utility within the software that helps the user, in a step-by-step fashion, perform a particular task. For example, the layout wizard allows the user to choose (from a graphical menu) various aspects of layout and design elements which are then automatically processed by the wizard. According to Sabella and Booker (2003), other features of PowerPoint that make it popular (and relatively simple to use) include:

- An AutoFormat function that automatically recognizes and maintains a presentation's layout. Similarly, the AutoFit Text feature automatically resizes text to fit into a placeholder so that it doesn't "fall off" the slide. This means that counselors don't have to spend time trying to make the text fit on a slide—it happens automatically.
- Automated and customized number and bullet outlining.
- Table drawing tools to quickly insert a table of any size. A counselor may then add a border, change the fill color, or customize a

single cell—just as you might do in a word processor or spread-sheet application.

- A host of topic-related templates that provide a uniform look throughout a presentation.
- A free PowerPoint viewer (available at www.microsoft.com/office/000/viewers.htm) that allows individuals who do not own the PowerPoint program to view presentations.
- Note pages with each slide that are automatically created in a separate frame for easy viewing. Speaker notes may be used for reference or for collaborating with others.
- Narration that can be recorded and played back in a synchronized manner with the original presentation and which includes all slide transitions and animations.
- AutoShapes features (e.g., arrows, starts, and callouts) for use in creating diagrams, flowcharts, or other conceptual diagram banners and layouts.
- Automated conversions to various formats for easy access from different platforms (e.g., World Wide Web, self-running presentation, and word processing document).

Following are several examples of how counselors use MMPs in their work:

- D'Andrea (1995) wrote about several activities, including music, art, food, and photos, that can foster both multicultural appreciation and technological literacy among elementary school students.
- One counselor scanned into her computer clients' art projects and shared them with appropriate others (e.g., faculty, parents, other consulting counselors).
- Counselors can create an MMP that describes their work so that others—such as teachers, administrators, parents, and community members—may better understand and increase their involvement for facilitating client progress.
- MMPs can also offer suggestions for how others may choose to support the agency or school, refer clients, and otherwise contribute needed resources.
- Similar to distance learning, MMPs can be used as professional or personal development delivery systems to help others learn important skills, knowledge, and attitudes to do their part in the client's progress (e.g., academic, personal, social, and career achievements).
- School counselors can conduct a very large group guidance for all students at the same time. After an MMP is created, it can be transferred to video and then shown on the school's television network (Sabella & Booker, 2003). For classes that have computers, the counselor can use the Internet to conduct a live chat about the topic. For classes that do not have a computer, the counselor can follow up that day and conduct live discussions.

- Counselors can provide MMPs to teachers-as-advisors to use with students, thus ensuring that they are presenting consistent and accurate information to students.
- Counselors can provide MMPs to peer helpers (e.g., peer mediators) to aid them in learning relevant helping skills and attitudes as part of a homework assignment.

Web Page Authoring

Great Web sites, like a great piece of literature, are easy to follow and enjoyable to partake. Both present ideas and stories that seem simple yet stimulate our resourcefulness and imagination. In addition to valuable content, both are popular because the authors worked very diligently to compose and orchestrate them. The technical side of creating a Web site has all but become a nonissue because of the powerful and user-friendly software now available to Web authors. Indeed, the hard part is getting the ideas right—that is, making sure that the words and pictures on your Web site represent the best of what you have to offer. Although not every counselor may find the need for them, Web sites generally help consumers and others learn more about your work, counseling resources, and what you have to offer. Also, an effective Web site may provide consumers a convenient way to communicate with you via e-mail forms or other similar Web site tools. Some more sophisticated Web sites may actually be the place where online counseling takes place.

In his book, *SchoolCounselor.com: A Friendly and Practical Guide to the World Wide Web*, Sabella (2003) suggested asking yourself the following questions when preparing to create and design a Web site:

- **What is your school or agency's acceptable use policy?** Your site must follow the guidelines set forth by your organization and by your Internet service provider (ISP) or Web host. An acceptable use policy governs the responsibilities of a school or agency administration, counselors, students, teachers and parents regarding software, the use of the Internet, and adherence to copyright laws.
- **Who will help create the site?** Even the best Web authors have an advisory group to assist in making important decisions concerning their site. For those who are just getting started, it is highly advisable to delegate Web authoring responsibilities among an established team or committee. Members of your Web development team can write content and assemble photos for the various sections of the site. Luckily for school counselors, many schools have computer courses and labs where, as part of an assignment, students can help design various parts of your site. No matter what type of counselor, however, you can summon the assistance of students who stand to gain a valuable experience as a result. You might also include talented parents and nearby college students who would like to provide a com-

munity service. Your school or organization may also consider including Web authoring skills as a criteria for hiring staff or seek community volunteers to help do the job. In this instance, you might take the role of editor: the person who guides others into developing appropriate and fitting material, makes any needed changes, and integrates the material with the total body of information in a way that is logical and easy to follow.

- **How much time will I need to maintain my site effectively?** Develop a schedule for site updates. Perhaps twice per month allow yourself a couple of hours to make pertinent changes. Sticking to a predetermined schedule can be advantageous. If you do not limit your hours, you can easily become overwhelmed creating a perfect site, and spend more time than planned. Also, making minor changes more frequently is often more time consuming because of the need to set up for the task. Keep a file of any edits that need to be made, make them all at once during your scheduled time, and then upload all the changes.

• Technology Tip 3.3 •

To save some time, consider using databases to automatically add to a Web page by filling out forms instead of actually logging on and manually updating. Check out http://www.microsoftfrontpage.com/content/articles/datintro. html for some help on how to do this.

- **What will the site's directory structure look like?** Outline the various sections of your Web site and what would most appropriately be placed within those sections (i.e., content, writing style, length, etc.). Many people find it most efficient to develop this scheme in the form of a flowchart. Ask yourself what the top level sections should be (limited to no more than eight) and what sections would logically go under these.
- **What tools do I have available to me for maintaining my site?** To make life easy for you in your Web authoring endeavor, you will need tools to automate otherwise difficult tasks such as editing, scanning photos, uploading to a server, creating forms, and creating images. Survey your workplace for available resources such as computer software and consultants. Determine whether the available resources will be sufficient. If not, what will you require and what will be the cost? How can you acquire any missing resources through purchases or donations? There are free or inexpensive tools available online (e.g., www.tucows.com or www.hotfiles.com) that may serve you well in doing what you need to do. At a minimum, you will need a computer, Web authoring software such as Microsoft FrontPage or Macromedia Dreamweaver, a word processing program, a scanner, and graphic editing software. Several notable Web authoring programs (HTML editors) exist and are available for free to anyone, such

as those found at http://www.notetab.com and http://www.coffeecup.com.

Although somewhat advanced, other important questions to consider when developing Web sites include:

- **What kinds of online interactive tools may I need to include on my site?** Online tools increase the possibilities for computation, communication, and collaboration. Many tools are achieved by using a bit of computer programming of which the most common are CGI scripts, ASP, Javascripts, applets, and ColdFusion macros. Fortunately, many scripts have already been written and are relatively simple to install such as those available at http://www.dynamicdrive.com, http://www.free-scripts.net, http://cgi.resourceindex.com, and http://www.freescripts.com/scripts. Such scripts add pizzazz to your words, graphics, and could also afford you a highly attractive menu/button system for you site.

- **Where will my site be housed?** Web site files must be located on a computer that is connected to the Internet and has the needed software to "serve" Web pages to those that request them. This specific computer is referred to as a Web server. Although it is possible to set up your own server, it is difficult and may be costly to do. Thus, you may want to use a Web host that can do this for you. Your school or agency may already have a server set up, or you can purchase Web hosting services for only a few dollars a month. If you don't mind some casual advertising on your site in exchange for free Web hosting, you can use a service such as those found at www.freeservers.com, www.tripod.lycos.com, or geocities.yahoo.com.

- **What will be my site address?** Your site's address, also known as the URL (universal resource locator) or domain name, is a unique identifier that points people to your site when they type it in the address field of a browser. Your address should be one that is short, reflective of the kind of site you have, and easy to remember. Most Web hosts also provide domain name registration services, which makes both of these processes quite painless. However, if you are interested only in purchasing and owning a domain name, you need to consult an online service such as www.register.com or www.networksolutions.com that will help you determine whether the name you have in mind is available and, if so, allow you to purchase it.

Web Authoring Tools

I (Russell Sabella) began Web authoring in 1995 by studying the source code of sites that I respected and by reading about HTML. Then, by using my word processor, I was off and running conducting the tedious task of writing, editing, and frequently rewriting all the HTML "tags" to properly show some basic text with a few graphics and a table. The procedure alone made me wonder why anyone would ever want to do such a thing. I'm extremely pleased to report that such programming efforts are largely foregone and have been replaced with sophisticated software that makes creating "eye-popping" Web pages a snap—without any knowledge of HTML coding.

Most popular Web authoring products come with site creation and management tools that allow you to create frames, draw tables, add rich graphics, and include support for an interactive database. Additionally, leading Web authoring programs allow you to view your site's navigational structure, directories of information, hyperlinks, hyperlink status, or all of your files at once. Some also include automatic hyperlink maintenance which allows you the freedom to make changes without worrying about broken links. With most programs you can start your page from scratch or begin with one or more of many professionally designed, customizable templates (e.g., see http://www.steves-templates.com or http://www.free-layouts.com). Other templates are reasonably priced, about $5-$25 dollars such as those found at OutFront (www.outfront.net). As if it couldn't get easier, virtually all Web authoring packages also include thousands of high-quality clip-art images, photographs, Web-art graphics, fonts, animated GIF files, color schemes, and many other design elements to create publications that reflect your individual needs and personality.

• Technology Tip 3.4 •

Web templates are highly formatted and precise. Don't make any significant changes to a template's structure (e.g., table width) or you may render it unusable.

Something else you should know before you go out to your nearest software store and spend between $50 and $1000 on Web authoring software: Today's leading word processing programs, especially Microsoft's Word and Corel's WordPerfect, will "mark up" or convert a document into HTML for uploading to your site's server. Different word processors make this happen somewhat differently, but basically, you either click on a menu item that says "send to HTML" or manually save your document in HTML format by finding this option on the [Save] menu. One word of caution however: Make sure that you make a backup copy of your document in case you find that your word processor writes over your original file and it vanishes forever. One way around this is to make certain to rename the file too. My experience is that this kind of conversion is not perfect and still has a way to go. That is, the way my document is laid out as a document does not exactly look the same when converted to HTML for the Web. "Cleaning up" the document while viewing it in HTML, though, is still easier than having to entirely recreate it.

How Do I Get My Site Noticed?

Once your site is up, running, and presentable, you will want to make your hard work pay off. There are several things you can do to publicize your new Web page and its offerings:

• 61 •

- Submit your Web site information to several popular search engines.
- Announce your new Web site to listservs with members who should find your site of particular interest. Realize though that many list-servs do not allow you to post messages unless you are a member of the group. Therefore, you will either have to temporarily subscribe or have the message forwarded by a member of the group that you know. Be aware that if your description sounds as if you are selling a product, this is considered to be "spam" and is virtually always con-sidered inappropriate. Some users who receive spam get angry and sometimes will try to punish you by filling up your e-mail box with tons of unflattering messages and files. Some users will log official complaints with your ISP, which can result in you losing your account. So be certain to emphasize that your site provides free and relevant information.
- Post your site information on relevant news groups. You can identify relevant news groups by conducting a keyword search of news groups using Google (http://groups.google.com/). Then, follow the instructions for posting information to the group. Again, be careful not to accidentally spam your audience.
- You can market your Web site by using flyers, cards, buttons, and so forth at various functions such as conferences, meetings, and in newsletters.
- Announce your site in the local newspaper and relevant community newsletters.
- Create a brochure about your site which can be handed to parents, clients, or interested others at the reception area.
- Include information about your site in your school's handbook, com-munity directories, or any other pertinent sources of communication.

Personal Information Managers

Personal information managers (PIMs) are a type of software application designed to help users organize random bits of information. Although the category is fuzzy, most PIMs enable you to enter various kinds of textual notes—reminders, lists, dates—and to link these bits of information together in useful ways. Many PIMs also include calendar, scheduling, and calculator programs (Webopedia, 2002c). The usefulness of this type of software lies in its ability to integrate data and provide feedback in the form of potential scheduling conflicts and event reminders. The more powerful PIMs can also help with important tasks such as coordinating mutual times of availability for meeting with important others, keeping a journal, managing a to-do list with repetitive reminders, publishing your calendar to the Web for others to review, or using your contact information for mass communication with others. Two quite popular PIMs are Microsoft Outlook and Lotus Notes, both of which provide fantastic tools for managing, collating, processing, and communicating personal (and professional) information. Several online PIMs exist too, some of which are free to use such as http://calendar.yahoo.com, http://planner. excite.com, and http://www.pimonline.com.

One feature of a good personal information manager is that it easily synchronizes all your information with any handheld computer. Of course, the advantage to doing this is that you can then keep your information at your fingertips when you are not at your desk. Also, you have the option of processing information such as adding appointments, contacts, notes, e-mails, or tasks on your handheld computer which you can later synchronize with your desktop computer.

Graphics Editor

In 1921, the idea that a picture is worth a thousand words was born as part of an advertisement agency's attempt to help a company sell baking soda (see http://www.cs.uregina.ca/~hepting/proverbial/history.html) by appealing to women who wanted to make their children happy by baking them treats. More than ever before, technology uses graphics as an integral part of communicating with others, eliciting emotion, and telling a story. Many popular news sources such as CNN, Time magazine, and USA Today maintain photo (and video) galleries to help us visualize and perhaps even vicariously experience various events in history. Capturing, manipulating, and publishing graphics or photos can help counselors in telling their stories, which may be a part of accountability and effectiveness, communication of services, or educating clients about counseling issues to name a few.

Graphics can come from many sources: traditional or digital camera, captured from video, created entirely using a computer, or from a digitized copy of a personal work of art. When creating a digital graphic or photo, you should pay special consideration to the file type in which you save it, which will be influenced by the purpose of your graphic (e.g., putting it on your Web site, including it in a professionally printed newsletter, or printing out an 8 x 10 glossy). To better understand the many different graphic file formats and the advantages and disadvantages of using them, the reader is referred to the following Web resources:

- **http://www.nycenet.edu/oit/multimedia/compare.pdf.** Graphic file format size comparison.
- **http://graphicssoft.about.com.** Graphics software from About.com.
- **http://html.about.com/cs/graphics.** Graphics for the Web—tools/ techniques.

- **http://builder.cnet.com/webbuilding/0-3883.html.** Graphics and multimedia guide from cnet.com.
- **http://members.aol.com/arendsart/pages/infopgs/filetype.html.** Your guide to graphic file formats.

Instead of accepting a graphic as is, you may want to change it somewhat, perhaps even applying some "special effects" to the graphic. To do this you will need a graphics editing program. Such programs allow you to manipulate graphics in thousands of ways from adding text, distorting elements of the graphic, to layering different aspects of many graphics into one graphic. Several top-rated graphics editing programs, many of which include both Windows and Macintosh versions, include Adobe Photoshop, Jasc Paint Shop Pro, Ulead PhotoImpact, Microsoft Picture It!, and Coral Draw.

Summary

Counselors who effectively use productivity software stand to gain valuable assistance, save time, and become more effective—essentially "doing more with less." When used correctly, productivity software can help the counselor to meet high work demands and provide high quality services to clients while facing shrinking resources. It is also quite important to acknowledge that these types of technological tools can help us to stay focused and balanced among our many personal and professional endeavors. In this sense, they can keep us on track to preserving the 40-hour work week as best as possible.

Internet Sites for Additional Information

- **http://www.cnet.com/webbuilding/0-7296-8-3706508-1.html.** This site provides tips and tutorials to help you master Microsoft FrontPage.
- **http://hal.lamar.edu/~luis/WebCT/WebCT_Excel.htm.** Opening a comma-delimited file in Microsoft Excel is explained on this Web site.
- **http://www.adobe.com/print/tips/pmk7boilerplate/main.html.** Readers can learn how to conduct a merge mailing with Adobe Page-Maker to create form letters, envelopes, or mailing labels from records.
- **http://www.macinstruct.com/tutorials/spreadsheets.** This site provides suggestions for sending Excel files to people who use a different spreadsheet or even a database program.
- **http://www.kde.state.ky.us/KDE/About+Schools+and+Districts/ Create+Labels+from+Comma+Delimited+File+Using+WordPerfe ct.htm.** As the address suggests, this site discusses creating labels from comma-delimited files using WordPerfect.
- **http://www.outfront.net/frontpagetechniques.htm.** This site provides great tips and how-to's for FrontPage 98 and FrontPage 2000.
- **http://www.builder.com/Authoring/FrontPage2000.** Tips are given to help you save time and customize FrontPage 2000.

- **http://www.outfront.net/index.html.** Outfront.net is a Microsoft Front-Page learning community with articles, tutorials, a discussion group, and a newsletter—all focused on helping FrontPage 98 and Front-Page 2000 users build sites.
- **http://www.freepolls.com.** A leading provider of free Web site polls.

Statistical Software

Competency: Be able to use computerized statistical packages.

For most counselors, the mention of "statistics" creates a well-conditioned response related to poor math teaching in the past. Today's technology offers the opportunity for anyone to quickly and painlessly analyze information to aid in the decision-making process. Importantly, the ability and willingness to use this technology may be the most important factor in being accountable to self, to clients, and to the profession. Our ability to demonstrate the usefulness or effectiveness of counseling services and programs seems to be, by far, the primary force that drives the allocation of resources needed to maintain our very existence.

Members of other professions, especially educators such as teachers and principals, are expected to demonstrate their accountability by raising achievement on standardized tests. In many states, the ability to demonstrate effectiveness in this manner is directly tied to raises, teacher tenure, and administrator renewal. Until recently, counselors have felt free to focus on their work without the threat of retribution from insurance companies, supervisors, or school systems. However, now counselors in all settings, agencies, communities, and in schools, are increasingly experiencing the effects of an outcome-based world, a world in which limited resources are given to those that can demonstrate the greatest effectiveness and efficiency.

As counselors become more skilled in demonstrating that their work directly affects their clients, budget cuts and layoffs will be more difficult to justify. The key in demonstrating effectiveness lies in the identification of important and relevant data, collection of that data, appropriate analysis, and persuasive reporting of the results. Counselors should not forget, however, that the practice of accountability is also critical to data-driven decision making. The results of data analysis can help counselors to be more confident in how they spend their time, the activities or interventions that they choose to perform, and the focus of those activities. Effective decision making in these areas based on sound information stands to help all involved: Counselors can rest assured that they are making a difference for clients and advancing their own job security; clients gain quality interventions in a timely manner; and the profession gains strength and prestige.

Technology Competency 3 from the ACES Technology Interest Network (1999)—"Be able to use computerized statistical packages"—was first developed with the intent that counselors had the knowledge and ability to collect or import data, analyze the data, use the data to confidently make decisions about their work, and/or report the data to others. The ability to perform these tasks is not limited to using software designed specifically for statistical analysis; in fact, these tasks can sometimes be more appropriately and easily performed by other similar software. Thus, this chapter shows how database and spreadsheet software, and other similar software such as treatment planners, can accomplish the same goals. This class of software will be referred to throughout this chapter as data processing software.

How Do Counselors Use Data Processing Software?

The following examples come from five main sources: the authors' personal experiences, our experiences working with other counselors throughout the country regarding technology in counseling, counseling-related listservs, the related professional literature, and from our ideas about how these tools can potentially be used. Counselors have used data processing software to:

- Analyze pre- and posttest data from psychoeducational group interventions to evaluate effectiveness.
- Analyze information about differences in standardized test scores between different grade level teams to determine whether the differences are statistically significant and a possible cause for concern.
- Develop empirically supported reports to demonstrate that students participating in peer helper programs have decreased referrals and increased grades after 6 months in the program.
- Determine optimal duration of treatment as part of individual counseling using a specific approach or as part of a program that espouses a particular counseling philosophy and accompanying techniques.
- Advocate for students who are systematically kept out of educational opportunities such as college preparatory courses (Stone & Turba, 1999).
- Conduct time and task analysis. For instance, Hughes and James (2001) wrote about how they created a report that demonstrated (a) how much time one school counselor dedicated to various tasks, including both direct and indirect counseling interventions, and (b) how the report caught the attention and promoted insight among site-based council members.
- Alert clients who may be at risk for failure. At the press of a button or perhaps automatically scheduled, school counselors, for instance, can set up an early detection system that alerts them to students who may be in trouble. A computerized statistical package or related database program can report data regarding discipline records, attendance, significant increases or decreases in GPA over time, or it can simply identify students who might require extra attention such as

new students to the school or students returning after extended absences from rehabilitation or incarceration.

- Use relevant data to reinforce and support student successes or special events such as birthdays, high test scores, or meeting behavior expectations.
- Consult with teachers. School counselors can identify teachers who may be writing a disproportionate number of discipline referrals or who have students with significantly lower grades, for instance.
- Select from their caseload individuals who may be good candidates for group counseling on the basis of certain criteria such as a diagnosis. Once selected, the same data processing software can then be used to schedule group membership on the basis of other variables to best meet membership criteria (e.g., age, sex, SES, race, grade level).

Types of Data Processing Software

In a survey designed in part to determine the types of technology being used and by whom, Lundberg and Cobitz (1999) reported that the use of both desktop-based spreadsheets (e.g., Excel, Lotus) and mainframe-based spreadsheets (e.g., SAS, SPSS; these programs are now available in popular desktop-based versions for Windows and Mac) was considered effective. The term "spreadsheet" (with appropriate examples) was chosen as a concise term, although it is not a perfect descriptor of all these statistical applications. According to Cabaniss (2002), although deemed quite important, the use of statistical packages and related software for accountability purposes seems to be the least used among all available technologies because of a lack of skill associated with using them. Therefore, she concluded, it is important first for counselor educators to include the use of statistical software in counselor training and second for counselors to make using such software a part of their professional development training. The good news is that collecting and analyzing data has become much easier since the not-so-long-ago days of punch cards, coding, and programming. Today's data processing packages allow users to easily enter or import data and then point and click to appropriate statistical procedures ranging from simple percentages, central tendencies (mean, median, mode), to full-scale regression models. Also, and perhaps more exciting, such software typically includes "statistic coaches" that help users determine the most appropriate procedures for analyzing data by asking a series of questions about the nature of the data and types of analyses needed.

SPSS/SAS

The most pervasive software tool today for analyzing data is Statistical Package for the Social Sciences (SPSS; www.spss.com) and Statistical Analysis Software (SAS; www.sas.com). Using powerful statistics, both of these programs can help you to understand and effectively present your results with high-quality tabular and graphical output and share your results with others using a variety of reporting methods including secure Web publishing. Because of the popularity of these programs, users enjoy a large array of technical support options that provide practical answers to frequently asked question, related tutorials including movies, and more (e.g., see http://www.ats.ucla.edu/stat/spss). One disadvantage of these programs is their cost, which, even with an academic discount, can total $600 or more. However, the cost may be justified if the program is centrally located and accessible by all personnel in an agency, community, or school. Better yet, an institution may choose to purchase a network version which can then be accessed by any computer over a network.

Spreadsheets and Databases

A less costly yet effective alternative to statistical packages such as SPSS and SAS are spreadsheets and databases. You probably already have a copy of both of these on your computer because these programs are typically a part of a suite of programs (word processor, spreadsheet, database, multimedia, and Web authoring) such as Microsoft Office, Corel Office, AppleWorks, or IBM's Lotus software suite that are usually included with the purchase of a computer.

Spreadsheets such as Microsoft Excel comprise tables of values arranged in rows and columns. Each value can have a predefined relationship to the other values. If you change one value, therefore, you may need to change other values as well. According to the Webopedia (www.webopedia.com), each value sits in a cell. You can define what type of data is in each cell and how different cells depend on one another. The relationships between cells are called formulas, and the names of the cells are called labels. Once you have defined the cells and the formulas for linking them together, you can enter your data. You can then modify selected values to see how all the other values change accordingly. This enables you to study various "what if" scenarios. More powerful spreadsheet applications (including all the ones previously mentioned) support graphics features that enable you to produce charts and graphs from the data. Most spreadsheet applications are multidimensional, which means that multiple spreadsheets can be linked together such that a change made in one spreadsheet will automatically be reflected in other spreadsheets.

Database programs operate similarly to spreadsheet programs but are more desirable when the user needs to quickly select desired pieces of data, such as if you were using an electronic filing system. Database programs are useful for organizing and managing large amounts of data and somewhat less useful than spreadsheets for performing calculations or statistics. More often than not, data is selected and exported from a database to be analyzed in statistical analysis or spreadsheet software. Relational databases deserve special mention because they allow the user to "link" pieces of data together so that, for instance, parts of a form are automatically completed because the database program will "look up" already available fields.

Qualitative Analysis Software

Qualitative analysis uses unstructured data (text, visual images, and interviews) to examine relationships that cannot be easily explained through quantitative analysis. The purpose of qualitative analysis is twofold: it allows the counselor to become familiar with the phenomena being studied, and it allows the counselor to formulate a new explanation by examining the phenomena's interrelationships. This process is conducted by data collection, coding according to given words or symbols, and then running analyses to make inferences. According to a George Mason University Library Web site, the following are popular qualitative analysis software programs and accompanying descriptions:

- **Nudist Nvivo**: This program allows the researcher flexibility in how information is stored and edited, provides a model component for those who are visually inclined, as well as coding and analysis systems that allow for maximum user-friendly applicants. It also includes hyperlinks to pictures or images, internal and external databites, and a memo system to store ideas and concepts while using it.
- **Decision Explorer**: Decision Explorer provides flexibility in models so researchers have a chance to explore phenomena as a whole or in parts visually through concept mapping. Concept mapping helps researchers obtain a better idea of phenomenon construction through identifying and linking concepts together: therefore, concept maps are used to examine an overall question or a question that may only appear at one stage during the investigative process. Decision Explorer has the ability to import data from Nvivo, export to Nvivo, or to create a fresh model.
- **Atlas-ti**: This program is a visually oriented qualitative analysis program. This program is similar to Nvivo. It is often used in group work and easy to learn.
- **C-I-SAID**: A multimedia qualitative analysis software. This program combines the analysis of text, video images, audio, and still images. It performs many analysis including lexical and rating scale.
- **Ethnograph**: Ethnograph is a text based qualitative analysis program. This program offers minimal options for analysis and is the easiest program to learn.
- **OmniPage Pro**: OmniPage Pro is used with a scanner to input printed text and images into the computer. This type of scanning is useful if the researcher is conducting open-ended survey for participants to write in their responses or if researchers have visuals that they wish to accompany a project. (From http://library.gmu.edu/srs/qualsoft.html#Nudist%20Nvivo; reprinted with permission.)

Clinical Record-Keeping Software

Today's clinical record-keeping software such as Therascribe (see http://www.wiley.com/legacy/products/subject/psychology/therascribe/) not only guides the counselor through each stage of the treatment process (e.g., intake and assessment, treatment planning, and progress monitoring), but also helps to conduct outcomes analysis. Dr. Martin Briscoe of the Royal College of Psychiatrists maintains the "Computers in Mental Health" Web site (http://www.ex.ac.uk/cimh), which includes a database of software, including data processing software, that promises to help counselors manage and process important information about their work.

• Technology Tip 4.1 •

Visit the Therascribe Web site at http://www.wiley.com/legacy/products/ subject/psychology/therascribe/ to download a free biopsychosocial history intake form.

Data Alphabet Soup

All data processing software files are created in a format native to the program used to create them. Using data from another source (such as an individual or your agency or school) that does not use the same software as you will require that you import the data. Similarly, you may have to save your data in a different format to share with others who do not use the same software as you. Fortunately, today's data processing programs can import and save data in a variety of formats. For example, in Microsoft Excel, you would choose File, Import, then select the file you want to import. Excel will run you through a wizard that will ask you to specify the type of file being imported and then help you to properly import it. After you complete the import wizard, you will be able to save and use the open file in Excel format.

• Technology Tip 4.2 •

If you have a comma-delimited text file, change the file extension to .xls to associate the file with Microsoft Excel. Instead of importing it, you should be able to simply open it as if it were an Excel spreadsheet.

Following is a description of several common formats that you can use with any typical statistical analysis, database, or spreadsheet program, and what you need to know to be able to use them:

- **Comma-delimited files**, also known as comma separated values, consist of pieces of data separated by a comma. When a data processor encounters a comma, it moves the next piece of data into the next field. Fields that include a comma in them, such as an address, are surrounded in quotes which let the computer know to ignore the comma as a field delimiter. These files often end in CSV, TXT, or DAT. The results from online surveys are often saved as TXT or CSV files.
- **Tab-delimited files** are the same as comma-delimited files except that instead of being delimited by a comma, they are delimited by a tab. These files also typically end in CSV, TXT, or DAT.

- **Fixed width files** are files with fields of information that begin and end in certain columns. For instance, columns 1–16 may include a client's name, columns 17–24 may include the client's birth date, and so on. To import these files, you must indicate in which columns fields begin and end. Programs such as Microsoft Excel allow you to view the data and simply move lines to the left or right that indicate in which column the fields begin and end. These files may end in TXT, ASC, CSV, or whatever the user chooses to save it as.
- **Database files**, usually ending in DBF, are rudimentary database files that can be opened and understood by most of today's database programs. Spreadsheets will recognize a DBF file and allow it to be imported similar to the comma-delimited file.

Other Methods for Collecting Data

In addition to importing existing data or manually entering the data yourself, technology has now afforded counselors several alternative and viable methods for collecting information. Although some of these methods are more advanced than others, they all continue to become more sophisticated, more user-friendly, and increasingly inexpensive.

Online

A school counselor was interested in conducting an ongoing annual survey about specific student competencies to better understand how her work was affecting student progress. Interested in the nature of his agency's clientele, a mental health counselor and his team conducted a survey given to all clients entering the building as part of the intake process. In both cases, the survey was available on a secure password-protected Web site. Survey participants sit in front of a computer connected either to the organization's intranet or to the Internet and answer questions by selecting from a menu of choices and entering any other comments. In the case of the school counselor, she e-mailed the faculty the Web site address and asked teachers to take students to the computer lab to complete the survey. After completing the survey, they then had a chance to take part in an online classroom guidance unit about career choices.

Online surveys come with many advantages. For one, data is stored and collated immediately after the respondent clicks on the Submit button. With one or two clicks of the mouse, the counselor can perform analyses or create graphs of the data at any time during collection, getting a snapshot of the results as they come in. Second, the time for the entire process is significantly diminished, especially if the same survey is periodically conducted over time. Third, an online survey can be conducted with only a few people in one locale or the entire planet over the World Wide Web. Barriers of space, place, and time become greatly lessened. Also, online surveys can include an array of multimedia elements including sound, animation, and photos, thus making them more interesting to the respondents and perhaps increasing response rates. Finally, copies of the results of an online survey can be sent to more than one person or place, which facilitates collaboration among the counselor and others such as interested researchers who can help with the analysis.

Some counselors have discovered that they can create an online survey if they have learned how to use the forms capabilities of a Web authoring program such as Microsoft FrontPage or Macromedia DreamWeaver. These programs make creating surveys as easy as word processing. Other counselors find that using online Web survey services, some free and some for a nominal fee, requires minimal skills and provide excellent results. Conducting an Internet search using the key phrase "online survey" will demonstrate the popularity of this method. Several companies have provided free online survey development capabilities, usually limited in power and scope as compared with the purchased versions. However, even the free versions have proven sufficient for counselors who want to survey a limited number of clients. Many of these sites also provide the ability to conduct analyses online or download the data for importing into your own software such as a spreadsheet. Such sites include www.zoomerang.com, http://www.surveymonkey.com, http://www.quia.com, http://www.freeonlinesurveys.com, and http://or.psychology.dal.ca/~wcs/hidden/home.html.

Several possible disadvantages exist for conducting online surveys. Of course, if the desired respondents do not have access to an Internet-enabled computer, they cannot participate. Because of limited access to computers and the Internet, another disadvantage might be that the sample of participants may not be truly representative of the population under study. Providing access in a mental health agency or school for instance would minimize this problem. Another possible threat to validity is the sometimes limited control over who responds to an online survey. For instance, without proper controls, participants could respond more than once or perhaps may more easily misrepresent their identity. Password protecting an online survey could help although may not solve this problem with exact confidence. Some online services may help with this problem by attempting to identify and track respondents to a given survey. Finally, respondents may encounter technical problems either with their computer, with access to the survey, or with a glitch in the survey itself that could hinder appropriate data collection procedures. In general, however, most people would agree that conducting surveys online provides powerful advantages that make this option quite attractive.

Handheld Computers

Handheld computers, also known as personal digital assistants (PDAs), promise to overhaul the way in which we collect and process data. What once could only be conducted over stationary desktop computers can now be handled by a device that literally fits in the palm of your hand. Handheld computers make data collection even more convenient than laptops because they are much smaller in size, significantly less expensive, and require a much shorter time to turn on and begin the survey process. For instance, during a measles vaccination campaign in Ghana in October 2001, the Ghana Red Cross was able to complete a complex survey of 2,500 caretakers, in 60 different sites, with no data translation errors. The objectives of the survey were to measure the impact of Ghana Red Cross social mobilization efforts and demonstrate the feasibility of using handheld computers for such surveys. The survey required two days of training and three days of field work, with in-country costs of less than $2,000. Analyzed results were given to the Ministry of Health at the end of the fifth day. This study demonstrated that community-based volunteers using handheld computers can quickly, accurately, and inexpensively conduct complex assessments. These results can be made available to decision-makers within hours of completion of the study. The secret of the Red Cross's success was collecting data on handheld computers and synchronizing them to a database kept on a laptop computer. After two days of training, the volunteers, many of whom had never seen a computer before, spent three days interviewing over 2,400 parents who had brought their children for vaccination (Donna, 2002).

Handheld versions of many of the popular database and spreadsheet programs already exist. Additionally, some software has now been developed for certain PDAs specifically designed for conducting surveys (e.g., see http://www.pocketsurvey.co.uk, http://www.handheld-systems.net, and http://www.pocket-surveys.com). Data collected using a PDA can easily be transferred to a desktop computer using the accompanying software and hardware for more extensive analysis and reporting. Today's handhelds can also easily upload data to another user hundreds or even thousands of miles away using a wireless Internet connection.

•   Technology Tip 4.3   •

Instead of purchasing expensive survey software for your PDA, consider setting up your own using a lesser expensive spreadsheet or database program such as the one found at http://5star.freeserve.com/Palm/BusinessandFinance/quicksheet.html.

Voice-to-Text Recognition

When survey respondents do not have ready access to computers, data is typically collected by paper and pencil and then manually entered, or "keyed," into a computer. Early attempts at data entry automation made use of machine-readable punch cards, although the process was replete with limitations and errors. In the last 30 years or so, many other methods for collecting data have become available that have ushered in new standards for automation and accuracy. These methods are important when clients, students, parents, or others do not have ready access to a computer. At the same time, counselors and researchers are finding that qualitative data, especially collected by conducting interviews, can sometimes better capture the answers to important questions. An emerging technology that facilitates obtaining qualitative data is voice-to-text technology. A counselor can use a digital voice recorder to record a participant's responses to a survey. Then, he or she plugs the recorder into his or her computer to create a transcript of the recording. After checking the transcript for accuracy, the counselor then uses special software to conduct appropriate analyses and reports. The accuracy of voice-to-text software has witnessed major progress in the last several years, boasting accuracy percentages in the mid to upper 90s. Also exciting is that digital voice recorders have come down in price and are currently available for under $200.

"Bubble Sheets" or Scantrons

If paper-and-pencil surveys are desirable and appropriate, technology still makes available another method for automated data entry. Instead of manually transferring data from paper to computer, you can have a scanner "read" input from a special sheet of paper often referred to as a bubble sheet or Scranton (this is technically called optical mark recognition, or OMR). These are the same sheets that you probably became accustomed to while in school, as many multiple choice exams are scored by using bubble sheets. Historically, using these bubble sheets required a specific piece of hardware, known as an OMR scanner or by the popular trade name "Scantron." For complete functionality, the Scantron machine must be connected to a computer that contains software allowing the two machines to communicate, and allowing the computer to analyze the data received.

Different scanners will work with different types of bubble sheets. Some scanners can read a great deal of data in a short amount of time because they simultaneously read both sides of a given bubble sheet. Other scanning software programs such as Remark OMR (http://www.principiaproducts. com/office) can read filled-in bubbles, check boxes and even bar codes. Of course, the obvious disadvantage of this method of data collection is that the requisite hardware, software, and blank bubble sheets can be quite expensive. Also, survey respondents may make errors when transferring their answers from surveys or questionnaires to the bubble sheets.

However, the industry has recognized these limitations and has arisen to the occasion by developing new software which allows the counselor to (a) design their own surveys on their computers including questions and room for responses, and (b) scan the created surveys using a simple and relatively inexpensive document scanner. For instance, the aforementioned Remark OMR allows you to design your own forms using any word processor, print them on your printer, scan and recognize data with your off-the-shelf image scanner, and then analyze or export the data to the application of your choice. A similar suite of software is Bubble Publishing from Scanning Dynamics, Inc. (see http://www.scantron.com/). Distinct advantages of these software products are that they are cost efficient, make creating customizable surveys very easy, and reduce the human error rate by placing survey items right next to the response bubbles.

PDF Surveys

Portable Document Format (PDF) is a file format developed by Adobe Systems which captures formatting information from a variety of desktop publishing applications. This software makes it possible to send formatted documents and have them appear on the recipient's monitor or printer as they were intended. In other words, people viewing a PDF file (or document) with the free reader (download the Adobe Acrobat Reader from www.adobe.com) see the document with the exact layout intended by the author. This is its main advantage over other electronic formats such as HTML, where the layout can vary depending on the software being used to view it. If your document contains particularities such as graphics, columns, tables, charts, and multiple colors, the PDF format is highly desirable. If so intended, PDF files can also contain hyperlinks that take you to specific locations on the Web or another place in the document. Advanced forms of PDF files may also contain forms that allow readers to enter customized information which is then integrated into a printable document. Using the Adobe Acrobat software, it is also possible to create forms containing form fields. After a user completes the form and then clicks on "Submit," the data can then be captured into a special file called a Forms Data Format (FDF) file. After the FDF file is created, you can let another application process it and enter the data into a database with the information. The primary advantage of using PDF files to collect data is that PDF files are popular and well-known to many users. However, a significant disadvantage exists in that the procedure requires a high level of skill to set up. Then again, some software now exists that makes the procedure easier and more autonomous (e.g., see http://www.pdfsoft. com/VPDFSoft/Products/plugins/XeMailing.html).

Tips and Recommendations

Accountability and data-driven decision making is a vital part of being a professional counselor. Technology is meant to extend our human abilities to collect and make sense of relevant data in an accurate and timely manner. Following are recommendations that we are confident will make your experience easier and more pleasant.

Choosing a Statistical Package

The range of applications available to assist the counselor in data processing activities is quite large. Many counselors will be best served by using software that meets their needs without going well beyond these needs. Although more powerful applications with greater flexibility may have greater utility in the future, they also tend to be more difficult to learn, are often more expensive, and may lead to a higher level of frustration for the beginner. Avoiding frustration and increasing ease of use are legitimate goals. Table 4.1 presents a number of topics to be used when considering purchasing or learning new statistical applications. By understanding your own needs, you will be better able to choose software that is appropriate. For a more detailed discussion of specific software packages in relation to these needs, visit http://iris4.chem.ohiou.edu/software.html.

Work with Your Local College

Counselor educators have several needs that lend themselves well to collaborating with counselors for conducting all types of research concerning your work. First, conducting research is an important part of many counselor educators' jobs. For many, it is a scholarly endeavor of particular interest, whereas for others it may be a less desirable condition of employment for which they are duly evaluated. Second, counselor educators are interested in providing their preservice students with valuable and realistic learning experiences. Helping you with the accountability and decision-making process can often become part of a supervised class assignment in which students and instructor collaborate with you by providing guidance and much needed help.

Plan Ahead

Although it is still possible to use data after the fact (e.g., conducting retrospective pre- and posttest projects; see Myrick, 1990; Sabella, Thomas, & Myrick, 1995), you should plan ahead for the types of data, both quantitative and qualitative, that you will require to answer questions about who you work with, how you conduct your work, where counseling happens, and so forth. Similarly, you should plan ahead for obtaining any instruments, permissions, facilities, or other needed provisions. Some types of

---

Table 4.1

Using Your Needs to Determine Which
Statistical Software Package to Purchase and Learn

---

1. Consider the class of data analysis to be performed. Do you require only simple statistics? Univariate or multivariate techniques? Do you require qualitative analysis?
2. Consider the level and type of data to be analyzed. Will your data sets be primarily continuous or discrete? Nominal, ordinal, interval, or ratio?
3. Consider the type of research. Do you primarily engage in survey or experimental research?
4. Consider the length of a typical project. Will you collect data over a long period of time and analyze it all at once, or will you need to analyze data at several points?
5. Consider your goals. Do you want to describe a phenomenon that is observed, or will you attempt to predict some future occurrence?
6. Consider your knowledge level. Do you have the background and skill set to collect and process data independently, or do you need software that will guide you through the process?

Note: This table was adapted from Currall, J. (1991).

accountability may continue on an ongoing basis such as studying the longitudinal effects of certain programs or treatments on relevant client characteristics. Similarly, you may have questions about your work that are relevant year after year such as, "How effective are my peer mediators at resolving conflict?" "What is the attendance rate for students in my school who have registered no more than three months ago?" "How does the stress level of counselors working in the crisis stabilization unit compare with those who work in other departments?" or "What are the top three presenting problems among clients or other stakeholders?" These types of efforts should only require minor adjustments, whereas other questions may require more forethought and preparation.

Use Relevant Existing Data

Agencies and schools collect ongoing data as part of their necessary daily operations. For example, schools routinely collect data about students' attendance, behavior, grades, test scores, teacher assignment, career interests, and demographics. Mental health agencies may regularly collect data by way of their intake procedures (e.g., biopsychosocial intake). The time-consuming and sometimes tedious work of data collection and input in these instances is already complete. Some institutions or agencies may already have, as part of a computer interface, a menu option to download specific data fields to disk.

Use Templates and Plug-Ins

Templates are files that serve as models or standardized formats for various applications—most commonly word processing and spreadsheets. In spreadsheet and database applications, a template is a blank form that shows which fields exist, their locations, and their length. In spreadsheet applications, for example, a template is a spreadsheet in which all the cells have been defined but no data has been entered (www.webopedia.com). They are meant to support consistency and data integrity, especially when data is being entered by more than one person in an organization or institution. Templates are also time-savers when they include macros or other programming that automates various data entry and presentation processes (e.g., the invoicing template that comes with Microsoft Excel allows the user to automatically add an invoice number). Templates can come from at least four sources: (a) you can create them, (b) you can ask other counselors to send them to you, (c) you can use the templates that come with your software, or (d) you may search and find available templates on the Internet.

After you have created a database form or spreadsheet that you anticipate using over and over again, complete with formatting and formulas, you should store it as a template. Templates are difficult to overwrite. That is, after you open a template and begin to add data, you will be forced to save it under a new name instead of saving it "over" the template file. In this way, your template will provide you with a standard look and function each time you use it. To save a file as a template, choose the template format in the File Type drop down menu which you see when saving your file for the first time (if you decide to save your file as a template after you have already saved it at least once, choose File and then Save As). If you need to make changes to a template in Microsoft Excel or many other programs, it will be saved as a new template.

•   Technology Tip 4.4   •

Check out Microsoft's Template Gallery at http://search.officeupdate. microsoft.com/TemplateGallery/ for downloadable Excel (and other) templates. For example, you can find detailed invoices, grade books, surveys, and expense reports too. Microsoft now also has a set of templates designed especially for health care workers at http://office.microsoft.com/assistance/ 2002/articles/healthcare.aspx.

If you are aware of other counselors (or noncounselors for that matter) who have developed templates that could be useful to you, you might ask to have them sent to you. If what they have is a regular spreadsheet file, for instance, you can save it into a template format file after you receive it. According to the Help program in Microsoft Excel, if you are using Microsoft Windows 95 or later, or Microsoft Windows NT version 4.0 or later, you can make a custom template available to others with whom you work by storing the template on a network location. For example, you might want all users in your workgroup to use a custom template for a special project without having to place individual copies of the template on each desktop. Instead, place the template in a folder in a network location that is accessible by all users in your group. Then create a shortcut to the folder or template, and have users place the shortcut in their Templates folder.

Finally, today's data processing software also comes with templates that many people find valuable, such as invoices, purchase orders, and expense reports. In addition, companies that manufacture office suites typically have available a library of templates and other helpful files for their products (e.g., http://officeupdate.microsoft.com/templategallery). Other software developers sometimes provide free and inexpensive templates (e.g., http://www.villagesoft.com/msprods) and plug-ins (e.g., http://www.mathtools.net/Excel) over the Internet. A plug-in is a software module that adds a specific feature or service such as increased number of mathematical functions to a larger system such as Microsoft Excel. Once you obtain and install a plug-in, the added features become choices on the main system's menu.

You Don't Have to Enter the Data

Why not get clients, students, and other stakeholders to enter data regarding their own progress in treatment or as part of a school counseling program? In fact, entering data and getting instant results in the form of graphs can be a significant part of the treatment plan. Clients can, quite immediately, view trends and other graphical depictions of changes over time that can point to progress or sticky points in treatment.

Use Online Tutorials

Attending a course or other training opportunity for learning how to use data processing software can take time and money, resources that counselors often do not have. Yet becoming competent in using these powerful tools can make a vital difference in how you can effectively and efficiently make decisions and be accountable. You can download practical tip sheets and fully illustrated guidebooks over the Internet, many of which are free. For example, the following Web sites provide valuable resources:

- www.unt.edu/training/Office2000/Excel2000.pdf
- www.nerdybooks.com/books/pdf/Excel_2000_25_pages.pdf
- www.immex.ucla.edu/ProfDevelopment/sec07-xl.pdf
- www.nahu.org/member/using%20excel%20to%20create%20lists%20and%20labels.pdf
- www.leeds.ac.uk/iss/documentation/tut/tut46.pdf
- www.microsoft.com/education/?ID=IOCTutorials

Use Data Processing Across Other Applications

Data that is included in spreadsheet, database, and statistical software can easily be used or imported in other applications to help make the best use of your work. Common applications may include using your word processor to print labels using name and address fields in a spreadsheet. You can also merge information from a data processing program into specific areas throughout a report that you create using your word processor. Data can be linked to graphs as part of your multimedia software for presentation to either a live audience or others to whom you send the file. When appropriate and desirable, you can even present aggregated data over a Web site by saving your file in the Web page format (i.e., HTML).

Summary

Technology can greatly assist counselors in collecting, managing, processing, and using data to make decisions and communicate to others how their work affects their clients. However, technology cannot compensate for resistance among counselors to perform this important function. Counselors must gain and maintain competency in basic survey design and methodology that works in their respective settings. Some counselors may be resistant because they have mistakenly assumed that accountability studies are aimed at evaluating them as either good or poor counselors. These counselors must realize that being accountable means taking more responsibility for evaluating objectives, procedures, and outcomes. It involves an explanation of what is being done and providing data to support any claims that are made. Accountability requires some form of evidence on which to make decisions or judgments (Myrick, 1990). The original intent of Technology Competency 3 was to make certain that counselors understand and know how to deal with data, especially analyzing data in a way that makes sense and is useful. However, modern off-the-shelf productivity suites such as Microsoft Office include all the requisite tools to collect, analyze, and report data. Such software even comes with "coaches" that can suggest procedures on the basis of your data collection design. This chapter provided an overview of various data processing software and included practical tips and suggestions for making these tools a part of your work day.

Internet Sites for Additional Information

- **http://www.mathtools.net/Applications/Statistics/Excel.** An excellent list of Microsoft Excel add-ons is provided to help with accountability.
- **http://www.mrexcel.com.** MrExcel.com is an entire community of Excel power users who are dedicated to helping you unleash the power of Excel.
- **http://www.j-walk.com/ss/index.htm.** This site has lots of great Excel references, downloads, and tips.
- **http://s9000.furman.edu/mellonj/spss1.htm.** Written by Gil Einstein and Ken Abernethy, this site contains seven tutorial lessons for SPSS 10.0.
- **http://www.hmdc.harvard.edu/projects/SPSS_Tutorial/spsstut. shtml.** Another wonderful tutorial for using SPSS, this one is from the Harvard MIT Data Center.
- **http://www.ace.net.nz/tech/TechFileFormat.html.** Almost every file format in the world is provided on this site!
- **http://www.ed.gov/offices/OESE/SASA/eb/index.html.** This page from the U.S. Department of Education is dedicated to Evidence-Based Education (EBE) and includes PowerPoints and PDFs.
- **http://www.microsoft.com/education/default.asp?ID=Excel97 Tutorial.** Explore the powerful features of Microsoft Excel 97 to simplify data research and organization by using worksheets and charts. This page will allow you to download a complete book (in parts) designed in Microsoft Word!
- **http://nces.ed.gov/nceskids/graphing/.** Create graphs online. Here you will find four different graphs and charts for you to consider.
- **http://www.mercator.co.uk/software/softwaresnappda.shtml.** Survey software: PDA Interviewer Module may be used to conduct surveys using PDAs.
- **http://www.syncsurvey.com/art/handheld-surveys.** SyncSurvey allows people to conduct surveys on their PDAs and then view results while connected to the Internet.

- **http://www.surveystudents.com.** Description of a variety of research tools including Web-based and intercept surveys as well as online and on-site focus group facilitation for schools, colleges, universities, and their business partners.
- **http://www.alliance.brown.edu/pubs/hischlrfm/datdrv_hsrfm.pdf.** This link is to Mary Ann Lachat's "Data-Driven High School Reform: The Breaking Ranks Model.

5

Technology and Assessment

Competency: Be able to use computerized testing, diagnostic, and career decision-making programs with clients.

Computers are particularly useful as tools to complete repetitive tasks, freeing the user to focus time and energy elsewhere. One area in the counseling process that involves a high level of repetition is assessment. Many assessment instruments involve time-consuming administration. Computer technology can be used to automate this process, resulting in substantial time savings. Further, the often tedious scoring process involved in some assessment work can be completely automated, resulting in fast, reliable scoring. In spite of these potential advantages, the application of computers in the arena of assessment has been slow to develop.

Perhaps this is due in part to the fact that the advent of computerized testing brings with it a host of new challenges as well as opportunities for counselors and other mental health professionals. Although there are a multitude of concerns related to using computerized test administration or interpretation programs, including ethical, technical, financial, and legal, there are many ways to address these concerns. This chapter will present an overview of these issues and make recommendations to help the reader address the issues in a professionally appropriate manner.

Computerized Versus Internet-Based Assessment

To begin, a distinction must be made between computerized and Internet-based assessment: Computerized assessment is a general term that is taken to include any form of psychological test or assessment instrument that is administered and/or interpreted by computer software. Internet-based assessment, on the other hand, is a particular form of computerized assessment that relies on computers or servers on the Internet for some component of the assessment process. Use of the Internet in this manner brings with it an additional set of considerations and opportunities.

A number of steps have been taken by various professional organizations to promote the ethical use of assessment materials that are computer and/or Internet based. The National Career Development Association (NCDA, 1997) adopted the Guidelines for the Use of the Internet for Provision of Career Information and Planning Services (available online at

---

This chapter was coauthored by Chris Abears at Wayne State University, J. Michael Tyler, and Russell A. Sabella.

http://www.ncda.org/about/polnet.html), which includes specific material related to online work and career assessment. The Association for Assessment in Counseling has made some efforts in this area as well (Lundberg, 2001).

The American Psychological Association (APA; www.apa.org) may currently be the best positioned to create comprehensive standards, having established the Task Force on Psychological Testing on the Internet. The purpose of the Task Force is to assess the current state of Internet testing and examine the issues raised, including test validity, psychometric equivalence, administration, confidentiality, test-taker authenticity, ethical interpretations of test results, copyright infringement, licensure issues when crossing state lines, and making interpretations on limited assessment information, among others. (American Psychological Association, 2002b).

The task force raises a number of important issues to be considered by practitioners, some of which are specific to Internet-based testing and others that are applicable to all forms of computerized testing. This chapter examines a number of issues that have been raised by the task force and others, and offers recommendations to address specific concerns.

Psychometric Properties of Computer-Based Assessment Instruments

When considering the use of computer-based assessment materials, as with more traditional materials, the psychometric properties of the instruments and procedures are critical. However, computer-based instruments may present additional issues related to psychometrics that must also be considered. Often the answers available from test publishers or Web sites will be insufficient, and individual practitioners will be forced to rely on their own judgment and knowledge of psychometrics to determine what instruments or services are appropriate for their needs.

In the rapid move to develop more computer-based assessment tools, there has in some cases been a willingness to forego standard validation and norming procedures. In other instances, computerized versions of instruments have been developed on the basis of the norms established with the traditional paper version of an instrument. In other cases, no attempt has been made to establish the psychometric equivalence between various formats of an instrument. This failure to establish the psychometric properties of these alternate versions of tests is clearly a weakness in much current practice.

• Technology Tip 5.1 •

Remember that not all clients are appropriate users of computerized testing and assessment, even if the assessment procedure would be appropriate in a traditional paper version. Always consider the combination of client and procedure together.

Following is a list of questions to ask when examining the psychometric properties of a computerized test:

- **Are the psychometric properties available for examination?** Practitioners need to always examine the psychometric properties of new instruments they are considering using to ensure that the instrument meets the claims of the publishers, meets the needs of the clinician, and is appropriate for the individual client. In many cases, particularly with Internet tests, psychometric properties are not readily available to the clinician. In some cases this information is only available for a fee, while in other cases the information is not available and may not exist. Anytime the practitioner cannot independently review the psychometric properties of an instrument, extreme caution should be taken. Generally, if this information is unavailable, practitioners are advised to seek alternate assessment materials.

- **Are the properties and norms presented based on the computerized version that will be used, or are they based on traditional forms of the test?** In clinical settings, it should not be assumed that a test that has been adapted for computer-based administration retains the psychometric properties of the original version. Changes in the user interface and user experience may alter responding in unexpected ways. Norms should be developed specifically for the form of administration being used, and for the specific client population represented.

- **Has there been any research published in peer reviewed journals on the test?** When the research is published in a peer reviewed journal *and* reports adequate psychometric properties, the clinician can be relatively confident that conclusions about the test based on the research provided are accurate. Single research articles should not be seen as definitive information about a test, however. The best instruments will have been used in multiple studies by multiple authors. Multiple studies will often result in slightly conflicting results. Clinicians must then use their own professional knowledge to understand the discrepancy in findings, and determine how these findings relate to their own professional needs. As with traditional assessment instruments, the more research available, the more confident one can be in using a particular online or computer-based instrument in clinical practice.

- **Will a computer-based version increase consistency in administration and scoring, or offer other advantages?** One advantage of computerized tests is that virtually all administrations of the test are identical. This reduces variability in test administration due to human error and therefore moves the consistency of administration to a new level. One of the exceptions to this increased reliability in administration, however, arises from technological difficulties such as the computer "freezing" or "crashing." Thus, maintaining well-functioning computer systems that are properly configured will reduce these problems significantly.

- **Does the client have the skills necessary to have a successful experience with a computer-based instrument?** A potential problem in administration may result from clients failing to understand responding procedures, or lacking computer skills. Clients will need to have a reasonable comfort level with the technology and appropriate skills if the assessment is to obtain accurate information. For a broader discussion of this topic, see chapter 9 and the discussion of helping clients use computers and the Internet.
- **Will the use of computer-based instruments contribute to spurious or inaccurate results?** If the test being administered via computer is a "state" measure—that is, sensitive to emotional states, such as the State Trait Anxiety Index (STAI)—then the test administration could be invalidated by technological difficulties. As an example, a slow Internet connection while taking an Internet test may contribute to a sense of frustration experienced by the test taker. In this instance, technological concerns may invalidate an otherwise valid and appropriate assessment instrument.
- **Has the integrity of the test been maintained?** Online and computer-based assessment instruments are more difficult to protect than traditional paper tests. Temporary files created on computers unintentionally capture information that can later be retrieved by computer users. More advanced users who are interested in obtaining copies of assessment instruments can use specific software designed to capture screen images, keystrokes, and passwords. This potential security threat raises the possibility that some assessment instruments may be available to clients long before they complete them as part of a therapeutic or counseling process. In many cases, there is no particular benefit to be gained, and it is hard to imagine reasons that clients would seek out such information in advance. However, in cases where clients have been mandated to enter counseling as part of a court proceeding, school disciplinary procedure, or other adverse circumstance, knowledge of assessment materials may appear to have great benefit. Additionally, where assessment materials are used to make placement decisions in school or employment settings, previous knowledge may be desirable by some to increase their sense of control over the assessment process. All practitioners need to be aware of these issues and watch for any indication that clients may have unusual knowledge or access.

Confidentiality and Security

An additional issue of concern is who has, or will have, access to the assessment data. In any setting, there are two groups of individuals who will potentially have access to any computer-based information: those with permission and those without. Appropriate policies and procedures must be maintained that recognize and respond to both groups.

The same confidentiality considerations that apply to paper files apply to computer files. The range of individuals who have access to the computer, and its information, can be limited by keeping the computer in a secure setting, and ensuring that the computer is password protected. Computers on an internal or external network, regardless of where they are physically located, are more accessible to others than computers that are not networked. Thus, there are additional considerations and precautions to be taken if the computer where the files are stored is connected to the Internet or an intranet. Following is a set of recommendations for maintaining confidential information on all computers, with additional recommendations for those that are networked.

When the computer that is being used in the assessment process (whether for administration, scoring, interpretation, or report writing) is not connected to the Internet or an intranet, the following recommendations apply:

1. The computer should be placed in a locked room in a locked building, where access is limited to those who have a reasonable need to access the information.

2. For added security and confidentiality, the computer should also be password protected. Depending on the operating system being used, the built-in security features may be sufficient. On some older operating systems, all files on the computer's hard drive can be accessed without having the correct password. Recent operating systems, including Windows 2000, Windows XP, and Mac OS 10, have better built-in security. If you are using an older operating system, and are unsure about the reliability of its security, then consider using an add-on product such as PClok (www.pclok.com).

    Password selection and storage are extremely important issues. A password does no good at all if it is something obvious. However, most people choose something quite simple to help in remembering the many passwords that are required to navigate life today. Anniversary dates, birthdays, a maiden name, or a pet's name are all quite common. Because of this, these all make poor password choices. It is important to choose a password that would be difficult to figure out. Most experts recommend a password that is a combination of letters and numbers. Passwords should be changed on a regular basis for the best security, and users should avoid using the same password for all of their computer activities. While maintaining separate passwords for home and work, client notes and client billing, and for all Internet transactions is difficult, it is the most secure approach. Finally, passwords need to be kept in a secure location and should never be kept in a list on the computer where they are being used. This is the first place an informed hacker will look. In some cases, if you lose or forget your password, it may be impossible to retrieve encrypted or password protected files. To protect yourself, a list of passwords can be helpful if properly protected.

• Technology Tip 5.2 •

If you keep your passwords in a file on a computer, be sure to password protect the file. Whenever possible, keep it on a separate computer, on removable media, or in a lockbox located at a location separate from your computer. Hackers know that users succumb to laziness and will often keep passwords in an insecure file on their computer. Never write passwords on post-it notes stuck to your computer monitor!

An alternate method of keeping track of your passwords is to use a program specifically designed for this task. One such program is Passwords Plus (www.authord.com). Passwords Plus is a shareware program that is designed to help users keep track of their passwords, and in some cases can automatically enter your password into other applications. This program will also generate random passwords and maintain all of your passwords in an encrypted list on your computer. This way, as a user you only need to remember the single password required to access this program. This approach is particularly useful if your computer is not used by other individuals, because it allows you to have many different passwords for the many programs and Internet sites you interact with. If someone discovers one of your passwords, they will not have access to all of your accounts, unless of course they find the password for this program. A similar program is Password Keeper (http://www.gregorybraun.com/PassKeep.html). Mac users can find similar features in VSE My Privacy (http://vse-online.com/my_privacy/index.html), This program goes beyond some others by helping users track, in a secure manner, PIN codes, bank accounts, and other personal data.

3. All files created with Microsoft Office as well as most other popular word processing programs can be individually password protected. This additional step will make it more difficult to open a specific file even if an unauthorized user obtains access to the computer's hard drive. It is also quite useful in settings where individuals share offices or computers. By password protecting individual files, multiple clinicians can share a computer and never have access to work created by others.

• Technology Tip 5.3 •

To protect files in Microsoft Office programs, go to **Tools > Options > Security**, then enter a password that will be needed to open the file.

4. Make sure your computer has an antivirus program (Norton Antivirus 2002, http://www.symantec.com/nav/nav_9xnt/; McAfee VirusScan, http://www.mcafee.com; Dr. Solomon's Virex, http://www.drsolomon.com/) that has *up-to-date* virus definitions. Most antivirus programs have the option to automatically check for virus

definition updates. If your antivirus program has this option, enable it to ensure that you always have the most current virus protection. A virus can do many different destructive things to your computer, including deleting important information, removing the operating system, e-mailing security data to the virus author, or e-mailing files from your hard drive to people on your contact list. This latter concern is particularly problematic as a virus might send complete client reports as e-mail attachments to everyone in your e-mail address book. While a mental health professional cannot be held responsible for the virus, he or she is responsible to ensure that appropriate security precautions have been taken.

•   Technology Tip 5.4   •

Failure to protect a computer against infiltration is as negligent as failing to secure client files in a locked cabinet.

5. Use encryption software to protect client files. Encryption software is designed to scramble the data in a file so that even if accessed, the data is nonsensical. A password and the proper encryption software are needed to restore the data to a format that the computer can use. Windows 2000 and XP come with the ability to encrypt files. This can typically be done by opening Windows Explorer, then right-clicking on the file you want to encrypt. From the menu that opens select Properties and Advanced from the General tab. Then choose the encryption option. On a Mac, simply Control + Click the file you want and choose Encryption from the contextual menu that opens. You will be prompted for a password. The next time you want to open the file, you must supply the password. If you use a different operating system or want a higher level of security, there are third-party encryption software programs available such as PGP (http://www.pgpi.org/) and DriveCrypt (http://www.drivecrypt.com/). See the end of this chapter for a list of encryption links.

Both Mac and Windows computers allow the user to encrypt entire folders. This approach ensures that all client data is encrypted every time it is accessed or saved. To encrypt a folder, follow the same procedure as encrypting a file except choose a folder instead of a single file.

6. Always be cautious of your surroundings, especially when using a laptop. In many settings, coworkers, clients, and casual visitors may be able to view your computer screen while you are working. The problem is even greater if you are using a laptop in a public place. Take care to position your computer so that others cannot accidentally see client information. Laptops pose an additional threat because of the potential for theft. A stolen laptop can easily reveal a counselor's entire caseload, including contact information, diagnosis, etc. By using encryption software to encrypt entire folders that

contain all client data, a stolen computer will be troublesome, but will not reveal client data, removing at least one of the concerns associated with a stolen machine.

When using a computer that is connected to the Internet or an intranet that contains client information, there are a number of ways to help ensure that confidential files do not fall into the wrong hands. Below are basic recommendations to be used on computers that contain confidential files and/or are used for clinical purposes. It might be beneficial to discuss the following recommendations with the network administrator in order to determine which options are best for your particular situation.

1. Check with the network administrator to discuss the appropriate precautions to be taken to ensure security. Expect that the system administrator, who is likely not a mental health professional, may not have the same regard for confidentiality as you have. System administrators generally will require full access to all computers over which they have authority. As well, they will generally want to allow all of their support employees complete access. While it is not feasible to set up computer systems that cannot be accessed by technology support staff, appropriate precautions, such as using passwords and encryption on specific files and folders will ensure that technology support staff have access to computers for maintenance purposes, but do not have unfettered access to client information.

2. Install a firewall such as Norton Personal Firewall 2002 (www. symantec.com/sabu/his/npf), McAfee FireWall 3.0 (www.mcafee. com/myapps/firewall/default.asp), Zone Alarm Pro (www. zonealarm.com), or BlackICE Defender (www.iss.net/products_ services/hsoffice_protection) or use the firewall built-in to some operating systems. Firewalls are designed to prevent unintended communications with your computer (i.e., hacking). This is especially important on computers that are connected to the Internet continuously through a broadband or network connection. MAC OS X comes with a powerful firewall that is difficult to configure, but you can use a program like Brick House (http://personalpages. tds.net/~brian_hill/brickhouse.html), available free for download, to help configure your system. In Windows XP, open Network Connections on your control panel. Then click the connection on which you want to enable the firewall. Under Network Tasks, select Change settings of this connection. Then, on the Advanced tab, under the section marked Internet Connection Firewall, select the Protect My Computer option. If you are using a third-party firewall, make sure that it is kept up-to-date to ensure the highest level of protection. If your computer is part of a network, ask your network administrator for assistance in setting up a personal firewall. To see how secure your computer is, go to http://www.grc.com. This Web site has very powerful tools designed to test the security installed on

your computer. If the firewall is not configured properly, this site will help you to identify the problem. Finally, while firewalls are an extremely good method to prevent hacking, there is no 100% fool-proof method of protecting confidential client information. Multiple safeguards are best.

3. Store important client information on an encrypted removable disk (floppy, Zip, CD-RW, etc.). By doing this, you can remove the disk from the computer when it is not in use, thereby making it impossible for a hacker to retrieve anything from that disk via the Internet or an intranet. Treat any computer disk with the same caution that would be applied to all client files. They should be stored in a locked area, and should never be removed from the office. By using encryption software, the files will remain protected even if someone unauthorized attempts to access the disk.

4. Keep your operating system up-to-date. If you use an older version of Windows, you can download a critical update manager that will notify you when updates are available. More recent versions of Windows as well as MAC OS X have features built in to alert the user of critical updates. In addition to maintaining a current operating system (OS), users must take care also to keep other software up to date. Hackers are constantly seeking access to computers through security flaws in popular programs. By keeping all of your software current, any security flaws found will be automatically fixed. One method to keep your system current is to use an automated process such as that provided by CNET CatchUp (cnet.com) or VersionTracker (www.versiontracker.com). These sites assist the user by tracking updates and security fixes so that you only need to visit a single site to obtain all the updates required for your computer. By keeping all of your software updated, you will minimize your susceptibility to malicious intruders.

Regardless of whether you plan on using computerized assessment tools, following the above guidelines is good professional practice. For those who do not plan on using computerized assessment tools, these security guidelines will help protect word processing files containing client reports or progress notes. It is a good idea to follow these recommendations on every computer you use, including your home computer and/or laptop. Once you have done the initial work to set up password protection, encrypted folders, and firewall security, then there will be minimal maintenance needed to remain secure, and the process of staying secure will become habitual.

Up to this point, we have focused primarily on protecting client information, but as much concern and care should be given to protecting your own information. If unprotected, it is possible for a virus or hacker to send your personal files to everyone on your contact list, including clients! Confidential information might also be surreptitiously sent to listservs or colleagues! While such concerns may create anxiety, once you have taken the appropriate precautions, you can ease your mind knowing that only the most highly advanced hackers will be able to gain access to your data, and those will generally be more focused on computers that contain financial data or those that will result in some notoriety for the hacker if infiltrated.

Choosing an Appropriate Computerized or Internet-Based Test

Choosing an appropriate computerized test for a specific need is an important decision and requires considerations not unlike those necessary when selecting a more traditional format. The Joint Committee on Testing Practices of the American Psychological Association has developed guidelines for choosing and interpreting tests in an informed manner (*Code of Fair Testing Practices in Education*, 2002). This set of guidelines is not intended to be specifically for computerized tests but is nonetheless a good beginning for our purposes.

Developing and Selecting Appropriate Tests

"Test users should select tests that meet the purpose for which they are to be used and that are appropriate for the intended test-taking populations. Test Users Should:

1. First define the purpose for testing and the population to be tested. Then, select a test for that purpose and that population based on a thorough review of the available information.
2. Investigate potentially useful sources of information, in addition to test scores, to corroborate the information provided by tests.
3. Read the materials provided by test developers and avoid using tests for which unclear or incomplete information is provided.
4. Become familiar with how and when the test was developed and tried out.
5. Read independent evaluations of a test and of possible alternative measures. Look for evidence required to support the claims of test developers.
6. Examine specimen sets, disclosed tests or samples of questions, directions, answer sheets, manuals, and score reports before selecting a test.
7. Ascertain whether the test content and norm group(s) or comparison group(s) are appropriate for the intended test takers. Select and use only those tests for which the skills needed to administer the test and interpret scores correctly are available."

Interpreting Scores

"Test users should interpret scores correctly. Test users should:

1. Obtain information about the scale used for reporting scores, the characteristics of any norms or comparison group(s), and the limitations of the scores.

2. Interpret scores taking into account any major differences between the norms or comparison groups and the actual test takers.
3. Also take into account any differences in test administration practices or familiarity with the specific questions in the test.
4. Avoid using tests for purposes not specifically recommended by the test developer unless evidence is obtained to support the intended use.
5. Explain how any passing scores were set and gather evidence to support the appropriateness of the scores.
6. Obtain evidence to help show that the test is meeting its intended purpose(s)."

Technology can help us meet these guidelines. When selecting a test (A1), most clinicians either limit themselves to instruments they have been exposed to through training or that are available at their place of employment. (In this section, these alphanumerical designations—A1, A5, etc.— refer to the *Code of Fair Testing Practices in Education* items.) Although it would be inappropriate to use any test without thorough review, supervision, and consultation, understanding the range of options is an important step in meeting client needs and provides a base for choosing areas in which to seek additional knowledge and skill.

• Technology Tip 5.5 •

Web sites such as *Buros Yearbook of Mental Measurement* (http://www.unl.edu/buros/) can help clinicians identify a much broader range of instruments to meet specific needs.

Many test publishers provide information about their products online. A publisher's Web site is often a useful site to obtain more information (A2). Buros maintains reviews online and is an excellent source of independent information (A5). Accessing PsycINFO through a local university library will provide clinicians with access to relevant research, and often full-text online articles as well.

Whenever considering new instruments, or a new form of an old instrument, clinicians should carefully study the material prior to having a client complete the test (A6). When working online, contact the Web site owner and make arrangements to complete tests online as part of the evaluation process. If sites will not allow you, as a clinician, access to the entire test for evaluation purposes, than alternate measures are suggested. It is important that clinicians are aware of exactly what the client experience will be so that they are prepared to answer questions, resolve problems, and determine whether a measure is appropriate for a particular client.

If a decision is made to use a computer-based test, and the norms provided are not based on this form with similar clients, this discrepancy should be clearly noted in interpretation reports (section B). Particularly when working with online clients at a distance, clinicians may find that they need to use online versions of instruments that are still in the development phase. In these cases it is critical to recognize the limitations of the instruments and seek alternate supporting information to aid in the assessment process.

In addition to these guidelines associated with all test selection, some additional considerations are important when selecting computer-based tests. First, as noted above, the clinician needs to take extra precautions to ensure that the decision to use computer-based tests is based on accurate information about the computer-based version of the test and not an alternate, traditional format (A7). Research into the impact that computer interfaces have on test outcomes is new and incomplete. Until more is known about this area, clinicians need to protect client interests by maintaining a conservative approach, using only those materials that have demonstrated their appropriateness through research and clinical use.

Additionally, the counselor must consider the skills of the individual client. If the client does not have appropriate computer skills, then the test may not present valid results. As well, the client's attitude toward using a computer must be considered. Some clients, regardless of their apparent skills, may be concerned about using computers. These concerns may emanate from concerns of security, previous frustrating attempts to use computers, or simply a lack of exposure. Any time a client is reluctant to use a computer, the impact that this attitude will have on the desired outcomes must be considered.

• Technology Tip 5.6 •

If a client does not want to use a computer, alternate methods should be employed. Client dissatisfaction with assessment procedures will almost always result in inaccurate information.

The Pros and Cons of Computerized Assessment

As with any new technology, or application thereof, a careful analysis should be done of the limitations as well as the benefits (see Table 5.1). If the appropriate steps are taken to respond to potential problems, computerized assessment will change the face of testing and assessment as we know it.

Counselors in all settings are facing severe budget restrictions brought about by changes in economic conditions, attempts to lower or reconfigure tax structures, alterations in insurance reimbursement and the continuing trend toward managed services. The use of computerized assessments may assist in responding to these budgetary concerns because the typical testing session will require less of the clinician's time. Additionally, as administration tasks are increasingly computerized, some tests may allow for less experienced assistants to "administer" them.

A cautionary note is important here. While administration of some instruments may become easier, and while clerical or support staff may have the computer knowledge to help administer a specific test, this does

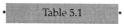

Table 5.1

Some Pros and Cons of Computer-Based Testing and Assessment

Pros	Cons
1. Computer applications may increase efficiency, thereby easing some financial problems.	1. The use of computer applications may decrease the amount of behavioral observation performed by the clinician during assessment, decreasing the overall level of data available.
2. Computer applications may allow more self-testing or testing by individuals with less training, freeing up individuals with higher levels of training for more direct intervention.	2. Not all clinicians have the skills, background, and confidence in technology to suitably use computer-based instruments.
3. Computer applications will decrease the amount of human error in scoring.	3. Computer-based instruments create new opportunities for security breaches, both of the instrument and of client data.
4. Test administrator bias may be reduced by more consistent administration procedures.	4. Clinicians will need to gain new skills and stay current in yet another area to successfully use new forms of instruments.
5. Clients may gain access to assessment instruments online before a counseling session, freeing office time for more direct interventions.	5. At least in the short-term, computer-based materials may be more expensive to implement than standard paper-and-pencil instruments.

not necessarily mean that it is appropriate for them to do so. The skilled clinician is aware that assessing a client as they interact with assessment materials can contribute important information to the assessment process. This information will be lost if all administration is turned over to support personnel. As well, support personnel may not have the skills to recognize client hesitation, frustration, or confusion that may result from interacting with computer-based instruments. In such a case, the clinician may never recognize the difficulty a client had in completing a procedure and may therefore misinterpret results.

Finally, it should also be noted that not every clinician is prepared to administer computer-based instruments. Having knowledge of the instrument and its properties is an important first step. But as new technology is used with clients, the clinician must also possess a high level of comfort and skill in interacting with computer technology to assist the client and recognize difficulties.

• Technology Tip 5.7 •

Clinicians who do not have appropriate technological skills will be better served by utilizing more traditional formats of appropriate assessment material until gaining a higher level of skill and confidence in dealing with technology.

As noted earlier, the use of computerized testing will drastically improve the consistency of the testing process, reducing human error of administration and scoring considerably. By automating nearly every aspect of the testing process, every testing session will be more consistent with every other testing session. This will allow certain tests and assessment procedures to move from an art, with wide individual differences in administration, to a science in which every administration is virtually identical.

This increase in the stability of administration has the important positive consequence of eliminating test administrator bias. Issues of bias related to ethnicity, religion, race, attractiveness, or other individual differences will no longer influence the testing process in the same manner as in the past. Although this change in administration will not reduce bias in norming procedures and test construction, it will have a positive impact in the area of administration and scoring.

Internet-based assessment tools can be put on a school's or clinic's Web site so that clients and/or students will have the ability to log in and fill out questionnaires online prior to meeting with a counselor or between sessions. This information can be saved in a secure database and made available to the counselor as a portion of the client's computerized record. This will save time as new clients can fill out demographics and background questionnaires online so that when they arrive for a session, a focus can be maintained on creating a relationship rather than on the mechanics of completing paperwork.

However, the outlook for computer-based assessments is not all positive. As alluded to previously, security issues, technological concerns, and client responsiveness must be considered. As well, the transition process to computerized assessment may be difficult, particularly in schools and offices where procedures are already established and materials have already been purchased.

All new technology requires some investment of time to master the skills necessary for success. Practitioners already in the field, often overburdened by heavy caseloads and a lack of support, will find learning new computer programs and becoming comfortable with their use time consuming. Some programs are easy to learn, whereas others will have a steep learning curve. Without appropriate support from the companies marketing these new products, as well as support from technology staff within the organization, frustration may run high and cause some to prematurely abandon attempts to incorporate these new technologies.

A second concern is cost. Many of the computerized tests that are currently on the market are expensive. The cost of purchasing software and licenses, along with equipping offices with the necessary hardware, will be difficult for many schools and organizations. Additional costs will be incurred as hardware and software is updated. This means that maintaining a current inventory of assessment materials and adequate hardware will likely be more expensive than past practices of maintaining paper versions of a test. In cases where these costs can be passed on to the client, they may not present an obstacle. However, in schools or nonprofit agencies where clients do not pay directly for their services, it may not be possible to absorb these increased costs. This may create real differences in the services that are provided based on the fee structure in place in a particular organization.

Finally, many of the computerized tests that are currently on the market are old and were originally developed to be used on DOS-based computers. With each succeeding generation of operating systems, these older programs become more difficult to run. Test developers must update their products to operate with current computer systems, and must either risk alienating some counselors by choosing to publish to a single operating platform (Windows, Mac, Unix) or absorb the additional cost of creating cross-platform programs.

Web Sites Offering Internet-Based Assessment

There are many Web sites that offer personality and IQ tests. However, there are very few Web sites that are intended for professional use. It is extremely important to determine whether a site is intended for fun or for professional use. There are a few signs to look for when searching for Internet-based testing services for professional use:

- **Does the Web site claim to be intended for professional use?** A claim by a Web site that it is intended for professional use does not ensure the quality of the material available, nor does it indicate that a site is necessarily suitable for a particular purpose or a particular client. Sites intended to attract a professional audience will generally provide the user with better information concerning the psychometric properties of instruments, applicable research, and the theoretical base on which instruments or procedures are based. These are important considerations in helping the professional determine whether a site is appropriate. Users are cautioned not to simply accept what a Web site offers, but to independently verify information by reading relevant research, test reviews, and so forth.
- **Does the Web site require that you register with them or pay a fee to access materials?** Web sites may require registration for several reasons. Sites that are built on a solid business model, that require registration and payment of fees, may represent work by legitimate test publishers seeking to market their products in a new way. On the other hand, sites that require no registration, are freely accessible to anyone, and have no way to generate revenue are more likely to be sites maintained by individuals for entertainment purposes. Such sites are less likely to offer assessment materials that have been appropriately validated.
- **Are credentials required to gain access to test results?** Most test publishers are careful to ensure that their tests are available only to individuals qualified to administer and interpret them. When purchasing tests, it is common practice to ask purchasers to supply information concerning their education and experience to determine

what types of tests are appropriate for the individual to purchase. Similar requirements can be expected from Web sites that are geared toward a professional audience and that are attempting to restrict access to their material to those with an appropriate background.

- **Does the provider store and back up assessment data?** If the provider does not store client assessment data, then you should have the option of downloading it yourself for storage. Be certain to identify in advance the form in which data is stored to ensure that it will be useful to you without the purchase of additional proprietary software. In all cases, it is important to determine how the site maintains data. It is appropriate to ask providers in advance how data is stored, if servers are secure, and what individuals have access to the servers within the organization. A quality professional site will have strong security measures to ensure confidentiality, as well as appropriate measures to ensure data is backed up in case of technical failures.

Included below are examples of Internet testing sites that are intended for professional use. A visit to each of these sites will provide the reader with a better understanding of how these sites operate and the services available. Taking the time to review these sites offers an opportunity for significant learning. In each case, it is helpful to review the material that the site provides to determine who the intended clients are, the site's procedures for security, and the quality of the service. These sites are included as representative sites, and their inclusion does not indicate endorsement.

- **ReadyMinds.com (http://www.readyminds.com/).** Ready Minds is a career and academic counseling service that provides online assessment materials. The customer is then matched to a counselor and one-on-one counseling sessions are conducted over the phone. After the counseling session(s) are over, the customer can correspond with the counselor via e-mail for one year. This is a full-service site that intends to provide individual feedback by qualified counselors after assessment materials are completed.
- **Assessments.com (http://assessments.com/default.asp).** This professional oriented site offers a wide variety of assessments available in several categories including adult justice, mental health, juvenile justice, behavioral health, school behavior, and substance abuse. To protect the integrity of the tests, test administrators are required to have certain credentials in order to use tests. The site offers users an option to complete assessments online or to purchase software so that organizations can install assessment materials on their own servers. This latter option will still allow clients to complete assessments online but maintains all client data on local servers, providing the organization with more control over who has access to client data. In addition, the site will convert locally created assessment materials to an online format so that schools and agencies can have any or all of their materials available in this manner. A concern that exists with this site is their

statement that they have psychometric properties of *most* tests available on request. Extreme caution should be taken when using any instrument, computer-based or paper-and-pencil, that does not have appropriate properties and norms available.

- **PsychTests.com (http://psychtests.com/).** PsychTests.com is a site that presents itself initially as geared to the professional, but also markets strongly to the individual. While its home page identifies professionals including therapists, human resources (HR) managers, and academics as the audience, the bottom of the page includes the invitation: "Take a test! Get to know yourself better with PsychTests' extensive battery of professionally developed psychological tests." (PsychTests.Com, 1996–2002). A review of the site identifies tests that were "inspired by" known instruments. It appears that all of the tests available were created specifically for use on this site. The psychometric properties of the tests are available upon request at $20 for each test. This site does not require professional credentials to use the assessment tools, a further indication of a mass market approach. You can view samples of some of the tests for free.

As the above three examples illustrate, there are wide differences among Internet testing sites that are intended for professional use. Some require credentials; others do not. Some have the psychometric properties available; others do not. Caution should be used in determining whether a particular Internet testing site provides the level of quality necessary for professional use. It can be anticipated that many more assessment sites will come online in the coming years. If professionals view these as viable options and are willing to pay the fees necessary, this approach to assessment will continue to grow.

By visiting Web sites not intended for professional use, the reader will be provided with a stark contrast and a better understanding of what clients may seek out as they struggle to address their own concerns prior to seeking professional assistance. These sites are included to illustrate the contrast between those intended for professional use and those that are not.

One example is TheSpark.com (www.thespark.com). This site has a large variety of "tests" that claim to measure all sorts of unusual traits. Many of the questions included are "tongue-in-cheek" and no real attempt is made to create valid tests. However, answers are immediately compiled and responses are compared with others who have completed the test online. Such "entertainment" tests may be used by individuals in an attempt to confirm or disconfirm self-beliefs, and the naive user may compare his or her reported results with others who have completed the test, with a potential for anxiety or confusion to result.

Another example of an entertainment site is Emode.com (www.emode.com). Emode offers a variety of tests in many areas. One example is a 41-item career test listed under the heading "Discover the career that's right for you." Unlike instruments at TheSpark.com, all items on this test appear to be legitimate, and the test would appear to be valid to many users. After completing the test, users are informed that they are analytical, creative, or some similar adjective, and a complete report is offered for a small fee ($14.95 at the time of this writing). No information is available about where or how these tests were developed, nor are any norms or psychometric properties available. This site, because it appears to have tests with reasonable questions, is likely to attract many individuals who seek quick answers to questions in their life.

Another similar site, geared to individuals seeking to know themselves better, is The Marriage Mentor (http://www.marriagementor.com/index.html). This site, developed by a marriage and family therapist, presents users with a 50-item test about their current relationship. A user report is then generated including sections on emotional maturity, marital passion, self-disclosure, acceptance, and commitment. The report goes so far as to suggest topics of discussion in which a couple might engage to improve their relationship. Additionally, the report provides advice about approaching your partner, things to pay attention to, and pitfalls to avoid. To the extent that the advice provided is general and not substantially different than might be read in many relationship enhancement books, the site appears harmless. However, such sites cannot help individuals identify and respond to serious problems in their relationships. If clients assume that such a site is a substitute for more direct intervention, then the site may decrease the likelihood someone will seek out the assistance they need. This type of site also presents a danger that a professional might assume that the test presented has good psychometric properties. In such a case, an ill-informed counselor might refer clients to complete the instrument, assuming that the report contained validated information. If a treatment plan were to be developed around such nonvalidated material, there is a high likelihood that client needs would not be well served.

Computerized Scoring Programs

Probably the most common use of computers in the assessment process, next to word processors for report writing, is computerized scoring programs. Although most calculations that are required to score common assessment instruments are fairly simple, a surprising number of mistakes and miscalculations are made in the manual scoring process. The use of computerized scoring programs drastically reduces errors in the scoring process. Typically, if there is a computerized scoring program available, it will be available through the test publishing company. Although they are often somewhat expensive, they save time and can decrease calculation errors.

Computerized Interpretations

Many computer administered and scored tests provide a canned interpretation of the data. Much caution should be used when reading these interpretations. Good assessment procedures require that the clinician seek multiple levels and types of information to complete the assessment process. This use of triangulated data helps to ensure that no single piece of data or assessment instrument, which may be inaccurate for any number of reasons, unduly distorts the outcome of the assessment process. Currently, computerized interpretation programs typically focus on a single instrument when reporting results. This lack of supporting data results in a computer interpretation that is very general and applicable to a set of norms, but not necessarily to an individual case. One approach to dealing with computerized interpretations is to not read them until you, the practitioner, have interpreted the results yourself in light of all of the other information obtained through interviews, medical and psychiatric records, school records, other testing, etc. By approaching interpretation in this manner, the practitioner is less likely to be biased by a single report.

Summary

The increasing use of computers and other technology to administer and interpret assessment instruments offers several advantages to the clinician. An increase in standardization of administration, less scoring error, and a potential for time savings are among them. However, not all clients are appropriate candidates for computer-based assessment, and clinicians must engage in appropriate assessment prior to use of these materials to make sure they are appropriate for a particular client.

In addition to ensuring that clients are matched to specific instruments, computer- based assessments may present new challenges for test security. Test questions may be compromised by poor security if they are available online, and test reports may be harder to keep secure if they exist in electronic format. Finally, computer-based interpretation may provide clinicians and clients with a false sense of reliability and validity. Even the best assessments should only be considered with collateral data appropriate to the specific assessment questions being asked.

However, with guidance from standards provided by professional associations such as the Association for Assessment in Counseling, knowledgeable counselors will be able to choose, administer, and interpret assessments using these new technologies in a manner that is beneficial to clients and that represents the highest level of professional practice. In conjunction with appropriate security efforts and ongoing training to keep skills current, these new assessment technologies will continue to move counseling services forward.

Internet Sites for Additional Information

- **http://psychology.about.com/cs/test.** This Internet guide contains links to a variety of information related to testing. Links are available suitable for clients as well as the professional.

- **http://psychology.about.com/msub_testonline.htm.** This site provides links to various online instruments. Much of the material is of the magazine quiz variety and is included as an example of information clients find online and mistake for accurate and valid material.
- **http://aac.ncat.edu/.** This is the official Web site for the Association for Assessment in Counseling (AAC). Information is available for and about members, the association, and various events.
- **http://www.ex.ac.uk/cimh/swaz.htm.** Computers in Mental Health is one of the oldest and most extensive sites of its type on the Internet. Links are provided to software reviews, journal articles, and other information of interest to the professional. Membership includes subscription to an active listserv where members discuss issues and trade advice.
- **http://www.ericfacility.net/ericdigests/ed446327.html.** An important ERIC digest, this site provides information on what information test developers should provide, how to ensure appropriate use and interpretation, as well as addresses for important organizations involved in the field.
- **http://ericcass.uncg.edu/digest/2000-02.html.** This site takes a brief look at the strength and potential weakness of technology-based assessments.
- **http://www.education-world.com/counseling/assessment/index.shtml.** A resource of links to other assessment materials, this site is a good starting point to view some of the range of what is available.
- **http://jtc.colstate.edu/vol1_1/assessment.htm.** This article from the *Journal of Technology in Counseling* provides an overview of how technology is actually affecting the assessment process.
- **http://www.intelbrief.com/compusec.htm.** This list provides a wide array of links to information on computer security. It is a good site for those looking for in-depth material.
- **http://www.netaction.org/encrypt/.** The purpose of this site is to help users determine whether they need encryption software, understand the options available, and learn to run encryption on their machines. A good starting point for the beginner.

6

Use of Database Information

Competency: Be able to access and use counseling related CD-ROM databases.

By using CD-ROM technology locally (installing a CD-ROM on your desktop), through a local area network (LAN) or over the Internet, counselors can access a level of information that is now at an all-time high and will continue to grow exponentially in the coming years. The current rapid change in technology and its impact is clearly represented in this single competency area. Between the adoption of the ACES technology standards (ACES Technology Interest Network, 1999) and the writing of this book, the lines between desktop, LAN, and Internet access have become quite blurred. In the recent past, many CD-ROM database programs of use to counselors, such as the Educational Resources Information Center (ERIC) and PsycLIT, were mounted on CD-ROM platforms with an interface known as SilverPlatter. Today, many individuals access these same materials over networks and are completely unaware of the technology that makes this possible. Thankfully, knowledge of the technology is not mandatory (Sabella & Tyler, 2001). However, because it is not easy to differentiate between technologies (and is largely unimportant), the remainder of this chapter will focus on the issue of accessing counseling related databases in general rather than CD-ROM specific databases.

The first and most important information counselors must be prepared to access are those databases that categorize professional literature. The two most common are the Educational Research Information Centers (ERIC) database and PsycINFO (formerly Psych-Abstracts and then PsycLIT). ERIC is a database maintained by the U.S. Department of Education through the Educational Research Information Centers. The ERIC system maintains papers from professional meetings, book chapters, unpublished manuscripts, and some journals. This database is now available online and can be found by pointing your browser to www.askeric.org. The ERIC system is also a good method for innovative counselors to disseminate information about their work. All counseling and psychology professionals can write papers or monographs about specific projects they are involved in and submit these materials to ERIC. They may then be added to the database and can be accessed by other professionals. Two specific ERIC offices to consider are the ERIC Clearinghouse on Assessment and Evaluation (http://ericae.net/main.htm) and the ERIC Clearinghouse on Counseling and Student Services (http://ericcass.uncg.edu).

PsycLIT has undergone various name changes over the years, but remains a critical tool in our work. Originally called Psych-Abstracts, this data set was a large, annually updated set of books which were intricately coded and cross-referenced. In only a matter of hours, the professional counselor could identify dozens of potentially useful articles on any topic in their field. Converted to a computer-based CD-ROM system known as PsycLIT, counselors with computer skills could accomplish the same literature search in minutes by visiting a local university library. In its most recent form, known as PsycINFO, the entire database can be accessed over the Internet by members of APA or for a small fee by nonmembers. Most university libraries also provide access, and in many states, dial-up access to universities is provided for professional educators. PsycINFO is often the professional counselor's first step to retrieve current data on any topic or area of professional concern.

While the above databases are among the oldest, they are not the only ones to consider. In some instances, newer services provide information and features not available on these traditional services. One example is EBSCOHost (http://www.epnet.com/). This service abstracts and catalogs over 1,000 professional scholarly journals. Once identified, many of the materials in this database are available immediately in full-text format, allowing the user to review the entire document to determine usefulness and then print a copy if desired. Additionally, many libraries, universities, publishers, and professional organizations are working to put large collections online. These series change daily so a complete accounting is impossible. One example is provided by the ERIC/AE Full Text Internet Library project (http://ericae.net/ftlib.htm). From this Internet site, professional counselors can access a wide range of materials related to assessment and evaluation in educational settings.

•   Technology Tip 6.1   •

When visiting the ERIC/AE Full Text Internet Library project (http://ericae.net/ftlib.htm), click on the Top Ten button to reveal the most frequently accessed titles.

Going "Under the Hood" of Online Professional Databases

The key to making online professional databases useful is knowing how to rapidly pinpoint and obtain relevant information. Most online databases have similar options and features and only differ in how they are accessed. As is the case for most software programs, once you become proficient on one of these databases it becomes much easier to learn the others. Following is an overview of general methods and guidelines for getting the most from your experience.

Searching

The simplest type of search is a standard search, which allows the counselor to enter keywords or phrases with the option of searching on any of the words, all of the words, or as an exact phrase. These types of searches can be conducted only on specific fields of information (e.g., only the title or abstract of an article) and/or within the full text of a document. The latter is especially helpful because one can search on the name of an author and retrieve articles written by that person or articles that reference the work of that person. Simple searches often make use of the Boolean operators AND, OR, or NOT which instruct the computer to conduct a very broad or narrow search. The AND operator combines search terms so that each search result contains all of the terms. For example, the words *counseling AND bipolar* will result in articles that contain both of these terms. The OR operator combines search terms so that each search result contains at least one of the terms. For example, *counseling OR bipolar* will result in articles that contain either term, which typically produces a much larger set of results. The NOT operator excludes terms so that none of the search results will contain any of the terms that follow it. The search terms *counseling NOT financial* will result in articles that contain the term counseling and exclude those articles that also contain the word financial. Terms that are surrounded by quotation marks are treated as a phrase, such that the search for *"career development"* will only provide results that include these two words in succession. Two other useful search commands are the wild card (?) and truncation (*) symbols, which are useful when your search may contain unknown characters, multiple spellings, or various endings. For example, the search for *counsel?or* will produce results including the words counselor or counsellor. A search for *counsel** will produce results with all forms of the word including counseling and counselor.

• Technology Tip 6.2 •

Save keystrokes: Google.com assumes the AND Boolean operator in between words, so there is no need to use it!

Advanced search options allow users to incorporate limiters and expanders. Limiters are typically a set of options that the user can check off to limit his or her search to meet criteria, such as only full-text articles, only peer-reviewed journal articles, or only articles published in a certain venue or during a particular range of dates. Other limiters may help the user to find results in specific media formats such as video, CD, DVD, audio, or software. Expanders, on the other hand, may for instance allow the user to include results using a database of related words to the search terms or search multiple disciplines.

Search Results

Results can produce documents in various formats that include a range of possible elements, all of which are represented by specific icons next to the article's link (e.g., an icon of a camera if the document contains graphics). At a minimum, results may include only text, sometimes an abstract, and other times the article's full text, depending on the options you select and on the specific database. Some text articles may also include a graphic that depicts a table or figure. Other articles are presented in PDF format, a very popular file format developed by Adobe that contains both text and graphics (as mentioned in other chapters, this file requires a free viewer to properly read the document which is available online at http://www.adobe.com/products/acrobat/readstep2.html). The PDF file is also popular because if the document is lengthy, it will often include a hyperlinked table of contents so you may quickly navigate to specific parts of the document as well as perform keyword searches within the document. Other files may be Web site links because the document is readily available on the Web.

Your results for any given article will also typically have links to other aspects of that article such as the subject, journal issue, or the author(s). Clicking on any one of these will take you to other articles of possible interest—other articles about the same subject, included in the specific journal issue, or written by the author.

Delivery Options

After viewing an article online, you may choose among several options to keep it. First, you may have the article e-mailed to yourself or others. This is advantageous because you may very well be at your local library while conducting research and require a method to store and access your results later. In a similar manner, you may elect to save your results to disk. Other times you may want to simply print the article to read at a later time. If you don't require the entire article, you can copy and paste parts of the article into your word processor, with proper citation, throughout the writing process. If you don't have time to read each article in your results, some online databases allow you to deliver your results list which you can then use to later continue your research.

Most online databases allow the user to import reference information or an entire article into several different bibliography managers. This is especially useful for counselors who may conduct the bulk of their professional development reading online or who do a great deal of research and/or writing for publication because these programs assist in organizing references, automatically formatting bibliographies, and searching remote databases. The most pervasive bibliographic managers include EndNote (http://www.endnote.com), Pro Cite (http://www.procite.com), and Reference Manager (http://www.refman.com; visit http://www.bibliotech.com for a review of others).

You can facilitate the procedure for importing data from a database directly into a bibliographic manager by using special filters such as those found at http://www.endnote.com/support/enfilters.asp, which are used with EndNote.

Bibliographic managers can help the counselor locate references in seconds with powerful searching options and save search terms and reuse them later. They can create reference groups to identify a specific subset of a database or help the counselor to use predefined sorting options. Perhaps the most useful feature of bibliographic managers is the ability to format bibliographies for hundreds of journal styles, certainly including APA, directly from your word processor. This means that while you are writing, you can link your references throughout your document and then automatically generate a formatted and accurate bibliography no matter how many times you edit your document. Across many documents, data entry and retrieval is greatly minimized. This is especially true for coauthors who collaborate on projects, because they may import each other's bibliographic databases.

Several online databases (e.g., http://www.amazon.com and http://www.elibrary.com) provide an alert system that allows counselors to have delivered to their e-mail addresses a list of newly published articles, books, or other materials based on keywords. Similarly, publishers of online journals (e.g., http://www.catchword.com) offer to e-mail to you the table of contents of new issues as they are published.

Online Database Issues

Although online databases provide counselors with unprecedented new power and convenience, several issues should be considered. For one, not all scholarly publications are available online because of negative financial consequences in the form of lost subscriptions. Online publications may not be representative of the entire relevant professional (or other) literature in any given area. Limiting oneself to only online material when reviewing the literature may provide skewed results that can lead to unbalanced or erroneous conclusions. The universe of online materials is not yet an adequate substitute for print materials available in a well-developed library system. Second, online materials are not always subject to the peer-review process and so may not stand up to the rigor of scientific inquiry. Indeed, included in online databases are articles from magazines, news reports, and other sources which may merely offer one person's opinion. Third, the power and convenience of online databases has contributed to the problem of plagiarism—one of the most serious offenses plaguing the academic and professional world (e.g., see http://www.plagiarism.org). Fourth, because subscriptions to the most powerful full-text article databases can only be afforded by large organizations and institutions, access to knowledge may be more limited now then ever before, especially to those who live in rural or poverty stricken areas. Libraries and educational institutions must continue to work with professionals such as counselors and others in their locales to provide unrestricted access to such resources. Further, communities must continue to find ways to provide hardware, software, Internet access, and relevant training to foster equity among every person. Finally, counselors may not always have or make the time to make reading scholarly publications an important part of their professional development activities. Credentialing bodies should look more at providing greater incentives in the form of continuing education credit for using online databases to advance knowledge in the field.

Other Online Databases

How might a counselor locate online databases of interest among the literally hundreds of thousands of databases available, a number that is rapidly growing? Probably the best method for actively learning about useful databases is to use your Web search skills to locate them (see chapter 9). You may also find that there are sites dedicated to locating, reviewing, and communicating to others about online databases such as Research Buzz (www.researchbuzz.com). Belonging to online counselor communities (see chapter 7) may foster awareness as people share their discoveries in this area. Professional associations now often include regular columns in their publications dedicated to this endeavor. Some counselors and counseling professors have developed ongoing lists of these and made them available on their Web sites. Following is a selective list of online databases of potential interest to counselors which we have generated after using all of these methods.

• Technology Tip 6.4 •

The creators of Research Buzz (www.researchbuzz.com) also provide a set of customized tools for conducting specific Google searches (e.g., businesses, recipes, movie information, poetry, etc.) at http://www.buzztoolbox.com/google.

- **Education World's Counseling Community (www.education-world. com/counseling).** This site contains many data sets including Associations & Organizations, Directories & Indices, At-Risk Resources, Career & College Information, Buros Assessment Test Lists, K-12 School Counseling Centers, Magazines & Journals, and Professional Development.
- **The United States Library of Congress (http://www.loc.gov).** The Library preserves a collection of more than 119 million items, more than two-thirds of which are in media other than books.
- **Research Buzz (http://www.researchbuzz.com).** This site provides news and information about search engines and databases which can be delivered to your e-mail as a free newsletter.
- **Buros Institute of Mental Measurements (http://www.unl.edu/ buros/).** This site helps counselors to locate information about a test, a test review, or a test publisher.
- **Lexis-Nexis Academic Universe (http://web.lexis-nexis.com/ universe).** Lexis-Nexis provides access to a wide range of news, business, legal, and reference information.
- **The Electric Library (http://www.elibrary.com).** For a nominal fee, this site offers the full text of a vast database of newspapers, maga-

zines, transcripts, maps, photos, and books. This site also offers a free tracking service which will search its database for new articles on your favorite topics and deliver the headlines to your e-mail address.

- **The Encyclopaedia Britannica (http://www.britannica.com).** The online version includes the complete encyclopedia, as well as Merriam-Webster's Collegiate Dictionary, and the Britannica Book of the Year. Advanced search and navigation capabilities and the power of the Internet make the Encyclopaedia Britannica an invaluable reference and research tool.
- **The Oxford English Dictionary (http://www.oed.com).** With more than 2.5 million quotations illustrating how words are used, the OED is a unique source of information on the evolution of words and meanings, from the earliest times to the present day.
- **The United States Department of Education Publications (http://www.ed.gov/pubs).** This Web site publishes a wealth of information for teachers, administrators, policymakers, researchers, parents, students, and others with a stake in education. Included is a searchable bibliographic database of more than 20,000 publications produced or funded by the department since 1980.
- **The ERIC Digest Database (http://www.ed.gov/databases/ERIC_ Digests).** This site contains over 2,500 digests published as of this writing and is updated quarterly.
- **National Center for Research in Vocational Education (NCRVE; http://vocserve.berkeley.edu/fulltext.html).** The NCRVE is the nation's largest center engaged in research, development, dissemination and outreach in work-related education and is funded by the Office of Vocational and Adult Education of the U.S. Department of Education.
- **(http://www.prairienet.org/~scruffy/f.htm).** Maintained by an individual, this Internet site seeks to link to sites containing full-text state constitutions, statutes (called codes or compiled laws in some states), legislation (bills, amendments and similar documents), and session laws (bills that have become laws).
- **The Journal of Technology Education (http://scholar.lib.vt.edu/ejournals/JTE/).** This site provides a forum for scholarly discussion on topics relating to technology education.
- **The Journal of Technology in Counseling (http://jtc.colstate.edu).** This journal publishes peer-reviewed articles on all aspects of practice, theory, research, and professionalism related to the use of technology in counselor training and counseling practice.
- **The Occupational Information Network (O*NET) and O*NET OnLine (http://online.onetcenter.org).** These services were developed for the U.S. Department of Labor and include information on skills, abilities, knowledge, work activities, and interests associated with occupations. The database used in O*NET OnLine is based largely on data supplied by occupational analysts using sources such as the Dictionary of Occupational Titles (DOT).

- **PubMed (http://www.ncbi.nlm.nih.gov/entrez/query.fcgi?db= PubMed).** PubMed is a service of the National Library of Medicine and provides access to over 11 million MEDLINE citations back to the mid-1960s as well as additional life science journals. PubMed includes links to many sites providing full text articles and other related resources.
- **The Catalog of U.S. Government Publications (http://www.access. gpo.gov).** This site catalogues records for documents published by federal agencies from January 1994 to the present.
- **The RECORD (http://psychwatch.com).** This is an online journal and news periodical with articles published, written, and submitted by Psychwatch.com readers and Web site visitors. The credentials of authors are listed following each article.
- **Technology Horizons in Education (T.H.E.) Journal (www.thejournal. com).** This is a free online magazine focusing on educational technology. Counselors may also sign up on the site for a free subscription to the hard copy of the magazine. Similarly, check out ConvergeMag at http://www.convergemag.com.
- **The Center for Effective Collaboration and Practice (http://cecp.air. org/promisingpractices).** This service helps counselors find information on what's working for children with serious emotional disturbances in systems of care.
- **The Cybercounseling and Cyberlearning Web site (http://cyber-counsel.uncg.edu).** Full-text information and resources are available on many aspects of counseling technology.
- **The Dictionary of Behavioral Terms (http://www.innerself.com/ Behavior_Modification/dictionary_behavioral.htm).** The site is useful in identifying names and concepts related to mental health and counseling needs.
- **The SchoolCounselor.com Newsletter (http://www.schoolcounselor. com/newsletter).** This newsletter provides practical answers to technology-related questions and information about related resources. The newsletter endeavors to advance counselor technological literacy.
- **The Office of Educational Research & Improvement's National Center for Education Statistics Web site (http://nces.ed.gov/).** This site collects and analyzes data that are related to education in the United States and other countries. Other useful tools exist on this site such as College Opportunities Online (COOL; http://nces.ed.gov/ ipeds/cool), which is intended to help college students, future students, and their parents understand the differences between colleges and how much it costs to attend college.
- **National Parent Information Network (NPIN; http://npin.org).** The purpose of this network is to provide information to parents and those who work with parents and to foster the exchange of parenting materials.
- **Practical Assessment, Research and Evaluation (PARE; http://ericae. net/pare/Home.htm).** This is an online journal published by the ERIC

Clearinghouse on Assessment and Evaluation (ERIC/AE) and the Department of Measurement, Statistics, and Evaluation at the University of Maryland, College Park. Its purpose is to provide education professionals access to refereed articles that can have a positive impact on assessment, research, evaluation, and teaching practice, especially at the local education agency (LEA) level.

- **The National Information Clearinghouse on Children Who Are Deaf–Blind (http://www.tr.wou.edu/dblink).** This site is home to a wealth of information.
- **http://www.psychologie.uni-bonn.de/online-documents/lit_ jou.htm.** This site contains a directory of psychology-related online journals.
- **The Internet Public Library (http://www.ipl.org/div/serials/).** This site maintains a directory of various related serials, including those of interest to counselors.
- **FindArticles.com (http://www.findarticles.com).** This site is a vast archive of published articles that you can search for free. Constantly updated, it contains articles dating back to 1998 from more than 300 magazines and journals.
- **The United States Department of Commerce U.S. Census Bureau (http://www.census.gov).** The Census Bureau site provides a sundry of searchable information.
- **The United States Department of Health and Human Services Substance Abuse and Mental Health Services Administration National Mental Health Information Center (http://www.mentalhealth.org).** This is a must-visit database of resources and articles.
- **The Medical College of Georgia's Mental Health Network (http://www.mcg.edu/Resources/MH/psychonline.htm).** This Web site provides a directory of online journals.

The Future of Counseling Databases

Counseling databases of the future can be expected to change in many ways. These changes include better integration across datasets, more intuitive interfaces, and more effective responses to natural language inquiries. Currently, performance of online databases on the Web are hindered because of translations between varying standards or protocols. Software engineers are making great strides in developing uniform standards and creating standards of interoperability such as with electronic data interchange (EDI). EDI is the transfer of data between different entities using networks, such as the Internet. As more agencies, schools, and organizations become connected to the Internet, EDI is becoming increasingly important as an easy method for them to trade information.

Another rapid development is combining many different databases across an entire enterprise, a process known as data warehousing. In business, data warehouses contain a wide variety of data that present a coherent picture of business conditions at a single point in time, which consequently supports management decision-making. The application of data warehousing in counseling will allow agencies, institutions, and schools to make more effective decisions about the management and delivery of counseling activities. In essence, data warehousing will empower counselors and the organizations in which they work to maximize the use of collected data to enhance their daily operations and perform comprehensive planning. Reports will be more easily accessed and even triggered by specific occurrences to reveal trends and establish connections between events more quickly. Data warehouses will help counselors more easily create a pool of knowledge for tracking themselves, clients, stakeholders, and their activities.

Data mining is a procedure that looks for hidden patterns in a group of data. Data mining software doesn't just change how data is presented, but actually discovers previously unknown relationships among the data. For example, in the medical profession, a combination of data warehousing and data mining supports hospitals to complete the process of formulating, managing, and publishing medical and nursing guidelines, laboratory protocols, and administrative regulations. The software also monitors "new evidence" published in journals and other sources. The results are matched to protocols, topics, and other documents, even patient records. Specialists do not have to formulate a query, only click on a "new" button to match patient needs with best practices (e.g., see http://www.sopheon.com/solutions_healthcaresols. asp). Advances in data mining technology in the counseling profession will help counselors interpret and use data in ways that they did not anticipate and help them answer questions which they did not originally conceive.

Peer-to-peer (P2P) computing is the technology currently being used primarily for "swapping" music files among millions of Internet users (also known as a distributed system). Essentially, one computer user or "peer" places in a shared folder the files he or she is willing to allow others on a network to access. The files are catalogued on a central database on the Internet. Computer users can search for and locate specific types of files available among P2P users on a given network system and download them directly from another individual's computer. If the same file is located on more than one user's computer, some systems can determine the fastest user or will even use many users at the same time to get the file to you in the shortest possible time. Anything that can be digitized (e.g., movies, photos, documents, and programs) can be shared. The most popular P2P networks as of this writing include Kazaa (http://www.kazaa. com), LimeWire (http://www.limewire.com), Gnutella (http://www. gnutella.com), and AudioGalaxy (http://www.audiogalaxy.com). Special P2P networks for counselors, currently not in existence, will open up a new world of data and other file sharing.

Summary

This chapter endeavors to help counselors recognize the power of data access and retrieval, especially in regard to scholarly publications, as it is available over the vast network of the Internet. Although at one time data was disseminated via CD-ROM, counselors can now access in one session, on their own or through universities, information in many relevant databases. As more counselors attend to their own levels of technological literacy and application, data available on the Internet stands to continue to proliferate. Developing technology will help counselors to integrate and more effectively manipulate data to learn and act in ways that ultimately better serve themselves, each other, and their clients. Sharing and discovering the best data-driven, research-supported practices in response to changing client issues and environments (i.e., accountability) can now be accomplished with a whole new level of confidence. Counselors of the future are sure to experience even greater confidence in how they work and how their work has, or does not have, a desired effect on their constituents.

Internet Sites for Additional Information

- **http://www.ncbi.nlm.nih.gov/PubMed/:PubMed.** A service of the National Library of Medicine, this Web site provides access to over 12 million MEDLINE citations back to the mid-1960s and additional life science journals. PubMed includes links to many sites providing full-text articles and other related resources.
- **http://www.psychcrawler.com.** PsychCrawler is a product of the APA created to provide quick access to quality content in the field of psychology.
- **http://etoh.niaaa.nih.gov.** This site from the National Institute on Alcohol Abuse and Alcoholism contains the Alcohol and Alcohol Problems Science Database.
- **http://library.stmarytx.edu/acadlib/indexes/psych.htm.** This list of open psychology and counseling databases is provided by the St. Mary's University Blume Library.
- **http://ericcass.uncg.edu/virtuallib/newlibhome.html.** The ERIC/ CASS Virtual Library is an online collection of full-text materials developed in order to provide access to relevant research and materials on current topics of interest. It is intended as a resource for anyone.
- **http://icdl.uncg.edu/.** The International Career Development Library (ICDL) is a free, online collection of full-text resources for counselors, educators, workforce development personnel, and others providing career development services.

7

E-mail and Listservs

Competencies: Be able to use e-mail and subscribe, participate in, and sign off counseling-related listservs.

According to Campbell (1998), only three or four times in recent history has a new technology been introduced that has fundamentally transformed human society by changing the way people communicate with each other. For the most part, the moments in which these new technologies come into being are preserved with a kind of clarity and drama that is both thrilling and unforgettable. There is Samuel B. Morse and the first telegram. Delivered on May 24, 1844, the message read "What hath God wrought!" Morse knew that he was making history. There was the dawn of the telephone era, heralded by Alexander Graham Bell's less grand, though still legendary, summons to his assistant on March 10, 1876: "Mr. Watson, come here; I want you." While the exact wording of Guglielmo Marconi's first wireless transmission in 1895 is not the stuff of legend, it didn't take long for Marconi to be heaped with honors and awards, topped off by a Nobel Prize for physics in 1909. Even 30 years later, the inauguration of wireless service between England and South Africa felt like an historic event to the participants. "We speak across time and space. . . May the new power promote peace between all nations," read the Marconigram sent from Sir Edgar Walton, high commissioner of South Africa, to General J. B. M. Hertzog, South Africa's prime minister, in 1924.

Campbell (1998) further wrote that sometime in late 1971, a computer engineer named Ray Tomlinson sent the first e-mail message. "I sent a number of test messages to myself from one machine to the other," Tomlinson recalls now. "The test messages were entirely forgettable. . . . Most likely the first message was QWERTYIOP or something similar." It seems doubtful that "QWERTYIOP" will make it into the history books. And Tomlinson's name hardly lives in the public mind. When he is remembered at all, it is as the man who picked @ as the locator symbol in electronic addresses. In truth, though, he is the inventor of e-mail, the application that launched the digital information revolution. Yet the breakthrough he made was such a simple evolutionary step that hardly anyone noticed it until later. At the time, it barely registered with Ray Tomlinson.

Clearly, the most pervasive and popular application of the World Wide Web is electronic mail, also known as e-mail. Beginning as a method for sending text messages across a network to other computer users, today's e-mail systems allow individuals to send anything that can be digitized or electronically stored to any one or more other users across various networks, including the Internet. E-mail gives people a very fast and inexpensive way to send information all over the world and to receive information through their very own electronic mailbox, or "inbox." E-mail is taking the place of many telephone calls, faxes, courier shipments, and traditional mail (often referred to among computer users as snail mail). Today, people use e-mail as a vital part of communication with colleagues and to keep in touch with friends and family. Perhaps the greatest e-mail advantage to counselors is the opportunity to participate in a network that enables participants to share professional ideas and information. Even more, there are many counseling professionals who are now offering advice, information, education, and therapy services over the Internet. These exchanges have been called therap-E-mail (Murphy & Mitchell, 1998).

How Counselors Use E-mail

Predominantly, e-mail seems to be used among counselors no differently than other professionals—for communicating ideas and information to colleagues and staff for the purpose of informing and collaborating during day-to-day operations. Communications range from trying to establish mutual times of availability for a meeting and sending reminders about events, to sharing ideas for cultivating policy, curriculum, or strategies needed to work. Some, if not many, communications may originate from sources well beyond the recipient's location. For example, e-mails may be sent to announce job openings, opportunities for professional development, new developments and approaches to counseling as shared by researchers, legislative alerts from professional associations, or opinions from other counselors concerning professional issues.

E-mail Therapy

Use the words e-mail and therapy as keywords in any Internet search engine and the results point to hundreds, if not thousands, of Web sites which counselors have created to work with clients. Tyler and Guth (in press) have shown that e-mail is the most common method of communication used by these counselors to provide "online counseling." For a slightly smaller percentage, the use of e-mail as a delivery system for counseling is only part of a more sophisticated system of interaction that includes synchronous videoconferencing, chat, and telephony. E-mail has become so pervasive and easy to use that many counselors and clients are anecdotally reporting positive results.

Murphy and Mitchell (1998; also see http://www.therapyonline.ca for the basis or context of this article) coined the term TherapE-mail to describe how they perform online counseling. In their article they propose compelling solutions to two challenges posed by using e-mail as the medium for therapy: (a) whether or not warmth, caring, and compassion can be communicated via text, and (b) dealing with the lack of nonverbal information in a text-only medium. The authors also delineate several advantages of using e-mail in therapy:

1. Removal of barriers of time and space may help clients gain access to counselors otherwise not available.
2. The entire text of therapy is available to both the client and the therapist.
3. Clients can read over and again their TherapE-mails, which allows them to reflect, recognize their growth, and especially identify their strengths and solutions for overcoming problems. Similarly, clients can also review the positive and encouraging comments that their therapist has made about them and their behavior, particularly when they are feeling down.
4. Because the e-mail exchange is asynchronous, a therapist can create an e-mail response and then send it to his or her supervisor before sending it to the client. In this way, the expertise of both parties can be brought to bear on the case after the client has presented issues but before the therapist has responded. Similarly, consultation may be easier, more rapid, and involve more professionals.
5. Clients can ask for specific clarification of terms or phrases that they do not understand. It puts an onus on the therapist to write in a language that is accessible to the client—an onus that is not present in an unmonitored face-to-face encounter.
6. Therapy using e-mail is portable—clients can take with them the entire sequence of sessions either as a printout or perhaps on their portable computers.
7. The very process of writing about their issues externalizes the clients' problems. As they type, the written representation of their issues appears before them on the computer screen. In other words, the recursive nature of writing has the power to effect change in and of itself.
8. Interacting over a medium such as electronic mail can further minimize any power imbalances and similarly decrease the negative impact of prejudices.

A reporter for a Texas A&M newspaper (Garcia, 2002) wrote about a study that examined the effects of written expression via e-mail on health among 150 undergraduate students. This study found that participants who wrote e-mails about their traumatic emotional experiences were healthier in the weeks following their writings than were those who wrote about nonemotional topics. Specifically, research participants reported being sick for significantly fewer days than their counterparts and were less likely to miss class because of an illness.

Some school counselors have found that e-mail allows them to connect with students in new and beneficial ways. For example, Bob Turba, a high school counselor at Stanton College Preparatory School, created a Cyber Guidance Office (http://www.cyberguidance.net) which allows students to e-mail their counselor for a review and analysis of records or for counseling for college admission, including recommended colleges, career advice, and even personal counseling. In addition to doing e-mail counseling, Turba's Web site allows students at his school to use e-mail forms to more efficiently request transcripts, apply for scholarships, and make appointments.

Cybervision

Many counselors take the opportunity to participate in a global electronic network that enables participants to share professional ideas and information, especially for receiving feedback about difficult cases. In this sense, e-mail communication offers counselors a unique and valuable opportunity for supervision and consultation. For example, Myrick & Sabella (1995) wrote about how they used e-mail as a supplement to practicum and internship supervision. The student counselors, during group supervision, first learned how to access the Internet through computers in their schools or with their own personal computers and modems at home. They could also access the system through computer stations at various locations on campus. Each person had his or her own e-mail address, which was known to the supervisor and other group supervision members.

Using e-mail, a student-counselor could send written messages to a supervisor asking for information or describing a case. When appropriate, the case was forwarded to other group members for their interest and reactions. The group supervision members discussed the best way to send an e-mail case. It would include (a) a brief description of the counselee; (b) the presenting problem, including the referral source; (c) the observed behaviors related to the problem or concern; (d) the counselor interventions to that point; and (e) any concerns or questions that were evolving. The authors concluded that e-mail supervision supplements the traditional modes of face-to-face meetings, telephone conferences, and fax transmissions. An ongoing group experience, it can take place in remote and diverse locations. Although the common once-a-week group meeting has its own value, group members felt that they were always within reach of assistance or encouragement. They felt closer to one another, and e-mail created a special bond that also enabled them to be more open about their situations.

E-mail Accounts

The requisite hardware and software that makes electronic transmission possible is now so relatively inexpensive that it is common for people to have at least one e-mail account or "mailbox," and many individuals maintain several. School counselors and community counselors who work for institutions are usually given an e-mail account as part of employment. They are also provided with the needed software (known as an e-mail client or application) to create, send, and otherwise process their e-mail. Although some institutions have set up e-mail as a way to communicate only among its employees, most recognize the usefulness of providing e-mail capability across the entire Internet so that counselors can achieve the full benefit of global networking, communication, and collaboration.

Across the Internet, counselors can gain valuable support by providing and receiving feedback about important counseling issues, cases, and resources. They can share documents, forms, multimedia presentations, or anything else that may facilitate increased effectiveness and efficiency. Perhaps e-mail has fostered the new and renewed sense of collaboration in the profession as is currently evidenced by the "open source" movement. In cyberspace, open source refers to programmers who choose to distribute the actual code to their programs so that others in the community may adjust or tailor the software programs to their individual needs. Providing open source material allows for the material to be improved on in the spirit of innovation. In counseling, this process is analogous to sharing forms, databases, brochures, lesson or treatment plans, and more. The remainder of this chapter focuses on answers to frequently asked questions that counselors may have about e-mail as well as tips for addressing a variety of e-mail issues.

Getting an E-mail Account

Even though counselors may already have access to an e-mail account at work, they may very well be interested in obtaining additional accounts. One reason for this is that the counselor may want an e-mail account to conduct separate, perhaps more personal transactions that are usually considered inappropriate by most organizational policy statements regarding appropriate e-mail usage. Or he or she may need an additional e-mail address to give out to those who request it in exchange for something else. This is often the case with companies that collect e-mail addresses for marketing purposes and are willing to trade your address for something else of value such as information or software. This secondary e-mail address may serve the purpose of a "junk mail" box which only gets periodically perused and emptied. One way to obtain your own e-mail account is to sign up for one over the Web from a company that provides this service. Most of the major Web portals or computer companies (e.g., www. yahoo.com, www.hotmail.com, www.fastmail.fm) provide limited e-mail services for free. Another way to obtain an e-mail account is to purchase Web hosting services (usually starting at $6 per month) which typically comes with several e-mail boxes. If you register your own domain name (e.g., schoolcounselor.com), your e-mail addresses can reflect your uniqueness (e.g., sabella@21stcenturycounselor.com).

• Technology Tip 7.1 •

Most free e-mail accounts are only accessible with an online user interface. However, you may be able to access these accounts using third party software such as the one found at http://www.boolean.ca/hotpop.

Retrieving Your E-mail

Most popular e-mail clients allow you to collect your e-mail from various accounts so that you may process it all in one place. This is achieved most popularly by a function called Post Office Protocol (POP). For instance, many people use free e-mail clients such as Microsoft Outlook Express (http://www.microsoft.com/Windows/oe/) or Qualcomm's Eudora (http://www.eudora.com) to collect and process their mail. You need to check your specific e-mail client's Help menu or complete the tutorials provided on their respective company's Web site to appropriately config- ure POP in your client. However, most e-mail clients will help you with this one-time setup task by asking several simple questions:

- **What is your name?** Whatever you put in this space will show up in the "from" field when others receive your e-mails.
- **What is your e-mail address?** Input the e-mail address that you are using.
- **What is your username?** This is the same username that you estab- lished when you set up the account. Many services consider this to be your actual e-mail address.
- **What is your password?** This is the same password that you estab- lished when you set up the account.
- **What is your server name (also called SMPT)?** This is the least understood of all. Typically, it includes everything after the "@" in your e-mail address although it could include more. Often times, the SMTP is the word "mail" plus your domain name. For exam- ple, if my address is counselorgeek@schoolcounselor.com, I would input mail.schoolcounselor.com as the server name. If this doesn't work, you will have to check with your e-mail or Internet service provider.

Some schools and community counseling centers provide a Web-based interface for you to check your e-mail. If you have this Web-based access, then no matter where you are in the world, as long as you have Internet access, you also have access to your e-mail account. Because this need is sig- nificant, some online services have surfaced, such as http://www.web2mail. com, http://www.pop3now.com, and http://www.mollymail.com, that provide this service if you do not already have it. These services allow you to receive and send e-mail from your real account just by providing your user- name, password, and server (SMPT) address. The trick is that your e-mail account needs to be set up to use the POP (check with your organization's/ district's computing person). Another way to check your mail is to actually sign up for an additional Web based e-mail account service such as Hotmail (http://www.hotmail.com) which also allows its users to receive and reply to messages from other POP enabled accounts. Setting these Web based e-mail accounts is quite similar to setting up a program such as Outlook Express (see above).

If you choose a Web-based service, it is important to ensure that the site is secure, reputable, does not save your account information anywhere, and is set up to automatically log you off your account after a certain duration of inactivity (i.e., timeout). This is a safety feature in case you walk away from the computer and forget to log out, leaving your e-mail account available for the next person that uses the computer. Even after logging off, you should always close your browser so that any account information temporarily stored will be deleted from memory. Even with these precautions, all Internet activity creates temporary files on the host computer. Unless specific software is installed to delete these files, they will remain and are accessible to anyone with the knowledge to retrieve them from their storage space. Because of the potential for a breach of confidentiality, public computers should not be used to transact any business where client's names or other confidential information is exchanged.

• Technology Tip 7.2 •

To automatically empty your temporary Internet files in Internet Explorer (otherwise known as clearing your tracks), Select Tools, then Internet Options, select the Advanced tab, scroll down to the Security section, then place a check mark in "Do not save encrypted pages to disk" and "Empty Temporary Internet Files folder when browser is closed" boxes. Click the Apply button, then the OK button.

The Basics and Beyond

Most counselors are already adept at the very basics of reading, responding, creating, sending, and deleting e-mail messages. Journeying further into e-mail capabilities may prove productive for sending unique messages, facilitating tasks, and enhancing collaboration. Let's now get "under the hood" and focus on several lesser known features of e-mail which have the potential to further effectiveness and efficiency. Most of these options are available under the "customize" or "setup" menu option of your e-mail client.

Read Receipt

When you want verification that someone received a package or letter you sent in the mail, you send the item via certified mail. The recipient usually signs a card which is then returned to you verifying a successful transmittal. This can also be achieved using e-mail by sending your message with what is called a read receipt. Before sending your e-mail, find this option among your menu items (usually under the menu item called Options) and activate it. The receipt is sent when the message recipient has displayed your message. This is useful when you are sending time-critical information, or any time you want confirmation that your message has been received. You should know, however, that many people find this at least annoying if not intrusive. In fact, many popular e-mail clients will alert the recipient of the read receipt request and give him or her the option of sending it or not. Sometimes a recipient may opt to simply not acknowledge any read receipts. If your e-mail client does not have such an alert or read receipt disabling system, there may be an add-on program available for you that you can find by doing some research over the Web.

Alphabet Soup of Sending

In the old days, one could only send e-mail in the form of basic text (i.e., American Standard Code for Information or ASCII) which is still desirable for several reasons. First, plain text or ASCII messages are fastest to download. When the message does not require fancy formatting or other objects such as photos or sound, this is still the best way to go. Second, there may be recipients who are using older e-mail clients that can only handle plain text—anything else comes in as gibberish. Third, plain text e-mail is easiest to save, store, and copy and paste into other applications. If, however, you would like to change fonts or add tables or bulleted lists for instance, your best bet is to send the message in Rich Text Format (RTF). Recipients that process their e-mail using clients that can handle RTF, and most of them now do, will be able to view the e-mail very close to or even identical to the format in which you sent it. E-mail sent in RTF format may also include symbols such as "©" and photos. Messages that look and act the same as Web pages can now also be sent and received because modern e-mail clients act very much like Web browsers. Such messages are created in the same way that one creates a Web page—usually with a Web authoring program or e-mail client that can generate HTML code. The advantage of HTML messages is that they offer everything RTF formatted messages do and more including sophisticated computer scripts, forms, animated graphics, and anything else that might also be included on a Web site. Most e-mail clients include HTML stationary, which can be added to enhance the message. Stationary can include graphics, animation, and sound (e.g., see http://www.thundercloud.net). Using HTML-based e-mail does have several disadvantages, though, including that they can (a) take a great deal of time to download; (b) more easily carry malicious code that can infiltrate your computer; and (c) also deposit cookies on your computer to track the nature of your e-mail activity (see http://www.cookiecentral.com/faq for frequently asked questions and answers about cookies).

Signatures

What would you think if you received a letter in the mail that had a cryptic one-line return address on the envelope and no closing or signature on the inside contents? How would you feel? You would probably be bewildered, frustrated, or even somewhat disappointed if the message were complimentary. Yet many e-mail users still send e-mails with the very same thing—their e-mail addresses leave no clue as to who they are and they do not end their message with any other identifying information. There exist two remedies for this. One, make sure to include your full name when setting up your e-mail account for the first time so that your name is displayed in the "From" field of the e-mail. Second, set up a signature, which is automatically appended to every e-mail you send out. Your signature should begin with several spaces to leave room between the message and your signature, a line which further separates the two, and then no more than 5 lines of text which tells the recipient who you are and how to contact you if necessary. Some users include an inspirational saying or Web site address to learn more. The ability to create a signature is a part of every common e-mail client used today. In fact, you may create and label more than one signature to use for various types of e-mails (e.g., personal or professional). In addition, some e-mail clients such as Microsoft Outlook allow you to automatically attach a "business card" or virtual card (Vcard) to every e-mail. Recipients who also use this product can then simply click on the Vcard to add a great deal of information, which you provide, to their electronic address book (and eventually their handheld computers, cell phone, or other communication devices).

• Technology Tip 7.3 •

There may be a time when, indeed, you do want to send an anonymous e-mail such as to report an indiscretion (e.g., sexual harassment). Although there is no guarantee that you will remain anonymous, there are several places on the Web that specialize in sending anonymous e-mails such as those found at http://directory.google.com/Top/Computers/Internet/E-mail/Anonymous_ Mailers/?tc=1.

Another way to sign a document goes beyond identifying yourself to the recipient of a communication and is meant to authenticate the sender of the information. Digital signatures (sometimes called certificates), we predict, will become increasingly more important as counselors find the need to electronically communicate, consult, and collaborate with others about sensitive and/or confidential information. Counselors will find the need to be sure that documents sent in e-mail are not forged and to be certain that messages they send cannot be intercepted and read by anyone other than your intended recipient. According to the Microsoft Outlook Help tutorial, using digital signatures or identifications can help the counselor prove his or her identity in electronic transactions in a way that is similar to showing your driver's license when you cash a check. You can also use a digital ID to encrypt messages, keeping them private. Specifically, a digital ID is composed of three different components: a "public key," a "private key," and a "digital signature." When you digitally sign your messages, you are adding your digital signature and public key to the message. The combination of a digital signature and public key is called a certificate. Recipients can use your digital signature to verify your identity, and they can use your public key to send you encrypted e-mail that only you can read by using your private key. To send encrypted messages, your Address Book must contain digital IDs for the recipients. That way, you can use their public keys to encrypt the messages. When a recipient gets an encrypted message, his or her private key is used to decrypt the message for reading. The trick, then, to sending encrypted messages between two people is that both must possess the other's public key.

Digital IDs are issued by independent certification authorities. When you apply for a digital ID at a certification authority's Web site, your identity is verified before an ID is issued. There are different classes of digital IDs, each certifying to a different level of trustworthiness. For more information, visit a certification authority Web site (e.g., www.verisign.com, http://www.privacyx.com, and www.thawte.com).

When you receive an e-mail that has been digitally signed, you will need to verify or authenticate the signature. This is achieved by a process known as revocation checking, which is a function of your e-mail software client. When you request a revocation check, your e-mail client will request information on the digital ID from the appropriate certification authority. The certification authority sends back information on the status of the digital ID, including whether the ID has been revoked. Certification authorities keep track of certificates that have been revoked due to loss or termination. Some companies have attempted to fill a need for private and authentic e-mail. For example, www.hushmail.com provides users with free encryption and digital signatures in a process that is transparent to the sender or the receiver of e-mail.

Filtering and Rules

Most commonly used e-mail clients have filtering capabilities or the ability to create rules that automate how some e-mails get processed. For instance, you may want all e-mails with a certain subject to be moved to a specific folder for later viewing. You may want all e-mails from a certain person printed or even deleted for that matter. Some e-mail filters attempt to intercept pornographic e-mails from the user's inbox and place them directly in the "trash" or "recycling bin." The Microsoft Outlook online help (Microsoft Corporation, 1995–2001) describes filtering as follows:

> In much the same way that retailers and businesses use mailing lists of postal addresses to send potential clients catalogs and other information, there is a growing business in using e-mail messages as a direct marketing tool. If you do not wish to receive these kind of messages, Outlook can search for commonly used phrases in such messages and automatically move them from your Inbox to a junk e-mail folder, your Deleted Items folder, or any other folder you specify. The list of terms that Outlook uses to filter suspected junk e-mail messages can be found in a file called Filters.txt. You can also filter messages based on a list of e-mail addresses of junk and adult content senders. There are third party filters, which are regularly updated, that you can add to Outlook. These filters have the latest lists of commercial and adult content senders.

The Rules feature goes beyond filtering and can help you manage your e-mail messages by automatically performing actions on messages. After you create a rule, an e-mail client such as Microsoft Outlook applies the rule when messages arrive in your Inbox or when you send a message. Examples of rules you can create (depending on your e-mail client) include:

- Assign categories to messages based on the contents of the messages.
- Set up a notification, such as a message or a sound, when important messages arrive.
- Move messages to a particular folder based on who sent them.
- Delete messages in a conversation.
- Flag messages from a particular person.
- Assign categories to your sent messages based on the contents of the messages.
- Delay delivery of messages by a specified amount of time.
- Redirect a message to a person or distribution list.
- Ask the server to automatically reply to a certain type of message by using a message you've created.
- Start an application.

As an example, you may want to use filters and rules to flag all messages from your supervisor or a particular client. Also, if a person who is a member of a counseling-related listserv is sending messages that are not useful to you although you do not want to unsubscribe from the listserv, you can have all messages from that person automatically deleted (moved to the delete folder).

Voting

Microsoft Outlook in particular allows users to send a poll (question and buttons for several possible answers) to two or more people. Recipients click on their answer and the response is sent to the originator of the poll while also tabulating who has responded and percentages of each response. You can visit http://www.exchangeadmin.com/Articles/Index.cfm?ArticleID=23304 to learn more about how to use the voting feature in Microsoft Outlook.

Folders

To avoid having a cluttered inbox, counselors should take advantage of organizing their e-mails into different folders and subfolders. Similar to maintaining an orderly filing cabinet, e-mails can be moved, stored, and then when necessary, easily located from pertinent folders. To do this, right click (i.e., use the right mouse button) over the root folder and choose "new folder" on the menu. Then, simply drag the e-mail into a specific folder. Some e-mail applications have a "Move to Folder" button on the menu which works just as well.

• Technology Tip 7.4 •

You may become too highly organized with your e-mail and will still have trouble finding a specific communication. In this case, use your e-mail client's Find function to search all your folders given keywords that can be found in all or certain fields.

Archiving

The contents of one or all folders can be archived into an archive file to help avoid clutter while still saving e-mails. For instance, the authors archive all sent messages by month and year as scheduled in their calendar as a recurring event. In Microsoft Outlook, one can automatically remove items of a specified age and transfer them to an archive file by following these steps:

1. On the File menu, click Archive.
2. To archive all folders, click "Archive all folders according to their AutoArchive settings."
3. To archive one folder only, click: Archive this folder and all subfolders," and then click the folder that contains the items you want to archive.
4. In the Archive file box, type a file name for the archived items to be transferred to, or click Browse to select from a list.
5. In the "Archive items older than" box, enter a date. Items dated before this date will be archived. Sometimes, dates for archiving are assigned on the basis of when an e-mail message was last viewed rather than when it was sent or received. As a result, archiving will at times leave messages in a folder that appear to have a date which would otherwise cause the message to be archived.

Emoticons

According to the Webopedia (2002d) an emoticon, also known as a smiley, is an acronym for emotion icon, a small icon composed of punctuation characters that indicates how an e-mail message should be interpreted (that is, the writer's mood). Smileys came about when e-mail correspondents felt the need to convey emotional content such as sarcasm, laughter, and other feelings as part of their messages. Without smileys, simple statements could easily be misinterpreted. These tiny pictures made from ordinary ASCII characters that are meant to be looked at with the head tilted to the left. For example, consider the following:

O:-)	Angelic smiley
B-)	Cool smiley wearing sunglasses
x-(	Dead smiley
:->	Devilish smiley
:-)~~	Drooling smiley
8)	Four-eyed smiley
:-(	Frowney
:)	Generic smiley
:*)	Intoxicated smiley
:-D	Laughing smiley
:O	Shocked smiley
:-O	Shouting smiley

:-)	Smiley, with nose
:-{}	Smiley with a mustache
{:-)	Smiley with a brush cut
:-o	Talking smiley
>:-(	Very angry smiley
:-()	Wide mouthed smiley
;-)	Winking smiley
|-O	Yawning smiley

Using a Listserv

An electronic mailing list, more popularly known as a listserv, allows messages to be communicated from one individual to many other individuals—hundreds or even millions of others—quickly and efficiently. Here is the analogy: When you sign up for a magazine subscription, your personal information is placed into a database. When it's time for the magazine to be published and mailed, you automatically receive a copy. Listservs are kind of like that except that they are usually free and everyone on the subscription list can be the "publisher." Specifically, you decide which lists to subscribe to depending on your area of interest. Once you subscribe to a list, you will receive any messages that any list member sends to the group. Other members subscribed to the list will receive messages you send to the group. In the case of a moderated list, messages first go to the moderator or list owner (i.e., the person creating the list) to be screened and then posted. So, listservs can be viewed as high-tech electronic discussion groups. On a popular list, you can literally receive hundreds of e-mails in a single day. Most lists offer digests in which individual messages are bundled together daily or weekly and sent to the list as a single, large e-mail with a table of contents constructed from all the Subject headings. These help prevent your mailbox from getting overloaded.

McFadden (2000) wrote about how listservs can serve as a powerful instructional tool for collaborative learning—especially critical, reflective, and deliberative thinking processes. He suggests listservs can expand student contextual understandings of culture and myopism while promoting equity among participants regardless of assertiveness or physical, regional, and cultural differences. Specifically, McFadden (2000) suggested that online discussion groups can help people in various roles:

- Counselors can gain ownership of issues as well as a deeper understanding of their own and others' perspectives and concerns.
- Counselor educators can develop course-based listservs for myriad projects including the assignment of simulation-based projects or design case studies that incorporate personal dimensions of culturally embedded activities and assess higher cognitive skills.
- Counselor educators and practitioners can increase international communication, exchange, collaboration, and research options.

- Counselor supervisors can participate in discourse of counselor skills and techniques developed in response to the needs for counseling with a worldview perspective versus those that reflect Western ways of life and concepts.
- Counselor trainees, via a course-based listserv, can develop skills for collecting, organizing, and integrating information and learn how to form and test clinical inferences and how to plan, implement, and evaluate interventions.

Also, counselors in particular might use a listserv to:

- Keep all members of a parent advisory group informed between meetings.
- Allow clients in a support group to communicate with the counselor and the other members between sessions.
- Answer questions from students that are part of a peer helper program.
- Send all clients valuable psychoeducational material in the form of a periodic newsletter.
- Communicate with other counselors about best practice.
- Keep stakeholders informed about important policy or fiscal developments in the community.
- Disseminate information about various groups pertaining to new services that are available to clients.
- Organize a local group of professional counselors to share continuing education opportunities, job openings, or funding availability.
- Alternately take turns allowing community professionals to introduce themselves and share information about their background to increase knowledge about referral sources within the community.
- Share information learned at professional conferences or create brief reports based on recent journal articles.
- Maintain contact with groups of clients to share information about ongoing education opportunities.

How Do I Find Relevant Listservs?

There are primarily two methods for learning about available listservs of interest. First, you might learn about a specific listserv as it is announced in professional or other publications such as journals, newsletters, or newspapers. Second, you may seek listservs of interest by querying a database of listservs maintained on some Internet sites. One comprehensive database of listservs can be found at http://www.topica.com. Others include http://www.lsoft.com/lists/listref.html, http://www.coollist.com, http://www.freelists.org, and http://www.tile.net/lists. Once at these sites, you can typically conduct a search using keywords or phrases and receive a "list of lists" that contain your keywords in the title of the list or in the body of the list's description. Moreover, these sites make it especially easy to then subscribe to the listserv by providing simple directions and a convenient link that automatically calls on your e-mail software and inserts the proper address for the listserv you want to join. Finally, you should know most of these sites and many others allow you to create your own listserv groups with little or no cost. A very popular site to create a listserv of your own is http://groups.yahoo.com. At this site, you can set up a group at no cost. Once set up, the group can be made public or private. If public, than anyone with an interest in the topic can join the list. If private, the group will be limited to those individuals you choose to add. A public list can be an effective tool to facilitate general discussions on professional topics, while a private list is better suited for any communication that may include sensitive information. Remember, however, that no online communication is completely secure, and even private lists should be cautious about the extent of information disclosed.

The International Counselor Network (ICN) is one of the most popular counseling related listservs to date. The ICN was founded by Ellen Rust (see Rust, 1995) in the winter of 1993 as an effort to use the Internet to lessen the isolation of school counselors from their colleagues. The list of subscribers has grown and seems to fluctuate between 1,000 and 1,300. Counselors and others on the ICN have shared ideas ranging from what should be covered in a comprehensive guidance curriculum, appropriate interventions for special counseling cases, to solutions for common challenges. Counselor educators on the list encourage their graduate students to join during the course of their studies. The students do not have to wait for a practicing counselor to address a class at the university; they can ask questions and receive feedback at any time. Some of the liveliest debates and discussions have been started by the students. To subscribe to the ICN, visit http://listserv.utk.edu/cgi-bin/wa?SUBED1=icn&A=1.

Netiquette

According to Sabella (2003), the Internet is a very busy place which, at least for now, is mostly self-regulated. Thus, there are certain commonly understood rules of "Net Etiquette" or "Netiquette" that users of the Internet and especially listservs should adhere. Following commonly established rules of discourse will help keep the Net a mutually respectful, viable, and flexible place to connect with others who may have different needs. Keeping peace and harmony on the Net is easier said than done, however. On one hand, a modicum of etiquette is needed to allow communication over listservs and newsgroups to function efficiently, without delving into unhampered and unbecoming discourse. On the other hand, there are issues of sheer volume that dictate frugal posting and replies. Finally, there are issues of freedom of speech and access control that many users are sensitive to and willing to uphold for themselves. Following are several well-established "rules" and/or guidelines for communicating over the Net (partly adapted from e-mailreplies.com, 2001, and Albion.com, 1994–1999).

When communication seems tense or unclear, consider an alternative way to more clearly communicate information and intentions. Sometimes, it's better to break the cycle of send and respond by picking up the phone.

- **Do your homework first**. Learn about the nature of the group before joining a listserv. It is very difficult to decipher the purpose and personality of a group simply by its title. For example, on first learning about one listserv named ECSTASY, you might be lead to believe that the group is sex-related or even pornographic. However, this listserv focuses on the role of spirituality in counseling. The title merely refers to the experience of higher order living. Similarly, you might join a listserv named SHEPHERD because of an interest in this type of canine. However, the group may actually be a small group of friends in Kansas who meet for lunch on Thursday and call themselves "the shepherds." It might be a softball team in Australia or perhaps a members-only group of religious crusaders. To learn more about a group, you can first try to find the groups' description on a Web site. If not available, then you might write the owner of the list, usually listed, and ask for a description. As a last resort, you might join and simply observe before making a decision to continue or unsubscribe from the list.

- **Lurk**. When you first subscribe to a list, it's good netiquette to practice the fine art of lurking. That is, spend a few days reading the messages to get a feel for the tone and the topic of the conversation (also known as threads) before jumping in with your own response. This is simply a "look before you leap" principle to see what kind of topics are deemed appropriate by current members of a listserv or newsgroup, to see how lenient others are of divergent opinion, and to learn about the overall culture of the group.

- **FAQs**. If available, review the Frequently Asked Questions (FAQs) file, which contains common questions and answers for a particular Web site or topic. This list is especially prepared to help novice users to more quickly adapt to new standards of practice, especially in a chat room or listserv discussion. It is important to locate the FAQ for a listserv or newsgroup and read it before beginning to post anything, especially questions, to the group for two reasons. First, it usually contains a bounty of information about the subject matter of the group. Second, many users of an electronic group are highly prejudiced of users who ask questions or post information that suggests they have not read the FAQs, and let them know quickly of their despondence in e-mail and postings to the newsgroups. It is expected that FAQ questions, having already been answered and placed in an easily accessible archive, will not be asked again within the newsgroup. Your question may have already been answered, many times over; asking it again will not get you off on the right foot in an electronic group.

- **Avoid flame wars.** A flame is a searing e-mail message in which the writer attacks another participant in overly harsh, and often personal, terms. A flame war consists of a barrage of personal attacks, usually targeting an individual or more than one member of the group. As do many real-life verbal exchanges, these virtual screaming matches are usually initiated due to a misunderstanding about the exact meaning of a message. What the sender may have intended as a gentle confrontation, the recipient may view as an outright attack. Much of this is due to the impersonal nature of e-mail. Without face-to-face contact, it is difficult to convey tone. Readers do not have body language to help decipher the meaning behind written words. We imagine, too, that those who flame may also get caught in the "heat of the moment" when adversely responding to a listserv message and, hidden behind the safety of distance, find it much easier to be very frank. Even worse, those who flame will often times do so by conveying contemptuous messages about an individual in front of the entire group which may stir up others to join. If you don't think this happens among compassionate, understanding, empathetic, and unconditional counselors, you're wrong. To our continual surprise and dismay, we have learned from participating in many counseling oriented listservs that counselors are not immune. Such conversation is embarrassing for individuals; puts a damper on spirited electronic discussion in the group; and for the counseling profession, runs the risk of tarnishing the reputation of a noble profession, especially among noncounselors who subscribe to counseling listservs for educational purposes.
- **Don't spam.** Particularly reprehensible to many is the practice of posting something to every group available, whether appropriate or not. According to the Network Abuse Clearinghouse (http://spam. abuse.net/), spam is the act of flooding the Internet with many copies of the same message, in an attempt to force the message on people who would not otherwise choose to receive it. Those judged guilty of spamming may be "flamed" so badly that their computer systems become frozen for a period because of the unadulterated volume of e-mail sent in protest to them and sometimes their Internet Service Provider. In some cases, an offense is unforgivable and may result in revocation of your account. Often though, material being posted is appropriate for several groups, and it is quite acceptable to post to multiple groups in that case. If you have a product such as a book or service such as consulting about a special topic that you really believe would be of benefit, you might post a sentence or two about the opportunity with instructions for requesting further details. A safe approach would be to forward a message to a listserv owner to evaluate and decide whether to forward to the group, which should soften the burden of responsibility for your message.

- **Personal versus private messages.** Before responding to a listserv message, make certain that your response will be received by those whom you intended. Especially be careful that you send personal and private messages only to individuals and not to the entire group. Having a private conversation over a listserv is similar to doing the same in a room full of other people who are trying to focus on the issues—it's annoying.
- **Give a pertinent subject line.** Most people like to know what the e-mail message is about to best decide how to process it (i.e., delete it without reading it, read it, save, forward, etc.).
- **Uppercase letters.** Refrain from using UPPERCASE letters unless you want to convey that you are shouting.
- **Be polite.** Use your best social skills: Compliment, use the person's name, be prompt with a response.
- **Humor.** Be careful when using humor or sarcasm as it might be experienced in a negative manner.
- **E-mail limitations.** E-mail is not a substitute for face-to-face communication. Don't use e-mail for communications that require tact and sensitivity (e.g., breaking up with someone or firing someone).
- **Proper English.** Use proper spelling, grammar, and punctuation. Sometimes e-mail communications can become the overriding factor that determines the impression you have on someone. Simple mistakes can easily chip away at your professionalism and credibility. Chat rooms have created an entirely new electronic language. Words are shortened, and symbols and numbers are often used to decrease the amount of typing needed. Generally, these chat room shortcuts are not appropriate for professional listservs. Many users will find these abbreviations indecipherable, and others will view them as a sign of laziness or unprofessional behavior.
- **Content.** The content of your e-mail may tell more about you and your background than you intend. For instance, occasionally we receive an e-mail sent over a listserv made up of hundreds of counselors which indicates that the counselor who sent the message is poorly trained (e.g., How do I deal with a client who refuses to listen to his parents?).
- **Do not forward chain letters.** We can safely say that chain letters do not add value to our work and in virtually all cases are hoaxes. Some chain letters are cruel pranks to try to fill up a victim's inbox with hundreds if not thousands of e-mails. Just delete the letters as soon as you receive them.
- **Copyright.** Although not necessarily supported by law, it is considerate to treat an e-mail from someone as copyrighted information. Therefore, you should cite the e-mail as a personal communication and, whenever possible, gain written permission to use the communication in a different forum.
- **Be forgiving of other people's mistakes.** When it comes to using technology, everyone is at the novice level at one time or another.

When someone makes a mistake—whether it's a spelling error, a less than intelligent question, or an unnecessarily long answer—be kind about it. If it's a minor error, you may not need to say anything even if you feel strongly about it. Think twice before reacting. Having good manners yourself doesn't give you license to correct everyone else.

- **Anonymity.** E-mail makes it easy for people to communicate unpleasant messages while masking their identity (e.g., www.anonymizer. com). Such communication is usually viewed as cowardly and unprofessional and should be avoided. Counselors should not use e-mail communication to relieve them of the work it takes to communicate with others.

Bulletin Boards or Usenet

A related technology tool for communication that can be used in many counseling interventions is similar to a listserv and is called a bulletin board. A bulletin board can be thought of as a place where individuals write an e-mail (as in a listserv) but instead of being mailed to everyone on a list the e-mail is posted on an electronic bulletin board, and whoever is interested may come and read what has been posted. In an agency setting, practitioners might use a bulletin board to report on an interesting journal report, an employer might keep employees informed about progress being made in preparation for an upcoming accreditation visit, or clients might share strategies they use to avoid overeating or succumbing to feelings of loneliness. Uses of bulletin boards in a school setting might include a discussion of limit-setting and discipline for parents, a spot for parents to ask questions and receive answers about school trips and events, and a discussion of activities parents can do to aid preschoolers in gaining skills necessary to enter kindergarten. Google (www.google.com) offers a complete 20-year Usenet Archive with over 700 million messages. Using this Web site, counselors can easily post questions or comments and receive ongoing feedback about counseling or other issues under many different categories of "conversations."

Chat Rooms

E-mail, listservs, and bulletin boards are powerful modes of asynchronous communication. This means that individuals can communicate with one another at different times. Asynchronous tools can be powerful because they allow for communication at times that are convenient for the participants. However, sometimes people need or prefer to speak more directly. Direct communication is considered synchronous. This reflects the idea that each participant has to synchronize or coordinate his or her dialogue with every other participant. Telephone conversations are an example of technology-mediated synchronous conversations. An increasingly popular form of synchronous communication is the electronic chat room. Chat rooms are Internet sites where individuals can speak directly to one or more other people in real time. It might be thought of as instantaneous e-mail. The synchronous nature of the chat room allows for a dialog that more closely resembles a face-to-face conversation than can be achieved in either e-mail or listserv communications. Chat rooms may be used by counselors to conduct brief meetings with parents and may work particularly well when both parents are not available as a result of time or distance constraints.

One step above text-based chat rooms are videoconferencing applications. According to the Webopedia (2002e), videoconferencing involves conducting a conference between two or more participants at different sites by using computer networks to transmit audio and video data. Multipoint videoconferencing allows three or more participants to sit in a virtual conference room and communicate as if they were sitting right next to each other. Until the mid-1990s, the hardware costs made videoconferencing prohibitively expensive for most organizations, but that situation is rapidly changing. Many analysts believe that videoconferencing will be one of the fastest-growing segments of the computer industry in the latter half of the decade. Counselors who can competently operate videoconferencing equipment will more easily attend ongoing professional development opportunities, collaborate with others around the world, and visit with parents and other stakeholders without leaving their desks, and they will enhance their work with students by conducting virtual meetings with them.

Chat room software has been explored as a method for providing counseling interventions. Tyler (2000) demonstrated how communication software could be used to conduct a counseling support group in a college setting. Delmonico et al. (2000) explored the use of chat room software enhanced with visual images as a counseling intervention. As counselors become increasingly comfortable and knowledgeable about these technologies, their use as tools of intervention will increase. This will allow counselors in many schools to share expertise and group students with specific needs into tightly homogenous groups run by experts. Numerous free chat room environments exist on the Web such as at http://chat. msn.com.

Dealing With Computer Viruses

A virus is a program or piece of code that is loaded onto your computer without your knowledge and runs against your wishes. All computer viruses are created by people, and most can replicate themselves. A simple virus that can make a copy of itself over and over again is relatively easy to produce. Even such a simple virus is dangerous because it will quickly use all available memory and can easily bring your system to a halt. An even more dangerous type of virus is one capable of transmitting itself across networks and bypassing security systems (see Webopedia, www.webopedia.com). The proliferation of messages and files transferred via e-mail can help malicious users spread damaging computer code to thousands, even millions, of people in a very short time. Counselors must be aware of methods for decreasing their risk of becoming victim to viruses (also worms and Trojan horses; visit http://service4.symantec. com/SUPPORT/nav.nsf/docid/1999041209131106 to explain the difference among these), unwelcome monitoring programs, and unauthorized access. Recommendations for securing your computer include the following:

- **Conduct regular backups of all critical data**. Keep all your documents and other irreplaceable files in one folder such as "My Documents" and back up this folder to a storage medium such as CD-ROM or a network hard drive. If your computer is attacked, files (or your entire hard drive) may become corrupt or deleted, rendering your files inaccessible. Making back-ups is also good practice because all hardware fails at one time or another. You may put a reoccurring appointment in your calendar or handheld computer to remind you of making these backups. Or, in a similar manner, you might use back-up software that uses a schedule.
- **Don't open suspicious files.** One of the primary methods that people use to disseminate malicious code is via e-mail attachment. An e-mail may actually come from someone you know and may use alluring messages (e.g., "Here is the document you wanted, don't show anyone else!") to get you to open an attached file which may cause you a range of computer performance problems. Some files may be designed to look like a Web site address because it ends in "com" such as your.file.yahoo.com. Such files may actually be a program that will run when opened. Instead, respond and ask the sender whether the file did indeed come from him or her and what the file contains.
- **Use antivirus software.** Make certain that your computer has an antivirus program running at start-up. Also, be sure that the program is scheduled to regularly update its database file because new viruses are introduced everyday. Most antivirus software includes a scheduler that can do this automatically.
- **Use antispyware.** Some e-mails (and especially Web sites) may trick you into accepting a piece of code (often referred to as spyware) that can monitor your activity for the purpose of marketing and advertising. Although this does not happen frequently, you may protect yourself by running programs designed to detect and delete such code (e.g., Ad-aware is available at www.lavasoftusa.com).
- **Use a firewall program.** A firewall is used to prevent unauthorized Internet users from accessing private networks connected to the Internet, especially intranets. In addition, all e-mail messages entering or leaving the computer pass through the firewall, which examines each message and blocks those that do not meet the specified security criteria. In all likelihood, your workplace network system probably already has more than one type of firewall installed. You

may need one, however, if you access the Internet from home. If you use a dial-up service and you are not online for extended periods of time, you are probably safe without one because dial-up services typically provide you with a random type of access which is difficult to trace to you. If you are accessing the Internet using a broadband or high speed connection, it is critical that you have a firewall installed on your computer. The reason for this is that broadband connections are "always on" even when your computer is not. It is much easier for hackers to find a security breach and gain access to your computer after you do turn on your computer.

• **Forwarding e-mails**. Some would consider certain e-mail messages a type of virus because they spread quickly and cause harm. For instance, a message that seems to summon help for a child and asks you to respond may actually be designed to flood an unsuspecting victim's e-mail box. Chain letters, some would argue, create unnecessary traffic that clogs people's boxes and slows down Internet traffic, sometimes causing harm to productivity.

The Future of E-mail

E-mail has greatly evolved since Tomlinson's first e-mail message in the early 1970s, from a simple text message to messages that include a rich array of information and interactivity. Communication over the Internet continues to evolve to include more synchronous or real-time communication, the use of video, and more ingenious ways to communicate specific messages to specific users based on their interests. Following are several current developments that will require continued monitoring, especially for how they may become even better tools of communication, collaboration, and treatment delivery among counselors.

Instant Messaging

Instant messaging (IM) is a type of communications service that enables you to create a private chat room with another individual or individuals. Typically, the IM system alerts you whenever others on your private list are online. You can then initiate a chat session with one or all the individuals. IM programs allow you to chat; send messages, files, and URLs; play games; videoconference; or just interact with your friends and colleagues while still surfing the Net. Several popular IM programs include ICQ, Yahoo IM, AOL IM (AIM), NetMeeting, and MSN messenger.

Videomail

As the name connotes, videomail (Yahoo.com, n.d.; see http://promo.yahoo.com/videomail) allows users to send a message that contains a video (including audio) of themselves or anything else for that matter. As the Internet is better able to process large files and as video file compression becomes better, videomail promises to be the next evolution in electronic communication.

E-mail Appliances and Wireless Communication

In an increasingly mobile society, people need to send and access e-mail from more than just their desks. The combination of e-mail appliances and wireless transmission are now the focus for helping make e-mail communication an "anywhere, anytime" application. E-mail appliances are small devices that can process e-mail in a fashion similar to your computer. Examples of devices that currently do this are some "Web-enabled" cellular phones, handheld computers, wristwatches, pagers, televisions, kiosks, and computer tablets. The potential for counselors to reach clients anytime and anywhere has powerful implications for many areas. For instance, a counselor could create an automated e-mail that is sent randomly to a client to signal him or her to write in his or her diary. Similarly, the client could complete a questionnaire on the same appliance and automatically send the results to the counselor for data collection and analysis. Clients can automatically receive reminders about appointments, access reading material to better prepare for a session, or continue to access the counselor even when on vacation, for instance. Some appliances may even monitor signals that allow others in close proximity to detect your presence and consequently send you an e-mail (known as push technology; i.e., sending data to someone without him or her requesting it). For example, when walking past your favorite coffee house, you may receive an e-mail entitling you to 10% off your favorite cup of coffee!

Summary

E-mail is the most widely used computer application today and is continually growing, with an estimated average of over 36 billion person-to-person e-mails sent daily by the year 2005. The number of e-mail mailboxes in use around the world is expected to grow by a compound rate of 138% until 2005, bringing the total to 1.2 billion, up from 505 million last year (ICD, 2001). Such rapid growth comes as no surprise when one thinks about the advantages that e-mail communication affords. For instance, according to Sabella (2000) and Myrick and Sabella (1995), several advantages include:

- The convenience of sending and receiving e-mails at any time of the day or night.
- Being able to think through a communication before making it.
- Not having to rely on a mutual time to communicate as one would with a phone conversation.
- Saving money in long distance charges when having to make only brief comments.
- Instantaneously communicating the same message to multiple people on a distribution list.

- Diminished inhibitions that face-to-face conversation may present.
- Whereas spoken words must remain in memory and are sometimes lost in a quick exchange, written e-mail messages can be reviewed.
- Large files, especially documents, can be instantly sent to others via e-mail, saving precious time and money as compared with printing and shipping the document via traditional postal carriers.

Perhaps e-mail developments in the future may take care of several known disadvantages of e-mail also noted by Sabella (2000) and Myrick and Sabella (1995), including the following:

- For some, typing can be slow and tedious.
- The absence of nonverbal communication such as gestures, facial expression, or tone of voice can sometimes lead to mistaken interpretations of an e-mail message.
- Although relatively very secure, sending an e-mail over the Net is sometimes like sending a postcard through the mail—others who desire to do so might intercept and read an e-mail. Therefore, issues of confidentiality and privacy are central to communicating sensitive information.
- If not careful, counselors can receive too many e-mail messages, which may lead to time and organizational management challenges. In this sense, counselors must be smart consumers of information and determine how much one reads, digests, and to which messages one should respond.

In general, e-mail has changed the way we work, play, and connect with others. Electronic communication, no matter what form or method it will take in the future, will certainly be an important part of how a counselor communicates, collaborates, and delivers counseling treatment.

Internet Sites for Additional Information

- **http://www.webfoot.com/advice/FindingEmailAddresses.html.** Kaitlin Duck Sherwood presents a useful article titled "Finding Someone's E-mail Address."
- **http://directory.google.com/Top/Computers/Internet/Etiquette/Usenet/?tc=1.** This links to Google's Usenet directory of Web sites.
- **http://www.faqs.org/faqs/usenet/primer/part1.** This site is titled "A Primer on How to Work With the Usenet Community."
- **http://www.cauce.org.** CAUCE, The Coalition Against Unsolicited Commercial E-mail, is an ad hoc, all volunteer organization, created by Netizens to advocate for a legislative solution to the problem of UCE (a.k.a. "spam").
- **http://www.smartgroups.com.** SmartGroups is a free service that combines Web-based group information together with e-mail messaging.
- **http://www.mcfedries.com/ramblings/email-primer.asp.** This site contains a brief e-mail primer, by Paul McFedries.

- **http://www.steve.maurer.net/email_primer2.htm.** This site contains more e-mail primers.
- **http://www.temple.edu/Listserv.** This brief listserv primer is furnished by some folks at Temple University's Office of Academic Computer Services.
- **http://www.gfi.com/emailsecuritytest/.** Is your e-mail system secure against e-mail viruses and attacks? Test the security of your e-mail system.

Evaluating Information on the Internet

Competency: Be able to evaluate the quality of Internet information.

Imagine a system of psychological diagnosis that can provide absolute insight into the personality and behavior of any client. A system that is more accurate than any other available, and one that is so responsive to events in the client's life it can, "in many instances, uncover repressed memories of molestation. No less important, the therapist would be able to distinguish between repressed memories and false memory syndrome." (PDC Profiles, n.d.). Such a system does exist according to the claims made on the associated Web site. The system is known as Psychodiagnostic Chirology (http://www.pdc.co.il/ind1.htm) and is a form of diagnosis through hand reading. By studying the shape of the client's hand, the length of various lines, the size of finger phalanges and other characteristics, the clinician can make absolute diagnosis with unparalleled certainty.

The system sounds fantastic, and certainly such a system would be a tremendous bonus to everyone in the field. Quick and accurate diagnosis that can immediately lead to an increased understanding of a client's complete history holds the potential to revolutionize the counseling process. The extent of its impact would be vast indeed, but relatively few people in the United States appear to know that this system exists, and fewer still appear to endorse the concept. A visit to the founder's Web site will provide the curious reader with articles, cases studies, and testimonials. The language of the site is quite compelling, and the results of a pilot study are offered to demonstrate support. As well, references for articles published in various journals are offered that purport to provide a basis for the underlying theory behind this approach. Provided with only the information offered by the author of this Web site, and a desire to believe in what we read, we are tempted to accept this system as a remarkable new approach to assessment. Many readers, particularly those with little background in psychology and assessment, may see this information and believe they too have discovered a remarkable new approach.

The reader of this book, as well as the reader of any material on the Internet, must decide what information to accept, what to question, and what to reject. As professionals in counselor education, we (the authors) have a bias concerning the need for all counselors to understand and be able to use available technology in their professional lives. Individuals who develop material for the Internet also maintain certain biases. In some cases these biases are consistent with mainstream cultural or political perspectives and go unnoticed. In the latter months of 2001 and into 2002, many published materials in the United States maintained a strong patriotic air. Such biases are often overlooked because they match our own values and beliefs. When materials run counter to our expectations and personal values or opinions, we are more apt to notice the bias displayed. In our professional capacity, however, maintaining an appropriate level of skepticism about what we read and hear in all things is a good idea. Material that supports our position should be carefully evaluated to ensure that our position is supported by current research. Material that does not support our position should also be evaluated to determine whether there is evidence to suggest a modification or change in a particular assumption or belief is in order.

Nowhere is this need for skepticism more evident than on the Internet. As professionals, counselors have historically obtained information from peer-reviewed journals, books written by professional leaders and researchers, or from universities or practice organizations where a level of expertise was expected. These arenas maintained various systems of oversight which, although imperfect, created some level of confidence in the information provided. The World Wide Web has no such oversight, and anyone can develop a Web site to promote any idea they happen to want promoted. Researchers are increasingly placing information on the World Wide Web rather than waiting for peer review because of the long wait that can occur in traditional paper publications. Universities are increasingly disseminating information over the Internet in an attempt to maintain a high public profile. And any individual who wants to be heard can create a Web page to express him- or herself in a matter of minutes, and potentially reach an audience of millions. The skilled professional must approach this seemingly unlimited amount of information with a questioning attitude and the skills to discern what information is likely to be most useful and what may be potentially misleading or damaging. Also, clients are increasingly turning to the Internet for information. The technologically literate professional counselor must be actively involved with clients as he or she seeks information in a manner that will help clients make good use of appropriate resources.

•   Technology Tip 8.1   •

Many "legends" exist on the Internet and are passed around via e-mail and in chat rooms. These often concern reports of destructive viruses, opportunities to make money, or requests to send e-mail to a particular individual. Before assuming any such reports are true, check them out at http://urbanlegends.about.com/ or http://www.vmyths.com/. Never forward an e-mail about a potential threat unless you know it is valid.

By now, you are well aware that the types of information provided on the Internet are quite varied. As well, the manner in which information is presented varies in innumerable configurations. In graduate school, where students are often taught to evaluate the quality of a research article, students are first presented with an outline or formula of what a research article is expected to look like. Based on this, the student is given or expected to formulate a series of questions that provide an evaluation template for most research. With slight variations for distinctions in qualitative versus quantitative research, or between research and theoretical manuscripts, the same basic evaluation template can be applied to almost all articles published in professional journals of interest to the counselor. Because of the widely varying styles of presentation found on the World Wide Web, the development of a template that can be widely applied is impractical.

Quality of Information

In their book on the evaluation of online resources, Browne and Keeley (2003) posed a number of questions that form the basis for their evaluation approach. This includes considering the argument presented on the Web site, the source of the information, included value assumptions, and the quality of the evidence. Overall, these topics appear to promote a critical thinking approach that is as valid in evaluating Web sites as it is in evaluating any new material that the professional might encounter. This approach of identifying a small group of relevant characteristics is common and is reflected in the work of others (see Sabella & Tyler, 2001). A more comprehensive approach was formulated by Kim, Eng, Deering, and Maxfield (1999). On the basis of their review of 29 separate rating tools, they identified 13 commonly used categories. These are summarized in Table 8.1. The remainder of this chapter reviews these concepts as a guide to help the counseling professional approach information on the Internet equipped with the skills necessary to critically evaluate material presented.

• Table 8.1 •

A Baker's Dozen of Questions for the Evaluation of Online Sites

1. Is the content of the site consistent with other known information?
2. Are the conclusions drawn warranted on the basis of the information presented?
3. What information is not available from this site?
4. Is the information that is presented sufficiently broad to adequately represent the domain of knowledge?
5. Has the content undergone a peer review process?
6. Who owns the Web site, and what vested interested do they have in a particular point of view?
7. Is the site developer/owner worthy of trust and respect?
8. Is the information current?
9. Do links provided connect to known, reputable sources?
10. Are the links active, or are there many "dead" links?
11. Are "facts" documented or cited?
12. Who is the intended audience?
13. Is the information useful?

Content of Site

A professor friend has often been heard to say that in her class, clip art on the title page of a paper is the key to a good grade. She makes the statement in jest, but it does carry an important, albeit hidden, message. The content of a Web site (or a student paper) may initially be judged on looks alone. But, to update an old saying, "Never judge a Web site by its home page." If the content does not present a compelling message, then all the factors that follow are of little importance. Also, if the argument presented is strong enough, then other factors like poor aesthetics or difficulty in navigation can be overlooked. First and foremost, the content of a site must be able to stand on its own.

To evaluate a site's content, a good starting point is to compare the information from the site with information at other sites, or information from other sources. Returning to the example referred to at the beginning of this chapter, the reader is presented with a site whose content is not supported by information presented in most books on assessment and diagnosis or on other Web sites presenting information on this topic. Immediately, the reader should be prompted to ask: What are the reasons that this information is available only from this single source? This lack of immediate corroboration is not necessarily a condemnation of a Web site. There may be many reasons that the information is not presented elsewhere. In some cases, the information may represent new research findings or proprietary information to which others have not had access. In these cases, the Internet user may have access to the most current information. However, in other cases information is not replicated because professionals or others with an interest in the topic have found the information unworthy of repeating.

A second step in evaluating the content of a site is to review the site to determine the conclusions that are drawn and then to identify the underlying argument that leads to the conclusion offered. An example of a site whose conclusions may not be well supported from the evidence is the National Association for Research and Therapy of Homosexuality (http://www.narth.com/). This site offers an article that suggests twin studies refute the link between biology and sexual orientation. In support of their argument, the site states that twin studies of sexual orientation have identified concordance rates (the rate at which both members of a twin pair are homosexual or heterosexual) between 30% and 50% (Whitehead, 2002). The authors continue by arguing that if sexual orientation were genetically based, then 100% of identical twins would share the same sexual orientation. Research scientists would generally disregard this interpretation, pointing to a variety of health factors known to have genetic influences but that never show 100% concordance rates in twin studies. A prime example is the diagnosis of schizophrenia, where concordance rates are below 50% (Barlow & Durand, 1999), but the genetic link is widely accepted. Statistics are often provided, as are tables, graphs, and charts of varying types to support a conclusion on a Web site. This information should always be carefully reviewed and considered. When in doubt, the reader should seek confirming information from other sources, or consultation from experts who can provide clarification.

A third step in evaluating the content of a site is to consider what information is omitted. Oftentimes information is omitted to maintain brevity or simply through an oversight of the developer or author. However, information is sometimes omitted that appears to be critical information, and the user may legitimately question why the information has been neglected. *Ask Dr. Judith* (http://members.aol.com/drjudith77/index.htm) is a Web site that offers online counseling and includes a brief list of the author's credentials. These include her education and various writings. Nowhere on the site does it mention whether she is licensed in the state where she practices. It is possible that this is an old site that predates licensure requirements in her home state of Indiana, or it is possible that the site is maintained by someone who is not required to be licensed to engage in some activities within the state. In this case, the lack of information available should prompt the user to seek additional information when trying to evaluate the Web site and its offerings.

Another consideration in the evaluation of the content of a Web site is the breadth of information available. Sites that provide a simple overview of a topic might be useful, but by their brevity risk failing to provide the full information that the professional counselor or their client may need. An article from CBS News (cbsnews.com) serves as an example (CBS News, 2002). In approximately 370 words, the article attempts to overview vagus nerve stimulation (vns) as a treatment for depression. In this short space, the reader is provided little factual information, although enough is provided to raise the hopes of many who might suffer from chronic and treatment-resistant depression. A similar article at Dr's Guide (www.docguide.com; Doctor's Guide Publishing, 1999) almost three times in length, provides a much better overview. Importantly, this longer article provides additional information concerning the populations that vns has been tested on, as well as information about test sites and outcomes. A more detailed overview of this approach is provided at Dr. Ivan's Depression Central (http://www.psycom.net/depression.central.html; Depression Central, 2002). Each of these sites has an important role and contribution to make. Readers must assess each separately to determine which best meets their individual needs. The final site, which includes citations for research articles and a more thorough explanation of treatment procedures, may be best for the clinician, whereas a client may be successfully directed to another site.

Sometimes information on the Internet has gone through a peer-review process, and in these cases, the reader may assume some level of quality exists based on this process. Increasingly, journals are providing access to their articles online, and some journals exist only as online writings. One such journal of importance to counselors is the *Journal of Technology in*

Counseling (http://jtc.colstate.edu/). This online resource provides a forum for counselors, counselor educators, and those with similar interests to discuss the use of technology in counseling and counselor education. This type of peer-reviewed resource is increasingly popular for a variety of reasons including lower production costs and much faster production timeframes.

Generally when we consider the content of a site, attention is focused on the informational text presented. However, many sites contain much more than text. The other content-laden material on many sites is the advertising that has become a tremendously large industry in recent years. These advertisements communicate a great deal of information about the site, its biases, and the purpose of the site developer.

DrKoop.com (drkoop.com) raises interesting issues about advertising on the Web. Dr. Koop was well known as Surgeon General of the United States as a strong and outspoken advocate of public health and access to information. The launch of his Web site was seen by many as an example of the positive contribution a public figure might make by becoming involved in the World Wide Web and information dissemination. The site continues today as a distributor of information on a wide range of topics, and for many is a first stop in accessing health information. However, in addition to information, the site has become a vendor of a wide range of products, including Dr. Koop's own line of dietary supplements. In addition, the site includes one of the more annoying features of the Internet, pop-up ads. As someone navigates through the site, new browser windows are automatically opened on the user's computer, each containing an advertisement for another product. In reviewing the site and searching for information on osteoarthritis, we reviewed six pages including information on various drugs and supplements that can be used to reduce symptoms. In this review process, we also had five new windows open on our computer, advertising debt elimination services, BonziBUDDY (a software program), a service to find high school classmates, and beauty products. This barrage of advertisements emphasizes the commercial aspects of the site, and diminishes the characterization of the site solely as a provider of medical information.

• Technology Tip 8.2 •

You can stop those annoying pop-up ads using a variety of software products. Visit http://www.raxarsoft.com/pop-up-killer.htm to find a list of software that can eliminate these annoyances from your life.

Disclosure of Authors, Sponsors, and Developers

A second area of interest or concern is the developer of a Web site. In most cases, the name of the developer or sponsor of a site is prominently displayed. This can be very useful information in determining what the agenda of a site developer may be. By considering the agenda of the developer, the Web user will be better prepared to determine whether a site may be biased in a manner that may misrepresent certain information.

The U.S. Department of Health and Human Services through the Center for Substance Abuse Prevention (CSAP) maintains a Web site known as For Real (http://www.forreal.org/). This unique site targets children between the ages of 13 and 17 and provides accurate and current information on marijuana. This well-designed site is engaging and provides a great deal of information. However, some users might be surprised to find this government site that does not have a .gov URL. By carefully reading through the entire page, including the footer at the bottom of each page, the reader will find information that associates this site with CSAP and the Substance Abuse and Mental Health Services Administration (SAMHSA). Casual observers may miss this connection and not understand the affiliation. Another online site, Yahooka (yahooka.com), a pro-marijuana site, is a popular resource site that provides a quite different view. Reviewing this site, the reader is left with two contact e-mail points, but no definitive declaration of who maintains the site or how the site is financed. In this case, the producers openly declare their agenda (to unite the marijuana community) if not their identity. Admittedly a reflection of our own bias, knowing who developed these sites and their agenda, we would tend to endorse the first as likely to contain more accurate medical information or current research.

It should be noted that some perceived bias should not necessarily be used to discount all that a site has to offer. Sometimes, seeking sites with a particular bias can help the counselor understand the world from a different viewpoint. There have been many news reports in 2001 and 2002 of Web sites that promote anorexia nervosa and bulimia as alternative lifestyle choices. Anyone who has worked with clients who have an eating disorder is aware of the secrecy and hidden world many such clients maintain. For some counselors who have never worked extensively with this population, there may be a lack of understanding of the thought processes that contribute to these disorders. While reviewing such sites is likely not appropriate for clients, counselors may find these to be informative sites to the extent that they reveal something of the hidden world of some clients. And while they may offer some insight into thinking patterns, they are likely not providers of accurate science and medical information.

Authority of Source

The next factor to consider when reviewing a Web site is the authority of the site author. In many cases, information presented on the Internet will have a clearly identifiable author. As in the case of journal articles, professional books, or other sources of information, the expertise and reputation of the author is always an important consideration when determining the value of specific information. A comparison of two sites will help illustrate the importance of the author's credibility.

The first page to consider is entitled *Children of Divorce* (n.d.), and is a first-person account of divorce and its impact on a child. The article includes citations but no complete bibliography, which means the citations cannot be reviewed and no follow-up is possible. Because of the included citations, there may be a tendency to assume that the information is accurate. However, with no included information about the author, it is impossible to judge the ability of the author to read, interpret, and represent another's work. In contrast is another page titled *Children of Divorce and Adjustment* (Nolan, 2000). This page is authored by Dr. Richard Nolan. A link on the page provides a brief biographical sketch of the author, including professional affiliations, work expertise, and something of his professional interests. On the basis of the information provided, the user can be more confident of the expertise of the author of this second page. In fact, the author of the first page may possess more expertise and knowledge, but, lacking information, the reader would be best served by taking a cautious approach and not assuming expertise.

At times, an author may not be noted. In these cases, the Web user may consider the authority of the sponsoring organization as one indicator of quality. Again, a comparison of pages will help illustrate the point. The National Institute of Mental Health (NIMH) maintains an online document titled "Depression in Children and Adolescents" (NIMH, 2000). There is no author attributed. A second online article, "Childhood Depression, Teenage Depression" is hosted by Symptoms of Depression.com (2002). The first paper is much more extensive and provides a broader array of information than the second. One important difference is in the sections that focus on risk factors or triggers. The NIMH document stresses the correlation between depression and gender, family history, significant loss, and trauma among other factors. The second paper notes triggers including divorce, a death, or family problem. No mention is made of family history or gender differences. Are these important considerations? In an earlier section it was noted that one way to evaluate content is to look for collaboration. In this case, these two articles do not provide collaboration on these specific issues. However, the authority of NIMH is well-established, so the information on this site may deserve to be given greater weight unless specific disconfirming information is identified.

It should be noted that the authority of a site is not absolute. In an important study on the reliability of information on the Internet, McClung, Murray, and Heitlinger (1998) looked at information on the Internet about diarrhea in children. This topic was chosen because the American Academy of Pediatrics has published specific practice guidelines for physicians concerning how this ailment should be treated. In their research, these authors found that only 20% of the Web sites reviewed contained information that met these important practice guidelines. Web sites that had been assumed to provide accurate information—including teaching centers, practitioners, and health departments—provided inaccurate information 80% of the time. This indicates that even those sites that might otherwise be seen as credible sources of information need to be viewed with a questioning attitude.

Currency of Information

As noted earlier in this chapter, one of the principal advantages of the Internet is the quick dissemination of information. It is not unusual for traditional professional journals to have a production time of 1 year or more between the time an article is submitted and when it appears in print. Adding whatever time the author spent writing and rewriting the work, the data is clearly dated by the time it is in print. Web pages on the other hand can be created in a matter of days. Authors can have their work online as soon as it is authored. Therefore, the potential for much more current information is available on the Internet when compared with most traditional print media.

However, this ease of providing data also creates another problem related to data remaining long after it is useful. An example of this is the National Association of Social Workers, Michigan chapter Web site (http://www.nasw-michigan.org/main.shtml). In an effort to keep members apprised of conference and training activities, this organization maintains a calendar on its Web site as well as a link to the NASW–Michigan state conference. On February 19, 2003, when the calendar was accessed (http://www.nasw-michigan.org/calendar.htm), the most recent listing was for January 1. No year was provided, but it was assumed the calendar was referring to events from the end of 2002 and the first day of 2003. On this same day, when the link to the annual meeting was accessed, information was provided for a meeting that had occurred more than 5 months earlier (http://www.nasw-michigan.org/annualconference.htm). Similar outdated conferences were found when seeking opportunities in Canada. Accessing the Counsellor Resource Centre (http://www.crccanada.org) on February 19, 2003, a list of conferences was found on its Web site (http://www.crccanada.org/english/conferences.html). Unfortunately, the list contained conferences dating back to September 2001. In fact, of the 13 conferences listed, 12 had occurred in 2001 or 2002. Although there is some value in maintaining information on the Internet as archival or historical data, these pages represent a common problem in Web-based material: a failure to keep information current.

A common practice on Web sites is to include a "last update" date. In fact, the practice is so common that most of the major software programs used to create Web pages have a function that will automatically add a new date every time the page is edited or modified. In most cases, this date can be found at the bottom of the site's home page. By reviewing this date, the reader can immediately determine the currency of the information provided.

In areas where information is developing rapidly, knowing the date a page was created is very important. A page titled "Subtle Brain Circuit Abnormalities Confirmed in ADHD" (NIMH, 1996) reports on the first comprehensive brain imaging study of boys with attention deficit hyperactivity disorder (ADHD). In the 6 years following, numerous additional studies have been completed and reported on via the Internet. Studies reported in 2000 (McLean Hospital, 2000) and 2001 (NAMI, 2001) have significantly advanced understanding in this rapidly changing field. Without appropriately dated material it would be difficult to compare differences in results.

The National Institute of Mental Health, Child Psychiatry Branch, maintains a Web page titled "Brain Development Study" (Giedd, n.d.). The page reports on a research study being conducted that images the brains of healthy children and adolescents to provide a better understanding of brain development, as well as control images for studies with individuals who have ADHD or other psychiatric illness. Unfortunately, the page has no date, so the reader has no immediate way to determine whether the page contains current information or reports on a study that has long since been completed. Fortunately, Netscape and Internet Explorer provide a feature which may be helpful in this situation. By viewing the page details in your browser, you can determine when a page was last modified. In this case, the page was last modified on February 22, 2002, 4 months before it was reviewed for this writing. This relative recency suggests the project is likely still active.

• Technology Tip 8.3 •

To view the details of a Web page in Netscape, the user can open the pull-down menu under the label "View" and choose "Page Info." In Internet Explorer, open the menu "File" and choose "Properties." These actions will open a small dialogue box that will provide the user with information on the page being viewed including the date of the most recent modification.

Links

One of the most positive aspects of the World Wide Web is the ability of site authors to link to additional information provided by themselves or by others at distant sites. Imagine the benefit we all might have experienced in graduate school if our textbooks had been electronic and we could simply point to a name we did not know and immediately be presented with a second book that presented all the information we wanted on this unknown person or construct. Of course, that is exactly what the Web is capable of doing. Users are not limited to what any individual author provides, but also have the benefit of links the author supplies to additional information.

Sometimes, the links that an author provides are quite limited and do not offer the reader a chance to move beyond the material the author provides in a significant manner. At other times, the links provided are relatively narrow in scope, and although they may provide additional information, they may suggest a particular audience to which the reader does not belong. This then may suggest that the initial page is also directed at an audience to which the reader does not belong. A page entitled "Sound Behavior" (http://www.soundbehavior.bigstep.com/; Sound Behavior, 2001) provides a useful example. When visiting the Resource Links section of this Web site, the reader is first presented with a page that contains links that redirect the reader to another page within the site. In this manner, the reader can click through a number of pages without ever accessing information from another site. The careful and patient user will continue through the list of links and the accompanying text to find at the bottom of the page a link to another page. This second page contains links to a variety of external Web sites. Starting with the first of these links, and continuing down the list, a pattern quickly emerges. The links are largely to commercial sites which maintain heavy advertising and are selling products ranging from supplements to books. These consumer-oriented sites may not provide information at the level that the professional counselor is seeking. This may also suggest that the original site (*Sound Behavior*) is also aimed at the nonprofessional.

Alternate pages, including Psychology and Counseling Materials (http://www.marshall.edu/library/psylist.htm; Marshall University Libraries, 2001) and "Counseling Resources on the Net" (http://www.uark.edu/depts/cned/web/orglinks.htm; Nisenholz, n.d.) are pages of more professionally oriented links. These sites are more likely to provide counselors with information that is geared to their level of knowledge and need.

The links provided on a Web site can also provide the reader with an indication of how well the site is maintained and if the information on the site is current. If the reader finds that many of the links on a page are no longer functional, this indicates that the links have not been maintained. Although it is certainly possible that the author has kept other information on the page current while ignoring the links, the likelihood of this scenario seems small. Current software packages for creating Web sites include tools to verify that links are working properly. While not everyone has these tools, they are quite common and easy to use. When a site has many links (internal or external) that are no longer functional, it suggests a lack of investment in site maintenance and raises some concern about the quality of other aspects of the site as well.

• Technology Tip 8.4 •

Sometimes you may want to share a link or a Web page with a friend or client. In Netscape choose File and then Send Page, and you can e-mail an entire Web page. In Internet Explorer choose File then Send then Page by E-mail.

Attribution and Documentation

In professional writing we are accustomed to having authors provide citations for their source material. Sometimes in footnotes, sometimes through a reference list, the reader of a journal article is informed of where the author's information comes from. By reviewing this information, the reader is assured of two important issues. First, the reader knows that the author of the work did not make up any statements of fact that are written. Second, the reader, if he or she chooses, has the option to track down source materials and review them to see if they draw the same conclusions or share the same interpretation of source material as the journal article author. This is an important step in the scientific process which seeks to extend knowledge in ever new and expanding directions.

The World Wide Web is seldom created on the basis of these same formal structural requirements. In part, this is because the majority of the Web is not aimed at professionals who are accustomed to this process of citations. Even those sites that seek a professional audience may choose to disregard the practice of maintaining a reference list or appropriate citations.

Working with individual clients, in small groups, and in large group guidance settings, social skills training is an important component of many counselor's duties. The Internet is a valuable resource in learning more about social skills training, what works, and the reasons that certain approaches work. A site titled "I'm Popular! Do I Need Social Skills Training?" (Lope & Edelbaum, 1999) is a well-written site that offers the professional counselor with valuable information about the need for social skills training. Well documented, the writing is peppered with appropriate citations and a complete reference list is provided for the reader. Because of this, the reader can maintain a sense of confidence that the site authors are knowledgeable and the information contained on the site is accurate. A different example is provided on a page titled "Social Skills Therapy" (http://www.family-connection.org/social_skills_training.htm; Family-connection.org, n.d.). This page also contains good information but includes no references or citations. The professional counselor who is seeking information may not know whether the information on this page is accurate and has no way to follow up. Additionally, if the page provides useful information, the counselor may choose to seek additional information. If references are provided, the counselor has an immediate place to turn for this additional information.

Intended Audience

As noted earlier, the World Wide Web is primarily geared toward consumers. Many information sites aimed at both professionals and consumers are funded through advertising and sales. Indeed, this overcommercialization of the Web has stimulated work aimed at the development of Internet 2, a faster network backbone to support research and academe (Internet2, 1997–2002). This commercial emphasis, along with the development of materials by hobbyists, enthusiasts, and seemingly everyone with an opinion, has created a virtual world of information that oftentimes lacks depth. As noted in the section on using search engines (chapter 9), one of the more overwhelming aspects of the Internet is attempting to sort through the millions of available sites to find those with relevance to the individual.

Although this is frustrating, it also provides great opportunity. Regardless of one's language skills, developmental level, educational achievements, or previous knowledge, there always seems to be some site available that matches the needs of each individual. The task of professional counselors is to seek information at their level.

It has been suggested that graduate students often skip the "Results" section of research articles and move straight to the Discussion section. This is likely done because the student finds the description and reporting of statistics difficult to follow. Unfortunately, the student who pursues this approach to journal reading is forced to accept the article author's interpretation of findings. To really understand and draw our own opinions, we must struggle to read and comprehend the difficult passages of research as well as the easy. The same is true of material on the Internet. On any given topic, material is available that is appropriate for clients as well as the counselor. In many cases, the type of information both groups require will be somewhat different. The counselor who does not seek out information geared toward the professional will be left reading the opinions and interpretations of others creating information for the mass market.

A quick search for information on dyslexia will provide an example. The site Dyslexia My Life (dyslexiamylife.org, n.d.) maintains a page titled "What Is Dyslexia" (http://www.dyslexiamylife.org/wb_dyslexia.htm). This is a very good page geared toward individuals who may have been diagnosed with dyslexia, or perhaps family members or friends of such individuals. The page contains some statistics and a few definitions of dyslexia. Armed with this information, a counselor would be aware that dyslexia is a specific language-based disorder that results in difficulty acquiring certain language skills. An alternate page maintained by the Greenwood Institute (greenwoodinstitute.org) is directed toward the professional (Lyon, 1995; http://www.greenwoodinstitute.org/resources/reslyon.html). This page offers a definition, but goes much further by discussing difficulties in creating a definition and the evolution of the term across time. Although this latter page may present more information than a parent or adolescent is interested in (or needs), this broader discussion will provide the professional with a more sophisticated understanding of the concept. As well, this latter page offers citation information on a complete article focusing on this topic that the professional may wish to pursue.

As professionals, we are charged with a particular role in society. That role includes an advocacy for others and comes with an expectation that we possess a level of knowledge on key issues that is broader and more sophisticated than that possessed by other, untrained individuals. To live up to the responsibility that this entails, we must seek out information beyond that which is geared toward lay audiences.

Usefulness of Information

The following characteristics of Web sites that one can use as evaluation criteria do not focus directly on quality. Rather, these characteristics address issues of usefulness. When evaluating a Web site, it is important to consider not only the quality of information, but whether the information will ever be used. As a professional, will you ever visit this site again? Would you recommend the site to a client or colleague? If the site is not useable, then it is not useful.

User Support

Issues of support are usually not of concern for most people as they surf the Web. However, there are times when unique features of a site create difficulty between the user and the site. In these cases, if support is not available, then the site will quickly be abandoned as the individual moves to another site with similar information but without usability problems. Historically, one example of this difficulty was the widespread use of frames during the mid-1990s. For a number of years, many Web sites used the convention of frames to divide the page into 2 or more separate panes. Often, one pane was used for navigation while a second was used to display content. This created a great deal of difficulty because many browsers in use at the time did not support frames, and users with these browsers were unable to properly view the site. While these issues have largely been resolved, it is still common to visit sites that have a link to a separate page that does not use frames.

Today, it is more common to have viewing difficulties because the site uses a "plug-in" to display some of its content. Common plug-ins include Macromedia Shockwave (http://www.macromedia.com/), RealPlayer (http://www.real.com/), and Apple's Quicktime Video Player (http://www.apple.com/quicktime/download/). Modern browsers are generally self-sufficient, and if you visit a page that requires a plug-in that you do not have, your browser will notify you that it needs to add this software, and then will proceed to download the software and install it with only minimal assistance from you, the user. Whenever viewing a site, if you have difficulty, look for a link to a Help page. Most designers are aware of the needs of their intended audience and will provide online documentation to assist with most common problems.

More difficult problems arise at sites that require registration, access codes, and password authentication. Very often, when a site requires registration, users will simply move on, choosing not to pass out personal information or to take the time necessary to register. Again, most sites will be aware of potential problems and will provide easy access to helpful information to resolve difficulties.

Accessibility and Availability

A more difficult access problem, although one that is less common, is access by sight-impaired individuals. Software is available and widely used that allows computers to read Web pages to those who have visual impairments. Unfortunately, few individuals take the time to test their Web site to ensure that it is compliant with these programs. As a result, Web surfing for individuals with visual impairments is much more difficult than it needs to be. Professionals who develop and maintain Web sites need to be aware of these issues and create sites that meet the needs of their audience. In some cases, federal law may require compliance. For a more complete discussion of these issues, visit Text Matters (http://www.textmatters.com/guides/visually_impaired_web.html) or Internetworking (http://www.internettg.org/newsletter/mar99/accessibility_lila.html). Disabled Accessibility (http://servercc.oakton.edu/~wittman/find/disabled.htm) includes information on design issues as well as access to federal laws and regulation. For additional information on technology designed to assist those with visual impairments, see the discussion in chapter 2.

Ease of Use

The latest software packages designed for creating Web pages incorporate sophisticated tools for the creation and customization of navigation tools within a Web site. Pull down menus, scrolling navigation lists, and similar features are increasingly common. As a result, navigation has become much easier on most well-designed sites.

Perhaps the biggest difficulty that Web users have related to ease of use is the potential to become lost. Because the Web is not created on a linear model like a book, where users move from page to page in a predefined sequence, it is easy to click through a number of pages and not remember how you arrived at your current location. Of course, becoming lost is not dangerous because we can always shut off our computer and find ourselves immediately back in the comfort of our home or office. Becoming lost can be frustrating, however. It is not an uncommon experience for users to find information of interest, click to a new location, and then find themselves unable to return to where they were previously. Some sites provide a system known as breadcrumbs to help the user understand where they are located. Breadcrumbs will usually appear at the top of a Web page, or in a navigation area in a column on one side of the page. The format generally starts with the title of the site's home page, followed by an arrow or dash, and then the title of a subpage that was moved to from the home page. This may be followed by another arrow or dash and the title of yet another page. In this fashion, the user can tell where they are within a given site at all times. In most instances, these breadcrumbs are active links, so the user has the option to simply click on the title of a previous page and they will immediately return to that page.

Another option in most cases is to use the Back or Forward button on the Web browser. Both Netscape and Internet Explorer offer this option, and each time the button is clicked, the user will be transported one page in the direction chosen. As well, both of these two common browsers display a small arrowhead next to the Forward and Back buttons. Clicking on this arrowhead will open a list of pages that were first visited prior to the current page, or after the current page was first visited. The user can then choose any page from this list and will be directly transported to the appropriate page.

Contact Address

In most cases, Web site designers are anxious to provide contact information. A common practice is to provide an e-mail for the Webmaster or site designer at the bottom of each page. Some organizations maintain policies that their address and phone number will be displayed on every page. In other cases, sites will choose to have a specific link in their navigation bar labeled "Contacts." Regardless of where the information is displayed, its availability suggests something about the site and its developers. And, because the practice is so common, when it does not exist its absence is seemingly more blatant.

At times, the omission of contact information is likely an oversight. Perhaps a novice Web designer has failed to consider this aspect of the site. In other cases this information is likely omitted on purpose. In some cases, as on sites that promote eating disorders or suicide, site developers will state they have chosen to omit contact information to avoid the harassment they fear they will be subjected to as a result of their beliefs. In any case, we believe that the omission of this information is a reason to legitimately question the quality of a site. Perhaps it has not been constructed with an eye toward details. If this is the case, then other important details may be missing as well. Perhaps the information is omitted on purpose. In this case, there may be reason to be concerned that other information, perhaps contradictory facts, will be omitted as well.

Design and Aesthetics

Finally, the issue of overall site design is important. Any individual who has spent more than a few minutes on the World Wide Web is aware that the visual appeal of sites varies greatly. It would be wrong to judge a site solely on the basis of its visual appeal, but there generally is a connection between a site's visual makeup and the level of the material presented.

There are a number of sites on the Web where individuals can build and maintain a personal Web site free of charge. Angelfire (angelfire.lycos.com) and Tripod (tripod.lycos.com) are two common sites. Sites created and hosted by these services often reflect the site builder's lack of knowledge about the World Wide Web. Such sites may contain poor contrast between backgrounds and fonts making reading difficult, very busy backgrounds that distract from the content, or poorly edited material with a great deal of spelling and grammatical errors. Such sites are easily recognizable as sites that individuals have created to express their opinions. The lack of professional quality may suggest a lack of professional content.

As noted earlier, another identifying design characteristic is associated with the advertising on a site. Sites created and maintained by educational institutions and many nonprofit organizations, sites whose purpose is the dissemination of information, will generally have no ads. These institutions have made a commitment to funding their Web presence through alternate means. This suggests that the content is not influenced by advertisers or specific needs related to revenue.

Over the past 8 years there has been a tremendous change in the manner in which Web pages are created and the basis on which they are designed. Today there is general agreement that pages should be free of distracting images, flashing graphics, or text of many sizes and colors. However, these practices were not uncommon in the past. Today, sites are much more likely to have more white space, areas on the page without any information. Fonts are chosen to be easy on the eye for the surfer who has been staring at a computer screen for extended periods, and graphics are carefully chosen to enhance rather than distract from the user experience. Sites that do not adhere to these current practices may represent older sites that have not been updated. In some cases, these may even be abandoned sites that have been forgotten by their original author. We ourselves have built pages and then as a result of job changes, new equipment installations at work, or other factors, have forgotten to remove pages for months or even years after their usefulness passed. An example is a course from 1998 which I (J. Michael Tyler) can no longer access to remove, so the site remains available, although outdated (http://ruby.fgcu.edu/courses/50171/6215open.htm).

• Technology Tip 8.5 •

Want to learn more about what a good page looks like, or just look at some really bad pages? Visit http://webpagesthatsuck.com/, a serious site that teaches through negative example. (If we're there please let us know!)

Summary

Over the course of our professional development—in educational settings, through supervision, and in clinical practice—we learn to evaluate information as well as behavior. Indeed, the ability to evaluate and draw inferences from this process is at the core of what we do as counselors. Vacc and Loesch (2000) and Gladding (2000) have identified a number of common elements of definitions of counseling, including an identifiable knowledge base "amenable to evaluation" (Tyler & Guth, in press). Learning to extend our evaluation skills to the Internet and the information found there is a requisite step for all professionals who want to be competent to practice in the 21st century. Without peer review and other oversight processes, the skills of the individual professional to evaluate are pressed into service like no other time in our history.

By focusing on a number of specific aspects of a Web site and the material presented, counselors will be better able to determine the quality of the information they find online. These include site content, the authority of the site developer, and the currency of information. As well, counselors need to focus on their specific need in seeking information to determine whether the information obtained is appropriate to meet the identified need.

Information is more readily available than at any other time. This affords the professional counselor the opportunity to be better informed, better educated, and more prepared than in the past. With this opportunity comes the responsibility to make sure that we invest the time and resources necessary not only to be consumers of information, but to be well-informed consumers, and whenever possible to help others responsibly use available resources.

Internet Sites for Additional Information

- **http://www2.widener.edu/Wolfgram-Memorial-library/webevaluation/webeval.htm.** This resource site provides information useful for those teaching others how to evaluate electronic information. It also contains excellent bibliographic material.
- **http://www2.vuw.ac.nz/staff/alastair_smith/evaln/evaln.htm.** This may be the only site you need because of its wonderful collection of links to other resources. Contains information on evaluating Web site design and content, as well as specific discipline information such as medical or education resources. The site also links to rubrics and checklists.
- **http://www.lib.vt.edu/research/evaluate/evalbiblio.html.** Another extensive list of sites on this topic, this list ends with a collection of sites focusing on Internet hoaxes. A great way to remind the reader that practical jokes and urban legends abound in cyberspace.
- **http://www.consumerwebwatch.org/news/report3_credibility research/stanfordPTL_abstract.htm.** This article reports on a study of Web users' behavior in evaluating online information. Not surprisingly, aesthetics carried as much or more weight than content.
- **http://www.pewinternet.org/reports/toc.asp?Report=59.** This report by the Pew Foundation focuses specifically on medical information. Its findings have implications for anyone helping others use the Internet.
- **http://www.library.kent.edu/internet/evalform.html.** This site contains an example of a form that can be used when evaluating Internet information.
- **http://www-personal.umich.edu/~pfa/pro/courses/EvalPtEd.pdf.** This is another sample form for evaluating information on the Internet.
- **http://www.hopetillman.com/findqual.html.** A full-service site with many links, examples, and excellent commentary, this site is a great primer, and for many will be all they need to read.
- **http://www.mentalhelp.net/poc/view_doc.php/type/doc/id/372.** This study evaluates sites providing mental health services or information and is an important step toward understanding services over the Internet.

Helping Clients Use the Internet Effectively

Competency: Be able to help clients search for various types of counseling-related information via the Internet, including information about careers, employment opportunities, educational and training opportunities, financial assistance/scholarships, treatment procedures, and social and personal information.

Increasingly, clients are seeking information for themselves directly from the Internet. The explosion of online information, along with tools that make accessing the information easy, means that anyone now has the capacity to seek out information once reserved for professionals. At the same time, tools to create Web-based materials have become exceedingly easy to use, making it possible for anyone to make information available online. Clients, particularly clients in emotional stress and turmoil, may not have the skills necessary to adequately sort through the available information, distinguishing accurate from inaccurate, and correctly understanding what is meant for a professional audience with a large foundation of discipline-specific knowledge. The result is that the well-informed client can easily become the misinformed client, and misinformation may, across time, be more harmful than no information.

As a portion of our role as experts in a specific domain, with advanced skills and knowledge, we have a responsibility for the relationship we maintain with clients. On the basis of principles of beneficence, we also have a more proactive responsibility to foster and promote accurate understanding and socioemotional development not only among clients but among those we can influence in other aspects of our lives as well. Helping clients and others gain access to, evaluate, and understand information is one portion of this responsibility.

Research has shown that clients enjoy and appreciate assistance in seeking medical information online (Helwig, Lovelle, Guse, & Gottleib, 1999). Most clients appear to find the information beneficial and report that they will change some health behavior as a result of what they have read online. Helping clients become empowered through educational activities has always been a role of the mental health professional, and the Internet and its seemingly endless array of information can be quite helpful in this regard.

However, clients cannot simply be encouraged to seek information. It is appropriate that we provide assistance and guidance, recommendations, and training where necessary to help clients in this aspect of their growth. To be able to do this effectively, we must possess concomitant skills and knowledge as professionals. The purpose of this chapter is to detail the skills necessary to help clients in their own journey.

Which clients should you encourage to use the Internet? As in other areas, build on client strengths. If a client is already Web-savvy and using the Internet, then it may be one more tool to foster personal growth, promote confidence, and increase knowledge.

When Is It Appropriate to Help Clients Seek Information Using the Internet?

The World Wide Web has just completed its first decade of existence. Its role as a tool in mental health and other arenas is just beginning to be considered, and is not clearly understood. Whenever possible we as professionals prefer to make decisions based on research. However, when it comes to the Internet and mental health, the research is just starting and little is known definitively. At the present time, there is no research that demonstrates with which clients the Internet can be used effectively, and with which clients it poses danger. However, several authors (e.g., Suler, 2001) have attempted to address the issue, and on the basis of these writings and our own professional experiences, some heuristics can be considered.

1. **Desire.** The first and perhaps most important characteristic a client should posses before being encouraged or assisted in seeking information online is a desire to do so. Although the World Wide Web has made accessing information convenient, there is no indication that it has improved the quality of information, or improved the learning outcomes of those who use it. In fact, there are some indications that learning may not be improved over more traditional forms of information retrieval. For instance, Cockburn and McKenzie (2001) found that individuals typically spend very little time on any single Web page, which may indicate that pages are often not fully read and comprehended. As well, they found that users in a typical online session view a wide variety of pages, many of which are not connected by a consistent theme or topic. This suggests that while attempting to find information, users may become distracted or potentially overwhelmed by unrelated and perhaps unwanted information on other topics. Therefore, gathering information online is not an end but a tool and should be reserved for clients who have motivation to engage in this type of activity.

   Professional counselors can use their assessment skills to understand the desire of their clients to work online. By understanding client activities and hobbies, the counselor can identify whether the client spends time online. As well, asking directly about sources of information in the client's life can be helpful. Consistent with good clinical practice, the effective counselor will find it useful to help clients explore the types of information they will find useful in their life, as well as options for obtaining that information. During such a discussion, clients who are interested and/or experienced in using the Internet to seek information will identify the Internet as one source of information. This approach will help ensure that the clinician is supporting the client by utilizing strengths that the client already possesses.

2. **Computer skills and knowledge.** The second requirement to help clients be successful online is to ensure that they have the skills and knowledge to achieve their goals. In this, as in all counseling activities, we do not want to create assignments that have a high potential for failure. Clients want and need success. Without some basic technology skills, clients are more likely to become frustrated than learn any significant information.

   As noted above, we can learn much about our clients' skills in this area by understanding their activities in professional and personal contexts. If clients use computers frequently in their work or school activities, than we can reasonably assume that they have at least a basic comfort level with computers. If they engage in e-mail correspondence with friends and family; chat room sessions with others who have common hobbies or concerns; or use instant messaging software to interact with friends, learning partners, or family, then we can be reasonably assured that their knowledge of computers and the Internet is somewhat above a very basic level.

   There is a potential however for common biases to cloud our judgments in this area, and caution dictates that we actively seek to collect information to ensure that our understanding is accurate. For instance, there may be a common belief that teens and young adults have better computer skills and more comfort than older clients. This may erroneously lead a counselor not to explore the possibility of Internet work with the elderly. However, many older adults have found that the Internet is a great tool to pursue hobbies and maintain contact with family and friends that are disbursed widely across the country or around the world. Similarly, many teens and young adults genuinely have little interest in computers and find that letters are still best composed on paper, and information best gathered in a library.

   Even clients who actively use computers in some situations may not have the skills necessary to successfully find information online. Many individuals engaged in clerical and data entry occupations never use the Internet in their professional capacity. Those whose exposure to computers is the public schools may have never actually been on the Internet, as many schools maintain closed-networks that do not provide access to the World Wide Web and its resources. In truth, most clients will have limited knowledge of software, including Web browsers, beyond what they use on a regular basis. Therefore, active assessment of client's skills and abilities are necessary before assuming he or she has the knowledge to succeed.

3. **Familiarity with online processes.** The more familiar a client is with the workings of the Internet and the World Wide Web, the greater the chances for a positive experience. Even clients with a high level of comfort and good basic skills often become frustrated when the computer fails to respond in a manner that is expected. By understanding how the Web works, as well as the processes necessary for successful navigation, the level of frustration can be reduced greatly.

One of the most important processes that clients must understand is how to successfully search for the information they desire. Although this may seem quite basic to those who are online frequently, the task of finding information can be quite daunting to the uninitiated. In fact, some clients who use certain Internet service providers may even discover that while they are online frequently, they rarely leave the services of their specific provider, and almost never actually reach beyond those services to access the wider World Wide Web. This is because some Internet service providers use software that directs their clients within service boundaries that are maintained by the provider. One excellent example is America Online (AOL). When using AOL software, customers are fed sites that are within the AOL structure to help keep advertising revenues high. Searches may result in sites within AOL, not listings from the entire World Wide Web. This practice on the part of AOL has the effect of helping to deliver to their customers an experience that is similar to being on the Internet, but in fact is not the same. Later in this chapter, searching on the Internet is given broader coverage. Here it is only important to know that clients may believe they are accessing a wider range of materials than they actually access. If you, as the clinician understand these distinctions, then you will be able to work with your clients to help them understand and successfully navigate the Web.

Another important process beyond finding information may be installing appropriate software. Increasingly, Web sites are enhanced with specific types of "applets" (small programs) that require browser plug-ins such as Macromedia Flash (http://www.macromedia.com/), Adobe Acrobat (http://www.adobe.com/products/acrobat/readstep2.html), or Apple QuickTime (http://www.apple.com/quicktime/download/). Clients who do not understand the processes involved and the software they are using may immediately leave these sites because they do not seem to function properly, or they may refuse to install the appropriate software to make the sites function as planned. Typically, computer users will assume that there is something wrong with the site rather than with their computer. Learning to tell the difference is a critical step in increasing access to material online and in decreasing frustration while on the Internet.

The most effective way to ensure that clients have an understanding of these processes is to spend time with the client on the Internet. Allow the client to show you, the clinician, their favorite search engines, how they find the information they want, and to show you the features of their favorite browser so that you become personally acquainted with their skill level. In most cases, sitting with a client for 30 minutes while they seek specific information is more than enough time to understand their skills and to provide some basic tutorial assistance if necessary. Pay close attention during this process to the client's comfort level and success. If they have difficulty performing a basic search on your computer (assuming it is properly equipped and functioning), then you can be reasonably sure that they are likely to have difficulty at home as well. In this case, some basic training is indicated.

• Technology Tip 9.2 •

If you sit with a client at a computer, make sure that confidentiality is provided. Computers at secretarial desks or other unshielded locations do not provide the privacy necessary to work with a client, even on educational tasks.

4. **Reading and writing ability.** The ability of clients to read, write, and comprehend varies greatly not only across settings but within settings as well. In addition to a wide range of abilities among clients, information presented on the Internet spans the entire possible range of reading difficulty. Because of these two variables, the prepared counselor will take great care to help clients find information that is suitable for their academic skill level.

Some clients will be reticent to share information about their ability to read or write. As in all cases, these skills must be carefully assessed in an appropriate manner to ensure that personal biases and presuppositions do not lead the counselor to mistakenly assume a client's reading capacity. Common mistakes may include inferring reading ability on the basis of an individual's job title, ability or inability to speak English, level of education, or daily activities. Many individuals, particularly those who are not primary English speakers and older clients, may not read and write well but have excellent compensatory skills. Through years of practice, habits and procedures often develop among those with reading difficulties that allow them to function quite successfully without ever revealing their true reading level. This may include actions such as appearing to read forms in a counselor's office prior to signing.

School counselors may have some advantage in that they have easy access to information that will define the reading and writing level of most students with whom they work. In settings where this information is not readily available, counselors should include some assessment in their intake if the course of intervention may include activities requiring reading and writing.

5. **History and previous experience.** Clients who have a history of using the Internet to obtain information may be good candidates to encour-

age to continue working in this fashion. However, simply having experience is not enough. It is important that the client's previous experience was successful. Clients who have had unsuccessful attempts in the past to obtain information, or for other reasons have had frustrating experiences online, may be better served in another fashion.

6. **Ability to critically evaluate material.** As noted elsewhere, the ability to put information on the Internet for others to read is quite easy and inexpensive. Organizations with particular political, religious, and moral views may choose the Internet as a way to reach a broad audience with little investment in resources. Indeed, it seems hard to imagine a controversial view or unpopular thought that does not appear somewhere on the Internet. This includes many sites that promise to deliver information on medical cures that the U.S. government wants hidden, sites that promote anorexia as a lifestyle choice, and sites that provide false or misleading information about genetic research in a variety of areas related to mental health and human development. As noted in chapter 8, even sites that may initially appear to be connected to reputable organizations may inadvertently provide incorrect information. Although no studies have been published that attempt to evaluate the overall quality of mental health information on the Internet, there is no reason to believe that the quality of mental health information is superior to that of medical information (The Fun Place, 1998).

   The lack of standards and oversight mean that clients must become their own evaluators if they are to seek information online. One way to help clients in this process is to provide them with the URLs of sites that the counselor has screened for quality and appropriateness. Another method is to provide the client with information and assistance in evaluating the quality of information obtained. Importantly, the counselor must be confident that the client has the capacity to consider the information provided critically and that the client will do so. At times, some individuals may be more interested in finding information that confirms their own beliefs and desires than information that is accurate. In such cases, a client may actually be harmed by finding information online that supports misinterpretations, inaccurate beliefs, or delusions.

7. **Ability to self-supervise.** Another area of concern with some clients is their ability to supervise themselves online. Some clients, because of their age or particular style of life, may be expected to have some difficulty setting boundaries for themselves related to their online activities. Examples may include individuals who have a history of online gambling, have shown tendencies for compulsive use of the Internet, have a history of involvement in unstable and unhealthy online relationships, or those attracted to the darker side of the Internet. While research is still in its infancy at this time, there are clearly indications that for some, use of the Internet is as compelling and destructive as alcohol is to some individuals. In such cases, it may be unwise to encourage clients to use the Internet for any reason.

Another group that may have some difficulty providing self-supervision are children and adolescents. Unfortunately, the Internet has become a vast repository of pornographic images and adult material. Purveyors of these materials are constantly seeking ways to make it easier for those who want this material to find it, and for those who may not be looking to accidentally stumble on it. For younger children, such an accidental finding may result in embarrassment, confusion, and a need to explain activities that the child is not developmentally ready to understand. For older children and adolescents, such an accidental occurrence may lead to a desire to seek out more adult material and raises the potential to shape adolescent views of human sexuality in ways that are not necessarily healthy and desirable.

Potentially worse are the increasing numbers of individuals online seeking to make contact with children and adolescents to meet their own sexual needs. Because anyone can assume any identity online, there is no way for a child to know with whom they are communicating. In all cases, children should be provided supervision in their online activities, and adolescents should be provided with enough oversight to ensure that the activities they are engaging in are appropriate.

8. **Part of a comprehensive approach.** Although many magic and wondrous expectations have been expressed for the Internet over the past decade, its primary purpose remains the simple exchange of information. Sometimes that information is in the form of text, other times video. The information may be exchanged almost instantaneously as in the case of e-mail and instant messaging, or it may be exchanged over a long period of time as in the case of articles that are posted and not retrieved and read for days, weeks, or even years. As a medium to exchange information, its impact on a client rests in the clinician's ability to incorporate the acquisition of information into a broader and more comprehensive approach to helping individuals resolve issues in their life.

Counselors must be prepared not only to help the client seek information, but then to reflect on and integrate the information into their lives. This is best done as a portion of a comprehensive approach to meeting any client's needs. If the seeking of information through any means becomes a secondary addition to the treatment process, clients will likely not engage in the process but instead will treat it as unimportant. This can be potentially damaging as a client may have collected some information and may remain only partially informed (or misinformed) on a specific topic. Another danger is that the client will determine that certain processes of self-education and reflection are unimportant and will be less likely to engage in education and reflection in the future. In almost all cases, such a process would hinder clients in their attempts to seek greater fulfillment and growth in their own life. These variables are summarized in Table 9.1 for quick review.

Table 9.1
Seven Characteristics of an Appropriate Candidate for Online Work

1. The client has a desire to work online.
2. The client has appropriate computer skills to be successful online.
3. The client already uses and understands the online environment.
4. The client has appropriate reading skills to succeed online.
5. The client can evaluate material online to determine quality.
6. The client can provide self-supervision to stay on task online.
7. The client's work online can be integrated with his or her treatment plan and goals.

Although these variables can be considered individually as components of the decision to encourage a client to seek information on the Internet, it will also be useful to consider them as a collective body rather than as discrete components. As is the case with many aspects of the work of a professional counselor, no single factor necessarily will lead to an answer on which client is best suited to which intervention. For example, while a client's reading level must be considered, just because a client has a low reading level does not necessarily mean that he or she is an inappropriate candidate to use the Internet. Rather, a low reading level suggests that if the client is to be successful, he or she may benefit from the use of specific supports. These supports may include having the client work with a family member or close friend to seek information. The information may then be brought to the counselor in session so that both may review the information obtained, discuss it, and consider how it may be useful in helping the individual client. Similarly, a client with poor computer skills may still be an appropriate candidate if supports can be provided or the work scaffolded in such a manner that the client's skills grow across time until they can reach their goals. For instance, clients may be encouraged to start by visiting specific sites that the counselor has identified. In this case, the client does not need Internet search skills, an ability to critically evaluate the material, or an understanding of online processes. However, while visiting these initial sites identified by the counselor, the client is developing skills. These new skills may be used at some future date to seek additional information. Even a lack of desire, in some cases, may not be an indication of a client's inappropriateness. Rational emotive behavior therapists often engage clients in specific activities that are designed to challenge a client's assumptions and ability to tolerate discomfort. If a client's lack of desire is related to lack of confidence or some mistaken belief, then the very act of using the Internet may prove to be therapeutic. On a case by case basis, the clinician must decide what each client needs in order to achieve his or her individual goals. If the Internet is seen as a tool to help achieve these goals, and if an appropriate structure is in place or can be provided to help the client use this tool successfully, then its use is recommended.

Addressing the Digital Divide

To this point, this text has advanced the view that technology (and the Internet) has become a ubiquitous component of life in the United States. On one hand, this view seems accurate. One need only consider the "Can you hear me now?" guy from television to know that companies are seeking to wire (or provide wireless service) every corner of the United States. We send e-mail with our cell phones and surf the net with our PDAs. Restaurants stop serving when electricity goes out, not because they can't cook but because they can't transfer the order from wait staff to kitchen. Refrigerators can be purchased that are wired to the Internet, and microwave ovens can identify the food being cooked and suggest accompanying side dishes (Williams, 2001). But this understanding betrays our cultural fixedness and personal bias.

In truth, a great divide exists in the United States between those who have a high level of technology in their homes and those who do not. Similarly, a divide exists between those who use the Internet and those who do not. Not surprisingly, these distinctions fall along racial (National Telecommunications & Information Administration, 2003a) as well as economic boundaries (Digital Divide, 2003).

In 2000, 56% of White households and 66% of Asian American households had a computer, whereas only 33% of Black households and 34% of Hispanic households had a computer. During this same year, only 30% of households with an income between $15,000 and $24,999 had a computer, whereas 73% of those with an income between $50,000 and $74,999 had a computer. The linear relationship between income and computer ownership is quite apparent at all income levels (NTIA, 2003c). In addition to race and income, education levels are also highly correlated with computer ownership (NTIA, 2003d).

Outside of the home, many children and adolescents have access to computers and the Internet in the public schools. Between 1994 and 2000, computer use and Internet access in the public schools rose dramatically in all schools, regardless of demographic differences. Currently, something close to 100% of public schools have access to the Internet. However, differences do remain. One report indicates that in schools with less than 35% of the student population eligible for free or reduced price lunches, 99% have Internet access. This number falls to 94% in schools where 75% of the student body is eligible for free or reduced price lunches (National Center for Education Statistics, 2003). Similar differences are noted in schools with minority student populations above 50%, and city schools when compared with urban fringe, town, or rural schools. Thus, those groups that may be least likely to have computer technology in the home are also least likely to have access to technology in the public schools.

Although some positive trends have been noted, deeper inspection suggests these trends are not necessarily favorable. Data indicate that all groups regardless of race, ethnicity, geographic location, or income have increased access to the Internet and are taking advantage of this access (NTIA, 2003b) over previous years. Unfortunately, between 1998 and 2000, the gap between Internet penetration in Black and Hispanic households compared with the national average increased. In 2000, approximately one third of all individuals in the United States accessed the Internet at home, whereas only about 16% of Hispanics and 19% of Blacks did so. Thus, although technology may appear everywhere to some in the United States, it is clear that there are large groups of individuals who do not have a high level of technology access and consequently are not likely to have a high level of technology skills or comfort.

This gap, referred to in the literature as the "digital divide," has implications for the professional counselor. The first may be the need to recognize that the development of technology-based services including education, information, and outreach may never reach certain populations. For those working primarily in economically depressed communities, communities with a high proportion of minorities, and those populations with low educational attainment, it is clear that simply creating technology-based services are inadequate. Professional counselors who identify the importance of these types of services must also become advocates in the community to create, fund, and maintain technology access and education. Public schools and private foundations must work together to ensure that computers are placed in areas where the client population can gain access. This may include libraries, homeless shelters, food pantries, churches, or other social service agencies. One way to achieve this is to work with corporations or large school districts that often have the capacity to donate older equipment as it is replaced with newer technology. Although this equipment, several years old, may not meet corporate needs, in most cases it will be quite suitable for accessing the Internet, running basic productivity software, and as a tool for technology skills education.

One social service agency with which we have worked collected older computers and taught courses where their clientele could learn to repair and upgrade equipment. This same equipment, once revitalized, was then used in classrooms to teach basic office skills as well as for technology education in the evening, while during the day it was used by other clients to write résumés and print application letters. In another agency, a program was established to place a number of older computers in a used RV. This mobile computer lab could then be taken to specific areas in their catchment area so that particularly poor communities, and in this case migrant work camps, could have some access on a part-time basis to computers and the Internet. Children became excellent teachers for their parents, as many children were exposed to the technology in school, while the parents often had never before touched a computer.

School counselors can become powerful advocates in this regard by working with administrators and others in their district to open up computer labs to the public during certain hours. In some cases, such programs may include restrictions that children may only come with their parents (or vice versa), creating the foundation for a family-directed technology literacy program. Opening up labs in the evening has a small cost associated, but that cost may easily be offset with some community support. Staffing can be provided by students in educational technology programs from local colleges or vocational education programs. In some cases, students from within the school can provide much, if not all, of the support.

A second impact of the digital divide that counselors must be aware of is a lack of online content that addresses the needs of low income or other groups marginalized by society (Taglang, 2003). One obvious example of this may be found when seeking employment online. Visiting most of the major online job sites, users will find that the majority of the information presented, as well as a majority of the jobs listed, is directed toward the professional. Even in categories associated with manual labor, job listings tend to be directed toward supervisors, leaders, or managers. Clients with very low levels of education may find that there are relatively few opportunities posted online that meet their skills and experience. Another example of an area where content may be lacking is low-income housing opportunities. Directing clients to seek information online when material is very scarce is likely to create frustration and may contribute to the client feeling even more marginalized and hopeless. It is critical that the professional counselor strive to find content that is appropriate for the individual at every level. In cases where appropriate content does not exist, then it needs to be created or alternate tools should be employed.

Similar to a lack of appropriate content is the issue of a lack of others with whom the client can identify. Many people use the Internet to find emotional support in chat rooms and other forums for a variety of concerns. Such support may be quite beneficial for many clients. However, clients who are already feeling isolated, alone, or different than others would be poorly served if they were to seek an online forum to connect with others sharing their concerns, only to find no one else like them online. Of course, it is not necessary that we seek support only from others who look like us or are in similar circumstances, but such similarities can ease the process of connecting and provide common ground for beginning discussions.

A third impact this digital divide may have is to foster the belief that some clients have that they are not a part of mainstream society. When television, newspapers, and other popular media outlets stress the role of technology in changing everyday life, and when individuals recognize they are not participating in this change, feelings of marginalization or hopelessness may be magnified. Although not all aspects of the technological changes in society are positive, these changes exist nonetheless. And, individuals who do not have the opportunity to stay current will find it increasingly difficult to function in many aspects of their lives. As an example, in many states individuals can electronically renew a driver's license or conduct other state business (see http://www.egovernmentaccess.com/Vehicle.htm). It is anticipated that increasingly individuals standing in line at the Bureau of Motor Vehicles will be those who do not have an alternative. Although such a change may seem minor, it clearly represents an increasing division in society where some individuals are provided with convenient methods of conducting business while others must continue to engage in rituals that many of us find exhausting and frustrating. Worse, often these same individuals who do not have alternatives are also the individuals who have greatest difficulty finding transportation and resources to conduct their business. As professional counselors advocate for technology access in their own professional and personal lives, we must also be advocates for technology access and education in our communities.

Finally, we must be prepared as professionals to address another aspect of the digital divide: the gender gap. According to the NTIA (2000), the rate at which men and women access the Internet is almost identical (44.6% for men and 44.2% for women). However, among children and adolescents, attitudes and behaviors appear to differ more significantly. A study by the American Association of University Women (AAUW, 1998) reports that girls are much more likely to enroll in data entry courses, whereas boys are more likely to take computer science and graphics courses. Additionally, girls rate themselves as less skilled than boys and use computers much less outside of school than their male counterparts. Projecting into the future, these differences seen in childhood may result in young women being less technologically prepared to enter the workforce upon leaving school. The concern of earlier decades when women were less prepared to enter science and math careers may be replaced by a new concern that women are unprepared for technology-related careers. Counselors, particularly in school and vocational settings, can have a genuine impact in these areas through their own advocacy efforts.

Searching for Information on the Internet

Looking for information on the Internet can be a daunting task. While no one knows how many pages actually compose the Internet, one search engine, Google (google.com, 2002), claims to have indexed over 3 billion pages. Certainly this represents more information than any single human could access or make sense of. Fortunately, an entire industry has arisen to help solve the problem. The primary methods of finding information include the use of search engines, directories, and databases. We now look at each of these, as well as some lesser used tools.

Search Engines

Search engines are computer programs that use other programs to index the Internet. The process starts when a special program known as a spider is run. The spider program goes to a specific Web page and then to every page linked to the initial page, then to every page linked from those pages and on and on. At each new page, the spider collects information about where the page is located and what words or images the page contains.

This information is all sent back to a database, where complex computer algorithms are used to index every page the spider visits. When a user wants to find specific information, the search engine looks into its database using these algorithms to find pages that may be connected to what the user wants. Although the process may sound simple, actually developing algorithms that return what the user wants without returning a lot of unimportant information or without failing to return the most important information, is a very complex task. Because search engines are computer-driven, there is no evaluative process, they return results based on their best guess, and they never evaluate the accuracy or currency of the information returned. Additionally, in most cases they return more potential sites for information than can be easily managed. The best search engines have developed algorithms that return only the most useful information, and have additional features that make them work even better.

Google (www.google.com). A favorite search engine among many users is Google. Since its introduction in 1998, Google has been seen as one of the best search engines available. Additionally, the site is continuously updated, allowing new features to be implemented and making searches easier.

• Technology Tip 9.3 •

While Google may have over 3 billion pages indexed, that probably is less than a third of the Internet. You can learn more about what they leave out at http://www.microdocs-news.info/newsGoogle/2003/05/10.html#a596.

The Google home page is a simple and uncluttered wonder with no advertising at all. Users are presented with a simple text box where they can enter words, phrases, or complete questions. Then the user may click one of two buttons: "Google Search" or "I'm Feeling Lucky." The "I'm Feeling Lucky" button will take the user to the first page on the results list. Very often, when searching for a specific site such as an organization or company, the "I'm Feeling Lucky" option takes the user to the exact page they need.

The "Google Search" button returns a list of potential sites based on the words input to the system. The results list includes a title for each potential page upon which the user clicks to be connected directly to that page. Also included in the results list is an abbreviated text passage taken from the page that allows the user to see some of the information on the page before actually deciding to visit. This helps the user decide quickly if the page looks like it contains the desired information.

Several additional features of the Google results page can be quite useful. For each returned site, an option is available to see a "cached" version of the page. The cache version is a copy of the page that the spider sent back to the Google database while it was crawling around the Web. Cached pages do not include images, but do include all text. This is a particularly useful feature to find information and Web sites that may no longer be available for any of a number of reasons. A second option, listed at the end of each result, is the "Similar pages" link. By clicking on this link, the user is letting the search engine know that a particular page contains the information the user wanted. The search engine can then use its algorithms to quickly find more pages that are like the page the user has identified. In this fashion, the results can quickly be narrowed to a more specific set of pages that are likely to be highly relevant to the user's needs.

•   Technology Tip 9.4   •

Use the "Similar pages" link on the Google results page to quickly narrow your search.

At the bottom of the Google results page the user is presented with another text input box. The user can enter new search terms into the box and choose the "Google Search" button to try again. This is convenient when the list of results does not seem to be exactly what was desired. Next to the search button on the bottom of the results page is the "Search within results" option. This is a very important and useful option with this search engine. By clicking here, the user is taken to a new page where they are asked to input additional search terms into a text box. These new terms are then used to search only those sites found in the original search to help narrow down the list. For instance, a counselor may enter the search term "depression" which will result in over 3.8 million potential sites. Then, by using the "Search within" feature, the new search term "treatment of" may be added. This narrows the search down to a more manageable 1.1 million sites! Continuing to use the "Search within" feature, additional search terms such as cognitive–behavioral and Michigan are added. The results list is narrowed still further to only 6,000 sites. By utilizing this process, the results list can be continually narrowed until a manageable group of sites on a very specific topic is identified.

These basic features, however, are only the start of Google's utility. On the Google home page (www.google.com) there are additional options. One of these is preferences. By clicking on the preferences link, the user can customize his or her experience with the Google search engine in very important ways. One option on the preferences page allows the user to change the language used in the interface. By choosing from a pull-down menu, the user can choose to interact with Google in over 70 languages, ensuring an interface compatible with the needs of most clients. Have fun. Go to google.com and change the language preference to Elmer Fudd or Pig Latin. A little silliness in your life is a good thing.

Another option instructs Google to search only pages in specific languages. By changing the language choice to Spanish, and entering the search term "depression," the user is presented with approximately 5000 sites written in Spanish. Suddenly, to a non-English speaker, there is an easy and efficient way to find information in a familiar language. With 35 languages supported, there is an option available for many clients.

Change the options on the "Preferences" page under SafeSearch filtering to automatically filter out explicit results. This way, when others use your computer, Google will automatically limit their search.

Yet another option allows the user to filter out of the results explicit images, all explicit materials, or no explicit materials. This option may increase the comfort level of some clients by helping to ensure that they are less likely to be exposed to material they find offensive. As well, with children and adolescents, this filter is one way to help block their access to such material. Note, however, that this filtering is easy to turn off (simply return to preferences and change the setting) and is not adequate as filtering software for those who want to block access to certain types of material. This type of blocking software is much more specific and is discussed more fully in Chapter 13.

Also on the Google home page is a link labeled "Language Tools." The language tools page allows the user to translate search terms into various languages to aid in the search process, or to search only pages from a specific country. As well, by entering a specific address, Google can automatically translate Web pages from one language into another. While quite useful, this feature does deserve some cautionary comments. As a useful feature, this might allow a non-native English speaker to navigate a Web site for your organization to find your name in a directory, to find addresses for satellite sites, or to understand the titles of upcoming community events. However, the translation process is not exact, and some information may not translate well. A paper written at a high level on the side effects of medications may translate poorly and not provide a client with the necessary information. Thus, although this is a useful tool, it cannot be assumed that simply pushing the "translate" button will provide an accurate and useful translation. It is best to find someone who speaks the language in question and have them review any translated sites before presenting them to a client.

Another option from the Google home page is the "Advanced" Search. By clicking on this link, the user is presented with a detailed form allowing the choice of many specific options in the search. From the advanced search page, the user can enter phrases that are specified to return only results containing all of the search terms, an exact phrase, with at least one of several words, or to not return pages with a particular term. For example, the user might choose to search for the exact term "treatment of depression" and to exclude the term "medicine." This search will allow the user to be more specific about the results he or she obtains. In this case, eliminating potential sites that focus on medication as a treatment for depression.

Another feature of the advanced search page is the opportunity to search for specific types of files (e.g., only PowerPoint files, only Word Documents). In this manner one can seek out very specific types of information. Other features on the advanced search page include changing language, setting dates to eliminate pages before a certain date, or searching for the search terms only in a specific portion of the page such as the title or the page URL.

The advanced search page also allows the user to input a specific URL and find other pages with similar content. Thus, if a user is aware of a page that provides parents information on specific developmental stages children go through and wants to find similar pages, the URL of the first page can be entered and a results list will be generated. Finally, a user can enter a specific URL and Google will find all pages that link to that page. Thus, a counselor might identify all pages that have been linked to their organization's Web site. This may be useful in discovering how others are using the Web, and who has found your site useful.

To be fair to Google's competition, many of the search features available on the advanced search page at Google can be performed using Boolean search terms (discussed in chapter 6) with almost all search engines. However, the Google interface makes this process easier and does not require the user to learn to use Boolean operators. This is particularly beneficial to the casual user who is not interested in the more subtle aspects of search engine behavior.

Returning once more to the Google home page, there are also options to seek only for images, groups, or directories. These options are listed at the top of the Google page and provide additional flexibility. By choosing images, Google will take any search term and seek images associated with that term. This can be a quick and convenient way to find images of all types. When searching for images, the level of filtering provided as indicated earlier in the preferences section should be considered. This will help ensure that offensive images are less likely to be displayed inadvertently on the screen during the search process. Using the groups option, Google can search 700 million messages posted to Usenet groups over the past 20 years. These groups are discussed thoroughly in chapter 7.

All The Web (www.alltheweb.com). All The Web is a search engine that in many respects is similar to Google. The basic features of the site are standard for a search engine, and the advanced search page contains many of the same features as Google. However, this site goes a step further by offering options to search for specific file types including MP3 files, videos, and files at FTP sites. FTP (File Transfer Protocol) sites are generally repositories of shareware, freeware, and demonstration versions of software. Although these same files can be searched for on most engines, this site makes the process easier by allowing the user to select just these file types with the click of a mouse. All The Web also contains excellent help pages that offer the user a great deal of information and tips on searching.

On the customize menu of All The Web, users can choose their language and many options that most people will never take the time to complete. However, taking the time to click through the sequential menus is helpful in understanding the search process and may reveal settings that individuals will choose to change on the basis of personal preference. For example, by default this engine collapses multiple pages from a single Web site into only one listing. However, the user may choose to change this option. By default, if a user searches for Rational Emotive Behavior Therapy, the search engine might find 20 different pages at the Albert Ellis Institute (rebt.org). By collapsing results, All The Web will display only one link to this domain. However, this may limit the results and make it more difficult to find the exact page within the Web site that the user seeks. By turning off the collapse option, the search engine will display a separate entry for every page it finds, increasing the potential for duplication but also providing a more thorough search. Another option that users may choose is to open all results in a new window. If checked, when the user clicks on a page from the search results list, a new window will open to display the link. This makes it easier to look at multiple pages and quicker to return to the search list rather than repeatedly clicking on the back button.

• Technology Tip 9.6 •

To search for specific file types in most search engines, simply include the phrase "filetype:ZZZ" where ZZZ is the type of file you are seeking. For example, entering "filetype:MP3" in the search box will result in MP3 files as the result of the search.

Alta Vista (altavista.com). A third search engine that is well-known is Alta Vista. Compared with the two previous engines, the Alta Vista home page is somewhat cluttered with category listings. However, some users will find these categories a helpful way to explore new sites. Like the others, Alta Visa has separate links to make searches for images, directories, news, audio, or video very simple. The advanced search option of this site is slightly less complete than the others but still provides a very good set of options. Customizability is also somewhat more limited.

Many people believe that the best choice of search engine is largely determined by personal choice and by which site individuals are most familiar with. While Google claims to have indexed the most sites, this does not necessarily make it the best. Other factors come into play as well. For example, Alta Vista has been reported to have more dead links (links that no longer work) in their results than Google (Notess, 2000) suggesting that the search experience with Alta Vista may be more frustrating than with Google. On the other hand, one report indicates that Alta Vista was able to find more unique sites (sites that other search engines did not find) than did Google. This suggests that Alta Vista may be better able to find a broader array of sites, particularly those that may not be well publicized or popular (Notess, 2002). In the end, it may be necessary to run searches on several engines to ensure that the sites you want are found.

• Technology Tip 9.7 •

No single search engine can index the entire Web. For the most thorough results, always run your search using multiple engines or a metasearch tool.

An alternative to choosing a single search engine is to use a metasearch approach. Metasearch software allows the user to simultaneously access a number of different search engines, then combines the results, removing duplicates and presenting the best results from each engine. One common metasearch tool is Copernic Agent (http://www.copernic.com/desktop/index.html). It is available as a free download in a basic version, or personal and corporate editions can be purchased with additional features. Copernic has the capacity to access over 1000 different search engines. Then, using proprietary technology, Copernic chooses the most relevant sites found by each engine and presents its own list. By accessing many different search engines, each with a unique way to find and catalog information on the Web, Copernic Agent attempts to offer the best of all without missing anything.

An additional tool called Copernic Summarizer (http://www.copernic.com/desktop/products/summarizer/index.html) adds another tool to make finding information online easier. Copernic Summarizer will summarize Web pages on the fly, identifying key information and providing a concise and readable abstract. By using this tool, Web users can quickly identify the information that is available on a Web site, and if it is relevant to their needs, they can then visit the site to view all of the information provided. Copernic Summarizer integrates with a Web browser and can summarize Web pages as well as PDF files, Microsoft Word documents, and e-mail messages. It can also be used on the desktop to summarize complex reports, full-text articles, or other material.

Directories

An alternative to search engines for finding information on the Web are directories. Directories are lists of Web sites, broken into categories, that have been compiled by human beings. The advantage of course is that each site has been reviewed by a real person to determine what exists. This can be a great benefit, in that search engines may misinterpret information, providing results that appear to have no relation to the information sought. Directories, on the other hand, almost always return results closely associated with the topic of interest. Some of the best directories are annotated by the organizations that maintain the directories. Directories exist for a wide range of subject areas and vary in size. None have the capacity to index the amount of pages that a search engine such as Google can index.

One very useful index is the Librarians Index to the Internet (http://www.lii.org/). Librarians have a great capacity to know how to find the information that their users need, and this site reinforces that reputation. Boasting over 9,000 annotated sites, this directory is a convenient and quick access to a wonderful array of reference materials. Carefully catalogued and reviewed, the material here is all quality content.

Another useful directory is Infomine (http://infomine.ucr.edu/). This directory, compiled by the librarians of the University of California, contains over 23,000 annotated listings. This directory lets the user search by keyword, title, author, or full text (or in any combination). Individuals familiar with standard library research tools on the Internet or CD-ROMS will find the interface quite familiar. Although searching by term is allowed, the user can also simply click through menus to get to recommended sites on a variety of topics.

Academic Info (academicinfo.net) is a subject guide geared toward the advanced high school student or beyond. The goal of the site is to provide access to premier educational materials. The site maintains that a current priority is the addition of full-text resources, as well as digital material from museums, libraries, and academic organizations. The precise size of this index is unknown, but they claim to add 250–500 new sites every month.

Reportedly the largest of all Internet directories is Yahoo (www.yahoo.com). Yahoo is an extremely extensive site and allows Internet searching as well as navigation through its own directory structure. When searching, the top of the results page will display links in the Yahoo directory structure the user can click through. However, by scrolling down on the page, the user will find a section marked "Results from the Web," where traditional search engine results will be displayed. Staying within the directory provides the user with helpful annotations for many sites.

The best part of Yahoo may be a companion site, Yahooligans (yahooligans.com). This Web directory is specifically designed for children and is a relatively safe way to allow children to seek information on the Internet. Sites with questionable material are excluded from the results. By navigating through the structure provided, a child's (or adult's) ability to spell or think in terms that a computer can easily search becomes irrelevant. Yahooligans has sought out and links to the best sites for children, regardless of the information that they seek. Although the site may be too limited for adolescents or young adults, it is sure to provide a pathway to information and learning for any preteen.

Finally, there are many specialized directories available. The easiest way to find these is to search for them using one of the tools listed above. For instance, using Google, search for the phrase "mental health Web directory." This will result in a brief list of sites that are intended to be directories on this specific topic.

• Technology Tip 9.8 •

Include the entire search phrase in quotes to obtain only results that use this specific phrase on their Web site.

Databases on the Internet

The previous discussion has focused on the "visible" Web, those pages that are developed in the standard languages common to the World Wide Web and "served" to users from specific Web server computers. However, there is another and potentially much larger invisible side to the Internet. One portion of this invisible side of the net is the array of databases that can be accessed online but which are not indexed by search engines or directories because they are not Web pages. An example of this type of information is the "card catalog" of a library. The information in the catalog exists in a database maintained by the library. Using modern programming, Web pages exist that allow the user to search the database from any Internet connection to retrieve information such as whether or not the latest Harry Potter book is available. However, when spiders search the Web (to create indexes for search engines) they cannot find the information in the database; they can only find the page the user interacts with to retrieve the information. Therefore, the fact that your local library has a Web site is recorded, but what information is available from that site is not. Fortunately, we can find many of these databases by looking for them. Again, using any of the search engines previously mentioned, simply type in a search term followed by the word *database*, such as "counselor database." This will return a small number of databases, accessible via the Internet, that contain lists of counselors or other information that may be of use. This technique can be quite useful to find information that you believe others may have compiled into database form. A very useful list of searchable databases can be found at http://www.lib.berkeley.edu/TeachingLib/Guides/Internet/InvisibleWeb.html.

What Kinds of Information Are Clients Seeking?

Having made some decision about a client's suitability to use the Internet to obtain information, and having become an informed user of search engines, directories, and databases, it is time to consider specific information and sites to find that information on the Internet. Any discussion of specific sites is precarious at best. The World Wide Web is a constantly changing and evolving entity. Although this constant change in response to user needs is part of the attraction, it also creates difficulty in terms of educating oneself about its resources. What exists today may well be gone by tomorrow, and if it remains for more than a few months, you can be reasonably sure that its presentation and features will change. Difficulties in keeping up with changes in technology is one of the challenges identified in chapters 1 and 13. Nowhere is this constant change and growth more evident than in Web services. Therefore, counselors who intend to use the Internet regularly need to invest time in staying current with their favorite sites, search techniques, and advice to others. Those who use the Internet infrequently will need to spend even more dedicated time to keep up, as their personal time spent online will not suffice to keep them current.

The NBCC standards for Technical Competencies for Counselor Education Students (ACES Technology Interest Network, 1999) indicate that the competent counselor will be prepared to help clients seek information in several specific areas including career information, employment opportunities, education and training, financial assistance and scholarships, treatment procedures, and social and personal information. The remaining portion of the current chapter examines some of these areas, providing some general direction as well as Web sites of interest.

Career Information

Career information and job sites are one of the areas where the World Wide Web has had the largest impact. Hundreds of dedicated sites are available to help individuals find employment. Employers can easily reach out to an international audience, and potential employees can review thousands of potential openings easily. Like other aspects of the Web, these sites are constantly changing. Developments in technology, search techniques, and advertising revenues create a constantly shifting market where company fortunes rise and decline quite rapidly. Counselors who work with individuals on career issues should be aware of specific sites that meet their needs. For instance, if a counselor works in a relatively small urban area with a place-bound population, they will need to know local sites including newspaper classifieds, state employment agencies, and sites maintained by local service agencies, professional organizations, or employment support groups. Counselors who work with specific occupational groups will need to know about sites geared toward this particular group. Often these sites are run by professional organizations or by trade publications. As well, all counselors should be aware of some of the larger national and international sites. Although the specific job listings may not be as relevant to local needs as the hometown paper, the information on interviewing, preparing a résumé and company profiles can still be invaluable. Listed below are a number of large sites that make a unique contribution.

- **America's Job Bank (http://www.ajb.dni.us/):** This site, which claims to be the largest of the Internet job sites, was developed jointly between the U.S. Department of Labor and private concerns and lists over 1 million jobs in the United States. Job seekers can post their résumé for others to see, sort job postings by keywords, and set up automatic searches that notify the user when a new job of interest is listed. Listings can be sorted geographically and by dozens of categories. At the bottom of the main page are links to CareerInfoNet, the Learning Exchange, and Service Locator. These additional resources make this a complete career resource site.
- **Career InfoNet (http://www.acinet.org/acinet/):** This site provides a full range of career information for those new to the job market or those considering a change. Occupations can be found based on the fastest growing fields, careers with the most openings, highest paying occupations, and others. Additional criteria such as level of training can also be specified to help identify careers suitable for specific clients. In-depth career information can be found and specific demographic and career data by state is available.
- **The Learning Exchange (http://www.alx.org/):** This site is dedicated to helping individuals obtain information about training and educa-

tion opportunities. Users choose from a large list of potential subject areas, then choose a state as well as type of training (classroom, Web-based, self-study, etc.). Results display titles, costs, and provider. Links can be clicked to obtain more detailed information. One of the strengths of the site is the range of training opportunities listed, including those for individuals with little formal education to traditional undergraduate college offerings. Alternative training and certification programs are also listed.

- **America's Service Locator (http://www.servicelocator.org):** This site was developed as a partnership between the U.S. Department of Labor and various state and local governments and agencies. Its purpose is to provide information needed by individuals seeking career-related services. This includes access to information on unemployment benefits, job training, disabled workers programs, and so forth. This is an important resource site to counselors in need of referral information as well as for clients seeking to learn more about their options

- **BestJobsUSA.com (http://www.bestjobsusa.com/):** This commercial site is a full-featured job search portal. In addition to job postings, the site contains information on salaries, company profiles, and information on relocating. Basic services include posting résumés and reviewing job postings. A variety of premium services such as hiring a résumé writer or having your résumé bulk mailed are also available. The site is probably best for those seeking professional level opportunities.

- **Career.com (http://www.career.com):** This site focuses as much on the employer as the potential job candidate. The interface is clean and easy to use, and job seekers will find many opportunities. Although the additional career information is not as thorough as on some other sites, there is a specific link for women's resources (look under Resources and then Women's Resources) which is fairly unique. For women seeking specific information or ideas on how to compete in areas traditionally dominated by men, these links may be quite useful.

- **CareerMag.com (http://www.careermag.com):** This site contains sections for job seekers, employers, and those who are self-employed. Complete with strategies to help in the job search, résumé and interviewing tips, and employer spotlights, the site contains a wealth of information. On the site's home page, a listing of professions makes searching in specific areas quite easy.

- **Career Journal (http://careers.wsj.com):** This site, created and maintained by the Wall Street Journal, is a must-visit site for professionals and managers seeking new opportunities. In addition to the usual tips and ads, the site contains access to information on career seminars and job fairs. Links are also available to executive recruiters and other professional assistance.

- **CareerBuilder (http://www.careerbuilder.com):** This site allows users to search by city, state, or keyword. It also contains some international links and can be customized as a personal job search portal.

- **HotJobs (http://www.hotjobs.com):** This Yahoo service is one of the older and better established career sites on the Internet. Given Yahoo's leading technology, the site can be expected to stay ahead of others in terms of its ability to seek out and deliver information. Search by keyword or profession, post a résumé, use the salary calculator, or complete assessments to help identify the ideal position.
- **JobOptions (http://www.joboptions.com):** This site claims over 500,000 jobs from 50,000 employers, and 2 million visitors each month. In addition to help for the job seeker, the site also provides information for employers that job seekers may find helpful. This includes information on employment law, diversity issues, and salary and financial information.
- **Monster.com (http://www.monster.com):** Search over 800,000 jobs, build and post your résumé, and access thousands of pages of career information and advice.

• Technology Tip 9.9 •

Just as no search engine can index all the information we seek, no job site can list all the potential jobs available. Using several different sites will allow individuals more opportunity.

Education and Training

Online education and training has become very popular and continues to grow at a rapid pace. Identifying specific resources in the area is difficult because the options are so great and varied. Excellent skills using search engines as described previously will help the counselor identify specific information that will be helpful to individual clients. There are some general issues that are worth noting.

Many people have recognized the potential of the Internet to provide education that is easily accessed by anyone with a computer. Therefore, the market has appeared unlimited, prompting many individuals, corporations, and schools both public and private to become involved with online education and training. This proliferation has allowed the development of many sites that are new to the marketplace, many sites that will not last over any significant length of time, and many sites that offer no real value for the money invested. Everyone involved will benefit if consumers remain aware of the potential for unscrupulous operators to offer more than they can deliver.

Sites connected with long-established colleges and universities at least offer the appearance of quality based on the reputation of the parent organization. Similarly, sites connected to professional organizations may be better prepared to maintain high standards for training. In some cases it can be helpful to look for sites that maintain a certificate to provide continuing education units (CEUs) within a given profession and/or within a specific state. Consumers would be wise to make sure that CEUs collected will be accepted by local, state, and national organizations before they invest time and money.

As with most aspects of life, offers that appear too good to be true probably are. Opportunities to earn degrees or diplomas in a time frame significantly shorter than can be obtained elsewhere should be carefully investigated. As well, consumers should work hard to determine whether those they work with or for will accept the training that an organization offers. Often, corporate policies will limit training to that which has been accredited by specific agencies, or to education offered only in a certain format. Like a GED, a certificate from an online institution may prove something, but may not always be seen as equivalent to a traditional diploma or certificate.

Financial Assistance

For clients seeking training or additional education, financial realities are almost always a barrier. Finding appropriate financial support is often the most important variable in helping clients move toward training goals. Fortunately, a variety of Internet sites are available to help. Some sites charge for services while others are free. Some sites may appear to be free but offer "premium" services for an additional cost. At times, the free material available may not be sufficient for a client's needs. However, if the client is willing to invest the time required to search a variety of sites, he or she often will find that there is not a need to pay for premium access to any single site. In some cases, clients may choose to pay for services and then will be disappointed to find that these services offer no more than can be obtained elsewhere for free. Following is a list of some financial assistance programs:

- **FastWeb (http://www.studentservices.com/index.ptml):** This site claims to be used by one-third of all college-bound high school seniors. Listing some 600,000 scholarships, it is a necessary stop for anyone seeking financial aid. In addition to financial aid, this site also facilitates the college admissions process with online applications, reviews, and other services.
- **Colleges, College Scholarships, and Financial Aid page (http://www.college-scholarships.com/):** Another full-service page, this site offers information on schools as well as financial aid and test prep tips. Scholarship searches are free, and information is available on graduate school as well as undergraduate schools, community colleges, and special groups of schools such as historically black schools.
- **College Net (http://www.collegenet.com):** This site allows students to apply to over 1,500 schools online. Providing financial aid information, college searches, and college resources, the site is quite inclusive. This site also offers potential students the opportunity to create an online profile that schools can view to see whether they would like to actively recruit the student.

- **Students.Gov (http://www.students.gov/):** This site is an opening to U.S. government resources that students or potential students may find of interest. Links not only connect to financial aid but to career resources, the military, voting information, community service, and travel. This is a kinder, gentler government Web site, designed to attract young adults.
- **Scholarships.Com (http://www.scholarships.com/):** This site is another large database site for finding financial aid. The site also provides information on education loans for both students and parents as well as prepaid tuition programs, and it offers tips on how to receive financial assistance, such as how to correctly completion forms.

Treatment Procedures and Social–Personal Information

One of the more controversial uses of the Internet by clients is to obtain information on treatment for specific concerns. In addition to finding information that may be misleading, many counselors fear that clients will find information that is contrary to the approach taken by the counselor, leading the client to assume that their counselor is unskilled, out of date, or not qualified to respond to the issues raised. Of course, in some cases this may be true. But in most cases the information obtained by a client simply represents a reasonable difference of style or alternative approach. In some cases, the information obtained by the client may represent information that is simply wrong, and the counselor must be prepared to help the client understand the information in the broad context of professional research. In all cases, the counselor will best serve the client by maintaining open communication, responding with appropriate concern, and avoiding defensive reactions. To best help clients avoid misinformation, the skilled counselor must be prepared to help clients find accurate and useful information. Sites listed below can be helpful in this process.

- **Mental Health Bill of Rights (http://helping.apa.org/spreadtheword/rights.html):** This important site should be visited by all providers of counseling services as well as clients and potential clients. Posted here by the American Psychological Association, the document represents the work of a collection of advocates for mental health rights. Everyone should understand their choices, and counseling professionals can help clients by empowering them to know and use this information about their rights.
- **Ask NOAH About Mental Health (http://www.noah-health.org/english/illness/mentalhealth/mental.html):** NOAH stands for New York Online Access to Health and is a collaborative project of the City University of New York, the Metropolitan New York Library Council, the New York Academy of Medicine, and the New York Public Library. This site is a gateway to information consumers will find beneficial about all aspects of healthy emotional growth and development. Links

are available for specific disorders and concerns, as well as general links about human development, parenting, medication and wellness. The links are clearly labeled so the user can tell which ones are within the NOAH system and which lead to other sites.

- **American Counseling Association (http://www.counseling.org):** This site contains a variety of information for consumers and professionals alike. Consumers can click on the link labeled "Media/ Consumer Information" to obtain information on treatment, ethics, finding a counselor, and so forth. Topical information is also available connected to current events such as responding to crisis and trauma.

Summary

As clients continue to increase their use of the Internet to obtain information, the role of the counselor as "professional guide" will continue to develop. Like any guide preparing to take someone on a journey, however, our first task is to make sure that the client has the skills and other characteristics necessary for success. In addition to a desire to use the Internet, clients who are to be successful should also possess basic computer skills and familiarity with online processes. Other factors that need to be considered include a client's reading level and language skills. For some clients, additional characteristics may indicate that they are not appropriate candidates for online work. This may include a history of poor choices online or an inability to provide self-supervision.

Once an individual has been identified as an appropriate client, he or she will then need specific skills to search for the type of information that will be beneficial in helping to achieve personal goals. Three primary tools available for finding information include search engines, directories, and online databases. By understanding how these tools are accessed and how they operate, counselors can help clients find information on almost any topic.

Helping clients successfully access the Internet and acquire information is a way to extend our impact into clients' lives by using a tool that is increasingly a portion of their daily world. By shaping this behavior and helping to empower clients' self-development, counselors can foster personal skills that will last a lifetime.

Internet Sites for Additional Information

- **http://www.internet101.org/internet101.html.** This site is designed to be an introduction to the Internet for those with little knowledge who do not want to read extensive directions. A good starting point for anyone just beginning.
- **http://www.wmrc.com/businessbriefing/pdf/health3_2002/reference/Ref7.pdf.** This report looks at how individuals use the Internet to obtain information about health-related issues. It also looks at rea-

sons some professionals are not happy with this trend, presents barriers to access, and offers words of caution.

- **http://www.ncpa.org/ba/ba317/ba317.html.** Another medical-focused site, this one shows the reader how online information may alter the relationship between professional and client.
- **http://www.metanoia.org/imhs/history.htm.** This site provides a summary of the history of counseling services provided online.
- **http://www7.scu.edu.au/programme/posters/1914/com1914.htm.** A brief look at a project to introduce the Internet to clients with various disabling conditions, this site includes a look at assessment and accessibility.
- **http://www.indiana.edu/~librcsd/search/.** This is a good site to learn more about metasearch technology and includes links to a number of metasearch engines.
- **http://carbon.cudenver.edu/~mryder/itc/search.html.** This site provides information on search engines, Internet directories, and links to information on improving search techniques.
- **http://daphne.palomar.edu/TGSEARCH/.** This site reviews many popular search engines and compares them on a simple graphic showing which engines incorporate which search features.

10

Continuing Education
Opportunities on the Internet

Competency: Be able to use the Internet for finding and using continuing education opportunities in counseling.

Continuing education for professionals is a very large business in the United States. As more individual states have adopted licensure laws, the demand for continuing education by counselors has increased dramatically. Today, there are tens of thousands of individuals and organizations providing these services. Identifying the complete list is difficult, but it is possible to look at some numbers to determine the size of the market.

The National Board for Certified Counselors (NBCC), as a national certifying organization, is one body that represents a large group of professional counselors. Because of the requirements that individuals who wish to maintain certification through NBCC face, this organization is one place to look for quality continuing education opportunities. Through their own approval process, NBCC has a list of 951 approved providers of continuing education (NBCC, n.d.). This averages to about 18 per state (including Washington, DC). But this is only a small portion of the approved providers. Many other organizations also offer "approval" to CEU providers. The largest source of approval may be state regulatory boards. One example can be found in the state of Florida. In Florida, the Board of Clinical Social Work, Marriage & Family Therapy & Mental Health Counseling has an approval process and maintains lists of providers for practitioners within the state. Recently, this list contained 555 individuals and organizations (Florida Department of Health, n.d.) approved as providers of some type of continuing education to licensees overseen by the board. Indiana, a recent adopter of counselor licensure, lists 81 individual providers and an additional 85 types of organizations (e.g., national organizations such as the ACA; universities and colleges; or federal, state or local agencies) that are approved to offer services (Indiana Health Professions Bureau, 2002). NBCC lists only 39 approved providers in Florida, and 12 in Indiana (NBCC, n.d.). The discrepancy between the NBCC approval list and the state board lists indicates that there are indeed a huge number of options available, and no single source can provide anyone a complete overview of availability.

Among the thousands of providers registered with accrediting agencies and state governing boards, many are providing their services online. The promise of anyplace, anytime education that is sweeping postsecondary education in the early 21st century is also changing the continuing education industry. All counselors who wish to maintain their license or certifications will be responsible to engage in some continuing education activities. Some method to understand the options available and to identify quality opportunities that meet individual needs is necessary. This chapter focuses primarily on continuing education provided online. However, many of the guidelines provided may work as well for face-to-face and other home-study options.

• Technology Tip 10.1 •

Use the "Bookmark" or "Favorites" feature in your browser to set up a folder called Continuing Education. Then, whenever you are online and find a site that offers continuing education, you can add the site to your bookmarks. Your list will grow quickly and you will always have ready access. In Internet Explorer click Favorites, then Add, then New Folder. In Netscape, click Bookmarks, then Manage Bookmarks, then New Folder.

Understanding Your Needs

The first and perhaps most important task for the professional counselor is to understand his or her own needs in terms of continuing education. To assess these needs, counselors should review all certifications or licenses they possess. Each separate organization or credentialing board that oversees the credentialing process will have individual requirements that need to be met. In this process there are several important steps.

- **Review the requirements of each organization or accrediting body separately.** Although many states have adopted counselor licensure laws that mirror standards established by CACREP and NBCC, it would be a mistake to assume that no modifications in the area of continuing education have been made.
- **Check each credential individually on the basis of when you received it.** Many state boards oversee the credentials of multiple types of mental health professionals (e.g., licensed mental health counselor, licensed social worker, licensed marriage and family therapist) or varying levels of credentials (e.g., Licensed Professional Counselor, Licensed Professional Clinical Counselor), and although the continuing education requirements are often similar, they may not be identical. Additionally, as state laws and rules change, certain groups of individuals may be held to different standards on the basis of when a license or certification was received. These discrepancies are generally phased out over time, but during periods of transition the professional counselor needs to be sure not to be caught unprepared.
- **Create a list of what credentials the continuing education providers must possess for each credential you wish to maintain.** In some states, providers approved by major national organizations (e.g., ACA, NBCC, APA, NASW) qualify automatically as CEU pro-

viders. In other states, only organizations registered and approved by the state qualify. As a result, an individual counselor may have enough hours to maintain one certification, but not enough for another because the providers do not have the correct credentials.
- **Create a list of credentials that you wish to possess.** Many credentials in specialty areas (e.g., substance abuse, sexuality counseling) require extensive experience as well as specialty training. These can often be obtained concurrently. As well, if the provider of the continuing education has the right credentials, training received in anticipation of some future certification can also be used to satisfy requirements for current licensure or certification. There is nothing wrong with using a single training episode to meet the requirements of different credentialing bodies.

Having completed this review, you should now be knowledgeable of what your own continuing education needs are. Now it is time to begin to look for quality training opportunities.

• Technology Tip 10.2 •

A quick way to find a Web site for your state licensing board, or the board of another state, is to visit the American Association of State Counseling Boards at http://www.aascb.org/index.htm.

Identifying Quality Training

Given the wide range of individual needs, variance in learning styles, and multitude of delivery options available, identifying the best continuing education opportunities for you rests in part on knowing yourself and your own likes and needs. It is clear that there is no single model of education that works equally well for all individuals. Beyond these individual differences, however, there are some elements of quality that the individual can assess to determine if a particular opportunity is likely to be one of quality.

The first and easiest way to assess the likely quality of a continuing education program is to assess the quality of the organization certifying the provider. Organizations like the NBCC have a vested interest in ensuring that their continuing education providers offer a quality product to their membership. As a result, some level of confidence can be placed in providers who are affiliated with this type of organization. Compare, for example, the resources that NBCC can invest in overseeing continuing education providers with a small state or regional organization. There is nothing inherently wrong with a provider who has received approval through a small organization, but small organizations are less likely to have the resources to carefully review and oversee continuing education providers.

A second way to assess a provider is to consider the range of approval they have achieved. An organization that has been granted provider status by a number of different accrediting bodies has been through repeated

• 191 •

reviews. With each review, different aspects of the training have come under scrutiny. As a result, potential problems are more likely to have been identified and corrected than if the provider has only undergone a single review process.

A third characteristic to consider is the parent organization of which the continuing education provider is a component. Oftentimes, continuing education is provided through a university, a community agency, or a local advocacy and training organization. Although there is no guarantee that the reputation of one necessarily represents the other, there is a likelihood that a university known for high-quality programming in a particular discipline will also have quality continuing education in that area. Similarly, a local agency known to offer substandard care is likely to offer continuing education that is reflective of its own approach to addressing clients and the community.

Finally, assess the knowledge and background of the individual presenter. In some areas, local clinicians provide the majority of continuing education available. Although such practitioners often have valuable experience and knowledge to share, it is possible that they will reach beyond their own level of expertise to try to provide training to the local community. In such a situation, the training provided may be less than can be achieved through the careful reading of a good reference book. As a worst-case scenario, the local practitioner reaching beyond his or her expertise may actually deliver misinformation, creating a cadre of misinformed practitioners that are unprepared to meet client needs.

These same four criteria can be applied to any online continuing education opportunity that you may consider. Returning to the first point, review all online material to determine who has approved this individual or organization to provide continuing education. The computer savvy counselor is at an advantage here because not only can you review who has provided the credentialing, but now you can also review the Web site of the credentialing agency to determine what the procedures are to become a continuing education provider. Some organizations require little more than a simple outline of the proposed training, whereas others require a detailed outline, examples of training materials, and copies of all assessment instruments. Clearly, providers who have completed a more rigorous review are likely to provide more complete and well-planned training opportunities.

Reviewing a provider organization's credentials online is likely to provide more information than simply reviewing a flier or brochure received in the mail or picked up at a conference. Brochures aimed at the professional counselor are likely to mention approval to provide continuing education from organizations specifically linked to counseling, such as NBCC. By reviewing the provider's online materials, prospective students may identify that the provider is also registered in their state and has approval to provide continuing education from other mental-health-related organizations such as AAMFT, NASW, and APA. These additional credentials, which may not be directly relevant to the licensed mental health counselor or certified school counselor, do indicate that the provider has undergone and successfully completed multiple reviews. This multiple review process is one indication that the provider has invested significant resources in planning his or her continuing education program.

The astute prospective student will generally find that it is easier to obtain information about a parent organization online than from other sources. For example, if continuing education is being provided by an institute in a city geographically distant, by going online one can learn more about the institute. In some cases, going to an institution's Web site will provide very little information. A lack of information may indicate that the institute is quite small and perhaps only exists for the purpose of providing online continuing education. In some cases, this will represent an opportunity to engage in training provided by a respected and known expert in the field who has chosen to provide continuing education through his or her own resources rather than through a university, hospital, or other organizational structure. This can represent a significant opportunity at reasonable costs. At other times, however, an institute established for the sole purpose of providing continuing education may suggest that a single individual saw an opportunity to make money with seemingly little input. In this case, the wise consumer would continue with caution. Most organizations and institutes that are free-standing will list their directors, primary officers, and key personnel on their Web site. If the list includes well-known experts, it may be an indication of quality. Well-known authors and leaders in the field are often careful in creating partnerships. Wanting to protect their own reputation, they may be cautious and refuse to sit on a board or otherwise associate with an institution of poor quality. Also review any information provided about an organization's budget, scope of services, or total number of employees. These can be important characteristics by which to judge an organization's size. An organization that lists two individuals as officers who happen to share the same last name is probably of a different type than one that lists numerous prominent authors and researchers among its board of directors.

As in the other areas, assessing the qualifications of an individual online is likely to be easier than simply referring to a printed brochure. Typically, a brochure will list a small number of key attributes of the presenter. By going online, you are likely to be able to access a broader range of information. Sometimes, a biography of several hundred words will be made available online, particularly for key personnel in an organization, or for ongoing training. If this information is not provided, by using a search engine such as Google (google.com) or All The Web (alltheweb. com), the name of the key presenter can often be searched.

Many times this will result in additional information about the presenter. If the presenter is associated with a university, such a search will often result in a curriculum vitae that will identify specific research and publications of the individual, thereby reinforcing the person's status as an expert or suggesting that the training is being conducted in an area of relatively less expertise.

The ability to use the Web to seek information about a particular person has become so widespread that the name Google has been turned into a verb, as in "I'm going to Google Dr. Tyler to find out whether he knows anything about group behavior before I go to his lecture."

These steps can be quite useful in gaining an overall understanding or developing a general impression of the organization and the individual involved in providing continuing education. However, these steps represent an attempt to take information about traditional continuing education practices and adopt them to the online environment. This is a good beginning, but it is not sufficient. Educators are aware that quality online education is more than simply placing an instructor's lecture notes online or creating PowerPoint slides for a student to view. Increasingly, models of online education represent new approaches that build on traditional pedagogy while also adopting materials and utilizing the strength of the available technology. Therefore, although the previous steps represent some basic procedures, they are not enough to understand the specifics of online education.

Online Instruction in Counselor Education

In 1999, The Executive Council of the Association for Counselor Education and Supervision (ACES) endorsed a set of standards for Online Instruction in Counselor Education (ACES Technology Interest Network, 1999). These standards were developed to help guide faculty and training institutions in the development of online courses. A student will generally not have access to all of the information necessary to determine whether a course or continuing education program meets the guidelines, but by reviewing the major sections of the guidelines it is possible to develop a series of questions from which to judge online continuing education opportunities.

Course Quality

The first section of the guidelines is titled "Course Quality." Standards in this section focus on ensuring that distance students receive an experience equivalent to face-to-face students, that material is delivered in an appropriate manner, and that students have sufficient support.

It is rare today to go to any type of continuing education program that lasts for more than 1 or 2 hours that is entirely lecture-based. Presenters are aware that students need to interact with materials, that meaning needs to be created, and that opportunities for application and practice are essential. These types of activities are difficult to re-create in online learning, but not impossible.

The best online continuing education will make attempts to recreate these learning opportunities. For example, the simplest manner to conduct online continuing education is to have the student read text-based material and then respond to a small number of multiple choice questions to demonstrate understanding. However, this approach is not consistent with current knowledge of adult learning. A better approach would be to have the student respond in advance to several open-ended questions, thereby accessing previous learning. After reading some material, the student might be asked to respond to additional open-ended questions, some of which require application and integration of material. Additional information might be presented in graphical formats or through streaming media. Assessment, in the ideal online course, would be multidimensional, providing the learner with repeated and authentic opportunity to demonstrate growing knowledge. Many continuing education offerings are as simple as reading a journal article or book and responding to several questions. Although this may be the easiest and quickest format, it likely does not represent the best opportunity for learning.

Variety of presentation styles and assessment types is important. This variety needs to be connected to the type of content presented. Skills are often better learned through demonstration than through review of text-based material. Therefore, the best continuing education opportunities will use streaming media to demonstrate interactions rather than simply providing a descriptive overview. Using streaming audio, which is available to virtually anyone with Internet connectivity, the professional counselor can hear exchanges between counselor and client, allowing for a better understanding of pacing, client intonation, and counselor receptivity. Increasingly, streaming video allows the opportunity to see as well as hear these exchanges. The popularity of training movies such as *Three Approaches to Psychotherapy* (Shostrum, 1965) demonstrates the impact that audio and video have on the trainee.

The issue of access to the instructor is one of critical importance. It is not uncommon for learners at all levels to have difficulty understanding material they view or read. The opportunity to ask the teacher questions is a central component of most education provided in the United States, but one that is lacking in most home-based continuing education, both online and traditional correspondence versions. Many of these courses rely on preprinted materials, often journals or books that the student reads and attempts to comprehend. When the student believes he or she is prepared, a multiple-choice exam is completed, which is then returned to some unknown person, graded, and a certificate of completion is issued. If students have questions, they may attempt to contact the organization providing the continuing education but likely will not have access to the original author of the material. Although rare, the best online continuing education will provide some support opportunities, either with the author of the materials or with a qualified expert.

Course Objectives

The second general area of the ACES guidelines focuses on course objectives. In general, accepted educational practices begin with an explication of learning objectives in the form of knowledge, skills, or attitudinal changes the learner will achieve or acquire. In some cases, providers of online content will make explicit to the learner what these educational objectives are. This is important for several reasons. First, without a clear presentation of learning objectives, learners are left with incomplete information concerning whether a particular continuing education opportunity is appropriate for their needs. Too often we are attracted to lectures, presentations, books, and articles because of the title, only to find that the content does not meet our expectations. When learning objectives are clear and available in advance, learners can make an informed decision about the suitability of a specific opportunity on the basis of their unique needs. Second, some popular and well-supported theories of learning (Gagne, 1985) see the presentation and review of learning objectives by the learner as a key component in effective learning. These theories suggest that the learner learns best what he or she expects to learn. By providing the objectives in advance, expectations are created and semantic networks are accessed that allow new learning to be easily created and stored.

Clearly defined learning objectives also speak to the overall structure of the learning opportunity. Although defined objectives do not demonstrate that the remaining portions of the experience will be well-planned, a lack of objectives does suggest a lack of preparedness overall.

The issue of clearly defined objectives raises some question about the popular practice of having the continuing education student read material that was prepared for another purpose as the primary means of teaching. Research articles are designed to present information based on some experience of the author, while other articles or books may be designed to present an opinion, educate about a cause, or simply to entertain. Few books or articles are written primarily as learning tools that incorporate known principles of learning and pedagogy. As a result, while many texts contain important and relevant information, simply reading the text without ancillary support may not be the most effective way to learn information and change professional practice.

Learner Support

The third general area of the ACES standards focuses on learner support. In the context of computer-based continuing education, support has many facets. The first of these is support provided by ancillary materials that may be necessary to fully comprehend the primary materials. In traditional educational settings, students are expected to turn to support materials such as discipline-specific journals, reference texts, library resources, and so forth to supplement the primary learning tools that are provided in the classroom. Generally, continuing education assumes that learners will not use these types of support materials to complete their ongoing professional learning. Most continuing education is conducted as self-contained units with no additional outside materials needed for successful completion. Although this approach is convenient for the learner as well as the provider, it suggests that continuing education is substantially different from the education provided in the traditional classroom setting. This approach may lead to learning that is less connected to other aspects of the professional's life and less personally fulfilling because there is not an opportunity or expectation that the professional will customize the learning through additional reading or study. Quality distance education is built on the assumption that the learner must have access to the same support materials as the traditional face-to-face student. Generally this is provided in the form of access to online library resources, full-text article databases, and specially developed electronic materials. Although rare, the best continuing education programs will also make these materials available to the learner, allowing the learner the broadest opportunity to expand his or her learning in personally meaningful ways.

Support also needs to be provided to the learner for the variety of technical difficulties that may occur when accessing learning online. Professionals choose to engage in online continuing education for a wide variety of reasons: convenience, flexible hours, and lower costs are just a few. Many professionals choose this option in spite of the potential technical difficulties or their own lack of training or comfort using technology in this manner. Even the most basic forms of online education will create difficulties for some users because of browser incompatibility, a lack of knowledge of obtaining plug-ins to view specialized materials, or difficulty in navigating a Web site. Quality continuing education sites will anticipate the potential difficulties that users may have and will create systems in advance to help address these issues.

Perhaps the most common approach to providing a user with information to resolve problems is through the use of an FAQ (frequently asked question) file. By looking for the acronym FAQ, or searching the Web site for this or the keyword "troubleshooting," the user can often find information needed to resolve problems. But even the most technologically proficient individuals occasionally cannot resolve an issue on their own. In such a case, a point of contact with the provider is critical. It is most useful to have this contact available by telephone as well as e-mail. Using a telephone (sometimes a cellular phone if the regular phone line is used for Internet access), the continuing education student can speak to technical support while he or she is also viewing the Web site of interest. This allows the student to directly describe what is occurring and to resolve any problem with the support of someone in real time.

Finally, prospective students need to know in advance all expectations for their completion of any work to obtain continuing education credit. In almost all cases, some form of test will be required to demonstrate completion of the education materials. Students should identify in advance whether a test can be repeated without charge if the initial performance is poor. Although this is a common practice, it is not universal. As well, some continuing education sites may charge based on access to each educational unit, while others will provide unlimited access for a period of time or to a large number of materials.

Faculty Qualifications

The fourth general area in the ACES standards focuses on faculty qualifications. In continuing education, faculty qualifications are often viewed quite differently than in university settings. Most mental health professionals holding a license have been trained in graduate schools by faculty holding at least a master's degree and in most cases a doctorate. Universities oversee faculty activities and ensure that they are engaged in scholarly works that keep their knowledge current. In the arena of continuing education, it is not uncommon for a higher premium to be placed on practical experience than on academic credentials. Many providers of continuing education have extensive experience in a particular area but lack significant academic training beyond that required for basic licensure or certification. Clearly, an experienced and talented clinician has much to share, and others can learn quite a lot from that experience. However, experience alone does not necessarily create a successful educator or trainer. Many professional counselors have experienced continuing education where the trainer had no apparent knowledge beyond that possessed by members of the audience, or lacked the communication skills to help others successfully acquire new knowledge. The ease with which continuing education can be created and placed on the Internet, and the lack of money necessary to start such an enterprise has contributed to an explosion of continuing education opportunities. Although many of these opportunities are positive, others lack substance. Learning as much as possible about the individual who developed the educational material to be used, as well as any tests to be administered or supplemental materials, will help the prospective student gauge the likely quality of the continuing education opportunity. Table 10.1 provides a list of 10 key questions to ask when assessing online education.

Finding Continuing Education Online

Using the Internet search skills you developed in chapter 9, you have the ability to go online and identify hundreds of continuing education sites. Indeed, a simple search on All The Web (alltheweb.com) identified over 350,000 sites, while the same search on Google (google.com) found over 400,000 sites! Such a large number of sites is truly overwhelming. Fortunately, there are some alternative techniques that can help locate continuing education that will meet your individual needs.

The best place to begin a search for continuing education may be on the Web site of the organization or government agency that oversees your cer-

---

Table 10.1

Ten Questions to Ask When Assessing
the Quality of Online Continuing Education

---

1. Does the agency that has approved the provider to offer continuous education credits (CEUs) have a rigorous oversight program?
2. Does the reputation of the parent organization providing the services suggest the CEU program is one of quality?
3. Has the CEU program received approval from multiple oversight agencies?
4. Are the presenter or developer's credentials available, and do they suggest a high level of expertise in the content as well as the ability to develop and deliver quality online continuing education?
5. Will the continuing education consist of reading text material and then answering a multiple-choice test, or will additional teaching and assessment materials be used?
6. Is the author, developer, or another qualified instructor available to answer questions or help with difficulties?
7. Are clearly defined learning objectives provided to the student in advance to assess the applicability of the course to the individual's needs?
8. Are any supplementary materials available for further research or inquiry?
9. Is technical support easily and freely available?
10. What activities will the student need to engage in to successfully complete the continuing education program?

---

tification or license. In professional counseling, the National Board of Certified Counselors (www.nbcc.org) is one accrediting body that represents many individuals in the profession. From the NBCC home page, you can quickly link to a list of providers that are approved by NBCC to provide continuing education units (CEUs) to those holding the NCC credential or one of the specialty credentials. On the continuing education provider page (http://www.nbcc.org/users/ceproviders.htm) you will be able to identify not only approved providers but also those who provide in-home education opportunities. All of these in-home providers have Web sites, and many provide their training via the Web. While reviewing the entire list is time consuming, this is a good way to learn about the wide range of education that is available. Often, by reviewing these opportunities, professional counselors will be reminded of areas they want to learn more about or will be introduced to entirely new areas they had never considered pursuing.

• Technology Tip 10.4 •

One method to find quality online continuing education is to ask others who have experience with online training. Sign on to one of the professional listservs mentioned in chapter 7 and ask others about their experience with continuing education. While positive reports may at times mean only that the work was not difficult or expensive (which says nothing about learning), negative reports certainly indicate that a particular opportunity may not be a good investment.

Counselors who are certified or licensed by a state entity may find that a Web site maintained by the state will provide information on continuing education opportunities. As noted earlier, the Florida Department of Health site associated with the Board of Clinical Social Work, Marriage and Family Therapy, and Mental Health Counseling (http://www.doh. state.fl.us/mqa/491/soc_home.html) provides a complete list of over 500 approved providers. This is not unique to Florida. The California Board of Behavioral Sciences (http://www.bbs.ca.gov/default.htm) lists over 1,700 approved providers in a document available as a PDF file.

•   Technology Tip 10.5   •

A PDF file is a file type designed to be opened and read using Adobe Acrobat (www.adobe.com). This file format can be read by almost all personal computers, regardless of the type of computer or word processing software being used.

Most local jurisdictions will maintain similar lists on their Web sites. A more complete list of Web sites for various state credentialing boards around the United States can be found on the Web site for this book: http://www.21stcenturycounselor.com.

Another option to obtain continuing education information is to visit the Web site of one of the professional organizations that represents your interests. For example, the ACA Web site (www.counseling.org) has a link to continuing education and online courses that ACA has developed or endorsed. The American School Counseling Association (http://www. schoolcounselor.org/) as well as the American Mental Health Counselors Association (http://www.amhca.org/education/index.htm) provide access to additional continuing education opportunities. Professional organizations have a very strong investment in ensuring that their members have adequate training and that the continuing education they endorse is of high quality. Therefore, starting with one of these organizations may be an easy way to access quality opportunities.

In addition to national organizations, state organizations may also be helpful. The Alaska Counseling Association (http://www.alaskacounseling.org/) maintains a list of continuing education opportunities on its homepage. One advantage of working with a local professional group is that local needs may be better met. The National Association of Social Workers–Alaska Chapter (http://www.naswak.org/cont.ed.htm) can help counselors obtain continuing education specifically geared to the needs of Alaskan Natives. It is doubtful that similar training will be advertised in any other state in the country. It should be noted that in some cases, training provided by or endorsed by organizations other than those that most directly represent the professional counselor may not satisfy specific requirements. Therefore, a professional counselor who obtains training through the Alaska chapter of NASW may find the training is valuable and professionally enriching, but still may not qualify to meet his or her specific licensure needs. Always verify with the oversight body if there is any doubt about what CEU providers are appropriate for a specific credential.

As has been shown, there are a wide number of organizations that provide CEUs. Depending on your specific needs and the rules governing your licensure or certification, there may be many opportunities available via the Web that are not specifically listed with your state oversight board or a professional association. This may be particularly true if your interests are quite specific. By knowing the rules that govern your continuing education needs, you will be able to identify many additional opportunities. A return to the World Wide Web, armed with good search skills and specific needs, will identify a wide range of opportunity. For instance, whereas a simple Google search for "continuing education counseling" found over 400,000 sites, a more advanced search for "continuing education sand therapy" found a more manageable 8,000 sites. Although 8,000 is still a high number, the sites found on the first several pages of the search were very relevant and immediately a number of online and home-study opportunities were identified. The even more specific Google search "continuing education REBT online NBCC approved" returned a small list of 21 possible sites, most of which were relevant for the prospective student seeking additional training in this area and who wanted to maintain NCC certification.

Finally, when searching for online continuing education opportunities, it would be a mistake to neglect more traditional information sources. Every member of the ACA receives on a monthly basis the printed newspaper *Counseling Today*. CEU providers are aware that this paper is circulated to their target audience, and many take advantage by advertising. Some of these ads are in the classified section, which can also be accessed online (http://www.counseling.org/ctonline/classified.htm). However, some ads are not available via the online version of this publication, known as CTOnline. Start with the printed version to find providers of interest and then visit their Web sites to obtain additional information.

Summary

All professional counselors are required to obtain continuing education to maintain licensure and certification. Increasingly, continuing education is being offered over the Internet. These opportunities can represent significant time and cost savings as they do not require missing work or traveling. Additionally, because they offer cost advantages to the provider, they can often be offered at lower rates than traditional classroom-based education opportunities.

Using the skills obtained elsewhere in this book, the reader is prepared to use search engines and directories to identify continuing education opportunities. Combined with knowledge about evaluating online information, new knowledge presented in this chapter focusing on evaluating education opportunities has prepared the reader to critically evaluate the opportunities to determine whether they meet personal needs and whether they are likely to be quality programs.

Continuing education is part of the lifelong learning process that professional counselors should be prepared to engage in. Using technology skills, counselors have a broader array of opportunities than at any time in the past. As a result, maintaining currency or gaining new expertise should be easier and more enjoyable than in the past. Although we all will gain individually as professionals, the real benefit from these opportunities will accrue to our clients and communities as we are increasingly able to meet specific needs.

Internet Sites for Additional Information

- http://www.m-a-h.net/hip/stateboards.htm. This valuable site provides links to state licensing boards and credentialing bodies throughout the United States. If you need to learn about licensure requirements in a particular state, this is the place to start.
- http://www.ccacc.ca/cocc.htm. This site provides certification requirements for Canada.
- http://www.nbcc.org/depts/cemain.htm. Designed for National Certified Counselors or others with a certification through NBCC, this site will keep you current on your continuing education needs.
- http://www.umdnj.edu/psyevnts/psyjumps.html. This intriguing list connects to more than 4,000 organizations worldwide with some connection to mental health or telemedicine. Included is an index of annual meetings of these organizations where CEUs can usually be earned.
- http://www.aascb.org/state.htm. Maintained by the American Association of State Counseling Boards, this site provides addresses to state agencies around the United States.
- http://dmoz.org/Reference/Education/Distance_Learning/Online_Courses/Healthcare/. This directory may be a good starting point to explore various online learning opportunities.
- http://dmoz.org/Health/Mental_Health/Professional_Resources/Continuing_Education/Online/. Along with the previous site, this directory provides a wide range of possible CEU opportunities.
- http://directory.google.com/Top/Health/Mental_Health/Professional_Resources/Continuing_Education/Online/. This directory of CEU opportunities provided by Google, while not exhaustive, is quite extensive.

Legal and Ethical Issues

*Competency: Be knowledgeable of the legal and ethical codes which relate to
counseling services provided via the Internet.*

In 1995, the National Board for Certified Counselors (NBCC) Board of
Directors appointed a Web counseling task force to examine the practice
of online counseling and to assess the possible existence of any regulatory issues NBCC might need to address. The task force established a listserv
composed of more than 20 individuals who had specific knowledge, expertise, skills, and opinions regarding the practice of Web counseling. It quickly
became apparent that counseling had a diverse presence on the Internet,
from Web sites that simply promoted a counselor's home or office practice,
to sites that provided information about counseling, and others that actually claimed to offer therapeutic interventions either as an adjunct to face-
to-face counseling or as a stand-alone service. No one knew if the lack of
visual input made a difference in the outcome of the counseling process. No
one knew about the legality of counseling across state or national boundaries. Few people knew whether there was any relevant research in any
field of communication that could shed light on these questions (Bloom,
1997). The relative newness of the use of the Internet for counseling service
and product delivery leaves authors of standards at a loss when beginning
to address the issue of ethical practices on the Internet.

However, through its work, the NBCC forged ahead and devised the
Statement for the Practice of Internet Counseling, available at www.nbcc.
org/ethics/webethics.htm. Similarly, the International Society for Mental
Health Online (ISMHO) and the Psychiatric Society for Informatics (PSI)
officially endorsed in January 2000 the Suggested Principles for the Online
Provision of Mental Health Services, available at www.ismho.org/
suggestions.html.

The American Counseling Association approved and published the
Ethical Standards for Internet Online Counseling (American Counseling
Association, 1999; see http://www.counseling.org/resources/internet.htm),
which are designed to establish appropriate standards for the use of electronic communications over the Internet in relation to the provision of
online counseling services. These standards are designed to supplement
the latest ACA Code of Ethics and Standards of Practice (ACA, 1995) as
stated in its Preamble. Other professional organizations have also adopted
specific statements referring to the use of technology in professional practice. The American School Counseling Association (ASCA, 1998) included in
the latest revision of its ethical standards a section specifically addressing

computer technology. The American Mental Health Counselors Association (2000) also addressed technology in a separate section in its code of ethics. Similar steps have been taken by the Association for Specialists in Group Work (ASGW, 1998), and the Commission on Rehabilitation Counselor Certification is considering adding statements on technology to a new version of the Code of Professional Ethics for Rehabilitation Counselors (CRCC, 2003).

Web counseling standards address important and difficult issues, such as educating clients about counselor qualifications and training; confidentiality and security of information; storage of sensitive information; verification of client identity; availability of the Web counselor; working in the event of technological failure; procedures for client crises; how to communicate offline; the limitations of counseling over the Internet; and more. This range of topics suggests the many dangers that are presented when technology becomes a part of the counseling process. While these guidelines were written with a view toward counseling services that are provided via the Internet, they also offer guidance about the ethical use of this technology to counselors and others in traditional counseling settings who use technology to support their work. Interestingly, whereas technology creates a number of concerns and new potential for ethical breaches, technology also provides us the tools necessary to guard against these possibilities. The remainder of this chapter examines various issues raised in the codes mentioned earlier (see Table 11.1) and discusses technology that can be used to protect clients and counselors. The chapter will not reproduce each of these codes or engage in a specific discussion of them. Rather, our intention is to present for the reader information about how to use technology to respond to ethical concerns to create best practice. Before continuing, the reader should review appropriate standards in their latest version. Web addresses have been provided at the conclusion of this chapter, and additional links can be found on this book's companion Web site (www.21stcenturycounselor.com).

Confidentiality and File Security

The threat to confidentiality brought about by the use of technology is likely greater than any other change in professional behavior in history. Reports of computer hackers accessing classified files within government agencies and infiltrating commercial sites to steal financial information has made everyone aware of the potential threat. The fact that many of these hackers are (or are perceived to be by the public) teenagers and young adults has added to the impression that hacking is widespread and relatively easy. In addition to being at risk from hackers, computer files are also vulnerable to unauthorized access by others on an agency or school network, susceptible to loss when stored on removable media, and susceptible to being accidentally viewed when left open on a computer screen. As with all client information, the counselor's responsibility to maintain confidentiality is paramount.

Table 11.1

Key Issues Arising from the Use of Technology in Counseling

1. Maintaining confidentiality in an electronic environment—Confidentiality may be compromised by intercepted communications, misaddressed communications, virus or worm attacks, or hackers.
2. Storage of electronic materials to ensure privacy—Materials stored electronically may be accessible to a wide range of people in an organization, or to hackers on the outside.
3. Helping clients become informed about online services and privacy concerns—Clients need to learn about the realities of the online environment just as they need to learn about the counseling process in traditional settings.
4. Verifying client identity—A key concern related to online services is verifying that clients are who they say they are.
5. Intervening in emergencies—Arrangements must be made to care for the emergency needs of clients receiving services from individuals or organizations at a geographic distance.
6. Transfer of information—As more information is transferred via electronic networks, appropriate precautions must be taken by both sender and receiver to ensure that all data is protected.
7. Licensure—A variety of legal issues still need to be addressed, including applicable laws. There remains debate about whether laws related to the geographic location of the client or counselor regulate professional practice.
8. Liability Insurance—As technology-based services are relatively new and remain a small portion of all services provided, insurers may not directly address these services in their policies. Professionals must be proactive to ensure that they are adequately covered.

Laws surrounding e-mail use and disclosure continue to develop. In most cases, however, e-mail communication is handled in the same manner as more traditional communication in a work setting. Understanding how the law applies to paper documents in your setting will provide a start to understanding how the law addresses electronic files.

In settings involving state or federal government, e-mail may actually be considered public documents and may be subject to disclosure under so-called "sunshine" laws, also known as "public domain" laws. These laws require that many acts of government and government institutions be conducted in full public view. As such, many documents created while conducting business in government settings are considered to be public documents and must be made available when properly requested. It is clear that this is true for e-mail that is related to operations of government agencies, including schools, that have been generated on or received by an e-mail server maintained by the state. It is less clear how these laws may apply to client records. In states where counselors have legally protected or privileged communication with their clients, an argument can be extended that e-mail communication with clients becomes privileged. However, in many states, counselors do not have the same level of protected communication that physicians or psychologists enjoy. In these cases, e-mail may not be protected. Similarly, e-mail communication between a counselor and a supervisor, even when containing client information, may not be considered a part of the client record but rather a portion of the supervisory record. Again, this may negate any protection. Counselors can protect themselves by working with local administrators and consulting attorneys to determine how local law affects privilege and e-mail communication. Additionally, schools and agencies can take proactive steps to protect clients by adopting written policies that describe how e-mail is to be handled, whether it is considered a portion of the client record, and who will have access to this information.

In most cases, a breach of confidentiality is more likely to occur as a result of poor handling of computer files, rather than through public disclosure of documents. To fully understand this danger, it is important to understand how computers handle various files and what occurs when files are deleted. By taking the time to become well-informed concerning computer operations, counselors as well as school and agency administrators will be better prepared to handle electronic information in a manner that will maintain confidentiality over the long term.

Many individuals assume that once an e-mail message has been deleted, it is gone and cannot be recovered. In truth, if you rely on the delete command that is built into most computer software, the deleted file is not actually gone, but may remain in several places. If your e-mail is Web-based, and you use a browser to read it, the process of reading the e-mail may create a temporary file on your computer. This file will often be stored in a folder labeled *Temp* or *Cache*. Even when the message has been deleted, this temporary file will remain on the hard drive. Although not accessible from the e-mail program, it may be accessible by navigating directly to the hard drive. Such temporary files are created by many software programs and are used to speed up the working of the machine. However, they also create security difficulties because they leave traces of your activity that others can access. The most effective way to respond to the problem of temporary files is to use a program such as IClean (http://www.aladdinsys.com/iclean/). This type of program can be configured to automatically erase temporary files, clean cache, and delete Internet histories when you log off your computer. In this manner, you can be assured that files are cleaned up and your activities will be more difficult to trace.

• Technology Tip 11.1 •

If you work in a school or agency setting, ask your network administrator or technology specialist to conduct an annual security seminar to train staff about security software, procedures, and local protection.

Another potential problem occurs because many e-mail programs do not actually delete a message when the delete button is used. In some cases, the message is simply moved to a folder called "Deleted Messages" where it will remain until the folder is emptied. If your e-mail client allows you to configure it to automatically empty the deleted messages folder when you exit, this is good practice. Other e-mail programs allow you to choose to delete a message rather than move it to the deleted items folder. This is also good practice.

To empty the deleted messages folder automatically when you exit Microsoft Outlook, go to Tools, then Options, then Other, and in the section called "General" check the box to "Empty the deleted items folder upon exit."

Finally, e-mail messages that are deleted from the user's computer generally remain on the server in some format. Some e-mail clients offer the user a choice to leave messages on the server or to download them to the local computer when they are read. When setting up your software, if you choose to leave messages on the server, the messages may remain visible to anyone with access to the server, such as technology staff or unauthorized users. The safest approach is to configure your software to download all messages to the local machine. In most cases, a desktop computer is less likely to be infiltrated than a network server. However, e-mail servers are increasingly well protected from external threat. In a school or agency, your e-mail administrator can help you to understand the level of threat your system faces and the best approach to protect your clients' data.

All computer users should also be aware that all files, not only e-mail files, generally are available after they have been deleted from a computer. Like e-mail, most computers are designed to simply move deleted files into a specific folder. Here, the files remain until the folder is emptied by the user. This feature is designed to provide safety and allow the user to retrieve files that have been accidentally erased. However, it also provides a starting point for anyone interested in determining what information a user has removed from his or her computer. Emptying the wastebasket on a regular basis is a first step toward protecting data.

Unfortunately, once the wastebasket or deleted file folder has been emptied, files that have been on a user's hard drive remain. For purposes of ease and to help users that have accidentally erased files, computers do not truly erase a file unless special software is used. Instead, when a file is erased, the computer changes a portion of the file's name. The computer is aware that the file has been deleted, and will no longer show the user the name of the file or any other information. However, common software such as Norton System Works (http://www.symantec.com/sabu/sysworks/basic/) contains specific components designed to identify these deleted files and retrieve them.

The only method to clear files from a computer in a manner that will ensure they cannot be recovered is to use a specific utility designed for this purpose. Not surprisingly, Norton System Works also contains a component, known as Wipe Info that is designed to make files unrecoverable. Once a file has been wiped or cleaned, it cannot be recovered. Other products available to clean deleted files include IClean (http://www.aladdin-sys.com/iclean/), Blackboard File Wipe (http://www.alberts.com/

authorpages/00000492/prod_403.htm), Mutilate File Wiper (http://www.
softandco.com/redir.html?u=http://home.att.net/~craigchr/mutilate.
html), and Secure Delete (http://www.aladdinsys.com/secure_delete/).
Even after the best software is used, files can be retrieved by very sophisticated procedures generally reserved for use by the police or other investigative agencies. However, for the purposes of the professional counselor, it
is unnecessary to try to hide files from these extreme recovery techniques.

Electronic communication in the form of Instant Messages or chat room
sessions are even more difficult to conceal than e-mail messages. A variety
of software standards exist for these types of programs, and most of these
products do not provide secure communication. However, efforts are
being made to resolve these problems. Link Arcade (http://linkarcade.
com/subportals/im.htm) is one instant messaging program that uses an
encryption feature to ensure that messages cannot be intercepted. VeriSign, a
well-known Internet company that provides security and privacy software,
has teamed with AOL to develop an encrypted version of the popular AOL
Instant Messaging software (http://www.nwfusion.com/news/2002/
0510veriaol.html). Clearly, in the coming months more options will be available for counselors and others who need secure communication.

Another potential avenue for a breach to occur is with computer administrators or technicians. In most settings, the individual who administers
the e-mail servers within an organization has access to e-mail that is passed
through the server. As a result, these individuals may inadvertently see
messages as they are performing various tasks related to maintaining
e-mail systems. In any setting, these individuals need to be aware of school
or agency policies concerning confidentiality and should be expected to
respond appropriately. In one unnerving situation, we overheard network
technicians in a school cafeteria discussing personal e-mail that faculty
had received via the school network. It was apparent that these employees
felt no need even to conceal their own behavior in reading these messages.

The ACA standards direct counselors to use encryption technology to
secure confidential information, and this clearly is the best way to protect
e-mail communication as well as any file that is to be transferred over a
computer network. The most commonly used encryption software is PGP
software. PGP was originally written in 1991 by Phil Zimmerman (PGPi,
n.d.). Since then it has become the standard approach to encryption, and
versions are available for every major computer operating system (http://
www.pgpi.org/products/pgp/versions/freeware/). For many, the best
part of this solution is that it can be obtained free of charge for most users.
PGP encryption works by generating a random *key* that is sent along with
the e-mail message to a recipient. The *key* to unlock the message can only
be obtained by the user who has a private key of his or her own. The process sounds complicated, but it actually works very smoothly. As long as
the individuals communicating do not share their private key with anyone
else, the message may be intercepted or overseen but will appear only as
gibberish. Without a key, the message cannot be interpreted.

Encryption software is also the best way to secure files that are contained on a personal computer. Using the password protection systems built into common operating systems works fine to keep out casual observers. However, password generators and other software designed to defeat these systems are available to anyone with an interest in accessing your files. Strong encryption software, however, ensures that even if files are accessed, they cannot be read. Fortunately, PGP software is also available to protect your hard drive as well as it protects e-mail. This software can be obtained from http://www.pgpi.org/products/pgpdisk/.

In addition to encryption software, the ACA standards also note that counselors may use "secured" Web sites as a means for collecting information or interacting via the Internet. A secure Web site is any site that is hosted on a server that uses any of a number of encryption technologies, including SSL, SHTTP, PCT, or IPSec. These servers automatically encrypt incoming information before it is stored locally. As a result, even if a hacker infiltrated the server, the information available is all encrypted and could not be understood. The best way to determine whether your server uses this technology is to speak directly to your network administrator. Be sure when discussing security issues that the administrator is aware of your needs. For instance, a server may use this encryption technology for certain folders on the system but not others. In this case, the administrator may inform you that the server is secure when in fact only certain folders on the server are secure. In such a case, Web pages you create and store in your personal folder may not have the same level of security as pages stored elsewhere. The more knowledgeable you are about these issues, and the better able you are to communicate your specific requirements, the more likely you are to receive accurate answers.

• Technology Tip 11.3 •

Your network administrator should always be your first contact in obtaining information or attempting to resolve security concerns. Every network is configured differently depending on the hardware in place, software version being used, perceived needs of network users, and knowledge of the network administrator. Never make assumptions about a specific network based on information about another network.

An area where the ACA standards may not support the best practice is an allowance that nonsecure forms of communication may be used for general communications. This includes "topical information on matters of general interest to the professional counselor's clients as a whole [and] third-party resource and referral information" (ACA, 1999, p. 1). Providing topical information to a client carries with it a suggestion of a specific need. Referral information for a local substance abuse facility suggests that there is a need for substance abuse services. If this information is obtained it can create a serious breach, as if the counselor had informed someone directly of the client's substance abuse needs. Extreme caution should be taken in all cases. We believe that sharing general information with the public can be appropriately done from a nonsecure site. A newsletter distributed by e-mail to a wide audience that covers a variety of topics is an example of communication with little potential for a breach. However, the same newsletter distributed only to clients publicly offers a very discreet list of client names, a clear breach. With quality encryption technology readily available, and secure servers increasingly used, there is no reason to compromise security.

Finally, counselors should be aware of their inability to maintain their own privacy in an online services model. Whenever counselors have the capacity to maintain copies of all exchanges between the counselor and client, clients have the same ability. The difference is that clients do not have ethical or legal responsibility to maintain the confidentiality of communication. A counselor may request that e-mails or chat room transcripts are destroyed, but there is no way to enforce such a policy. Clients can choose to forward e-mail to anyone at anytime. Clients are likely to keep copies of e-mail that they find particularly meaningful. Some clients will share this information with others to allow them to understand the client's world, and some will share this information with friends and neighbors they believe will also be helped by the communication. Some people love to share e-mail, forwarding large quantities of jokes, humorous sayings, sad stories, and scripture with long lists of acquaintances. Advice from counselors is likely to become a part of this mass of e-mail that is seemingly endlessly circulated around the world. Worse, the information can easily be abbreviated, paraphrased, and misrepresented, all the while maintaining a link to the original author. Although some counselors may gain notoriety for their wisdom, more will likely become the base for jokes and "Top Ten" lists.

• Technology Tip 11.4 •

Invest as much energy in protecting yourself and your reputation as you invest in protecting your clients.

Creating Informed Consumers

Throughout the ACA standards, counselors are directed to keep clients informed of all aspects of the counseling process and their work online. This includes informing clients of the limits of confidentiality, risks and benefits of working online, who has access to client information, and how records are maintained. Information is empowering, and because helping clients to become empowered and maintain control over their lives is a central component of the counseling process, it follows that providing clients with timely and accurate information is a part of all online services.

The information that clients need can be provided in a number of ways, each providing unique benefits and drawbacks. The most common method to provide this information is to develop a statement describing counseling procedures, limits of confidentiality and the like, and then including the information on a Web page that can be linked to the counselor's site. From a site-management perspective, this approach is the easiest because it requires the development of a single page that can easily be updated as necessary. By providing a link from all or most Web pages on the counselor's site, the material will be readily available. For additional security, a link can even be added to e-mail. The risk is that clients will not take the time to read this information. Most Web pages contain numerous links to other resources, advertisements, information, and sites that have no direct appeal. Individuals who spend a lot of time on the Internet learn quickly to ignore this barrage of links as they often detract from one's ability to find the most useful information. Therefore, a link that offers to explain security issues may be overlooked.

An alternate method is to provide this information on a Web page that a client must view before arriving at a more specific page. For instance, a link on an organization's home page for online counseling may connect directly to a security disclaimer. At the bottom of the disclaimer is another link that will allow clients to continue forward until they reach the page where they can request online counseling. By forcing this sequential movement through a series of pages, the counselor can be assured that the information was presented to the client. Further, to move from this page to the next, a button might be used that is labeled "I have read and fully understand the security information presented on this page." Such a step is an attempt to verify that the information has been read. However, in our years of experience as computer users, we have clicked hundreds, or perhaps thousands of such buttons, and rarely read the complete information provided. Anyone who has installed software on a computer has been confronted with an End User License Agreement (EULA) and verified that they have read the entire statement. Relatively few people actually have read these statements, and fewer have understood what they mean.

Another method to present this security information is to create a "pop-up" window. Pop-up windows are automatically opened when a user navigates to a particular Web page. In this case, when a user arrives at a page where personal information is requested, a pop-up window may automatically open containing a statement of security issues. Such a window might contain a button, as described above, which needs to be clicked for the window to close. The use of a pop-up may attract more attention than a standard Web page. However, users may install on their computers a variety of software programs designed to close these windows as soon as they open, resulting in a user that never sees the message offered.

• Technology Tip 11.5 •

While the use of pop-ups are a convenient way to present information to clients, these can easily be disabled through the use of various software products. See chapter 8 for additional information.

Finally, a security statement may be included as a portion of any e-mail that is sent by a counselor. As noted in chapter 7, most e-mail programs have the capacity to automatically append a signature to an e-mail. This same feature can be used to create a short statement about security and confidentiality that will be attached to every e-mail. The benefit to this approach is that the client will be reminded on a regular basis of the security issues surrounding their work. Normally, this information will be appended at the end of an e-mail. Clients will quickly learn where the personal e-mail response ends and where this standard response begins. We anticipate that clients will choose not to read this impersonal statement. It is possible to create a macro (described in chapter 3) that would insert this statement at the start of an e-mail, although beginning every exchange with this may interfere with the client's focus on the message that follows.

Clearly there is no single response that best fits all cases. Counselors will best serve their clients by using multiple means of providing information and working directly with clients to ensure that security issues are fully understood. Whereas the automated approach recommended by ACA should be followed, following up with a personal discussion will help to guarantee that everyone is fully informed.

Under the heading of "Professional Counselor Identification" in the ACA standards, counselors are directed to provide full disclosure to clients the names and identities of all persons who will have access to client information and client communication. Often, in the case of counselors working in school and agency settings, client cases are reviewed in staff meetings called case conferences, case management, or group supervision meetings. It is not unusual for these meetings to be attended by various professional staff in an organization, not all of whom may have direct dealing with a client. In school settings, these meetings may include school social workers, school psychologists, or other counselors within a building who do not have direct responsibility for a student. In agency settings, intake workers, nursing personnel, social workers, psychiatrists, and psychologists may all attend. Under these specialty guidelines, the counselor may need to inform the client of everyone in attendance, particularly if specific electronic communications are shared in whole or in part. Further, the guidelines indicate that the client is to be informed of who will supervise sessions or who will have access to session information and should be provided with detailed information including education, licensing, and areas of practice. It is quite easy to create and maintain a single Web page for every clinical staff member associated with a counseling site. Clients can then be informed in writing that others may have access to clinical information, and links can be provided so that the client can learn more about each individual. In the case of minors or those whose ability to consent is compromised, this same information should be provided to the individual(s) responsible for providing consent.

Informing clients of issues related to the counselor and the counseling site is not enough, however. Clients should also be aware of issues related to their own computer use which may create problems or compromise security. For instance, clients should be aware that if they use an e-mail account at their place of business or school, their account may not be secure. A study by the American Management Association (Diederich, 1999) indicates that 43% of large corporations regularly monitor employee behavior including e-mail and Web activity. This monitoring may be performed by reviewing e-mail on the corporate server, which is legal under current law. In other settings, so called spyware is used to unobtrusively monitor what employees do at their computers. Such spyware may capture an image of the users screen periodically, track Web sites that the user visits, or record keystrokes to create a complete record of everything typed. Clients should be aware of these potentials and take appropriate steps to ensure that their personal computers are secure as well. Software programs such as Pest Patrol (http://www.sunbelt-software.com/product.cfm?id=911), Spy Cop (http://www.detect-spyware.com/), and Cone of Silence (http://download.com.com/3000-2271-867725.html?tag=lst-1-9) are all designed to foil various spyware products. Unfortunately, many companies that create these products also create commercially available products for the purpose of monitoring, meaning that everyone is in a constant race to keep software updated and working better than the competition.

•   Technology Tip 11.6   •

Before installing any software on an agency, school, or corporate computer, be sure to verify with technical support staff that the installation of such software conforms to location policies. To learn more about spyware and how to detect it, visit http://www.cnet.com/internet/0-3761-8-3217791-4.html.

From a legal standpoint, client records in counseling settings are generally treated to a high level of privacy. While a court order can be obtained in certain cases, there is generally an expectation that a high level of need must be shown before such an order is issued. Internet service providers (ISPs) are not governed by the same legal standards as counselors. Police or others may be able to obtain court orders to review records, which may include information about an individual's online activities. In some cases, ISPs may be willing to share this information without a court order. Although it is not likely that a record of an online counseling session would be available from an ISP, it is possible that a record exists showing a client accessed a particular chat room (maintained by a specific counselor) for 50 minutes on a weekly basis. While not divulging the contents of any work, such a record clearly would indicate an ongoing counseling relationship. Federal law has made it illegal for corporations such as AOL to reveal contents of e-mail on their servers, and additional privacy measures are being reviewed continuously.

Verifying Client Identity

An ongoing concern that has been expressed about providing services over the Internet is the inability of the counselor to verify who the client is. Clear directions are provided by the ACA standards on this issue. Unfortunately, verification is not always easy. Creating an online identity may be as simple as choosing a name and setting up an e-mail account under this identity. While the e-mail provider may require some additional information, there is usually no direct attempt to verify an individual user. Then, when contacting a counselor, a legitimate e-mail account with a fake name can be used. Counselors may choose to seek additional verification by calling a telephone number provided by the client to speak directly to the client. However, such an attempt may not reveal the true identity of a client. Additional information may be even harder to verify. For instance, a counselor may collect demographic information including ethnicity, age, gender, and previous counseling experience, all common questions. With the exception of gender, a telephone contact will not necessarily verify any of this information, and even gender may be left unverified with some minor attempts to alter one's voice. One way to decrease the likelihood that a client has adopted a persona is the use of videoconferencing technology. Quality videoconferencing software will provide the counselor with a reasonable picture that will help to verify basic information about the client's identity. However, clients are not likely to possess high-end hardware and software, leaving the ability to view clients over the Internet unattainable for many.

Whereas those individuals working strictly via e-mail or in a chat room will have great difficulty verifying a client's identity, those who work in school settings or other environments where they have physical access to a client may be well served by verifying in-person that e-mail communications are legitimate. It is easy to imagine a school counselor receiving an e-mail claiming to be from a student that was actually sent by another student as a prank. In the school environment, a counselor can identify a reason to speak with the student and briefly verify that the e-mail was sent. Once verified, e-mail counseling may be conducted with more confidence about who is receiving the counselor's response.

Counselors may even consider requiring that copies of identification such as a driver's license be presented prior to the start of counseling. It is certainly possible for a client seeking to create a false identity to use a computer to generate a driver's license copy or even to copy another person's license. However, this requires significant effort, and will stop many individuals who might adopt a persona from proceeding with fraudulent plans. Collection of this type of information is not unusual, with many settings collecting student IDs, insurance cards, or other identifiers. As online services become more common, it may be possible in the future, with a client's permission, to contact professional referral sources or others as a step in the verification process.

• Technology Tip 11.7 •

By developing and following rigorous procedures for verifying client identity, counselors who do inadvertently work with minors or others who have provided deceptive information can show that they have followed best professional practices and will be less likely to be found negligent.

Intervening in Emergencies

In a traditional counseling setting, the counselor is a member of the community. If a client becomes involved in a situation and emergency services need to be contacted, or systems activated to provide protection to the client or others, the counselor simply opens a phone book and makes contact with known resources. In the case of online counseling, however, the counselor is not likely to be a member of the client's community. If emergency services need to be contacted, or a referral needs to be made, the counselor will not have this information readily available.

By obtaining emergency contact information from a client, counselors will be prepared to intervene should the need arise. Counselors will be well served by verifying that emergency contact information is accurate and current by testing it occasionally. If a client's phone number is provided, calling the number at least once to verify that the client receives the call can be helpful. In an extended counseling relationship, calling the number after some period of time to ensure that it is still in service may also be helpful.

Counselors should also take the time to locate phone numbers for emergency services, crisis intervention, and other referral sources in a client's community prior to providing services. In this manner, the counselor will be well prepared to respond to any situation that arises. Common contacts may also include physicians, clergy if the client attends religious services, family members, and employers. By requesting this information in advance from the client, the client will be aware that the counselor is putting in place information to provide support if it becomes necessary.

• Technology Tip 11.8 •

Clients are well served by counselors who obtain emergency contact and referral information in advance. Working with a client online demands that the counselor can respond to an emergency as quickly and effectively as if the client lived in the counselor's own community.

In addition to requesting this information from the client, there are online resources available to help obtain phone numbers. AnyWho (http://www.anywho.com/) is a Web site that provides telephone numbers and addresses for businesses throughout the United States. Users can search by keywords such as *crisis intervention* to find assistance in any city and state. In some cases, maps and driving directions are also available that may be provided to a client if needed. Similar services are provided by Switchboard (http://www.switchboard.com/). In Canada, services are provided by Canada 411 (http://canada411.sympatico.ca/), and in the UK by BT.com (http://www.bt.com/directory-enquiries/dq_home.jsp). Why Canada and the UK? First, we don't assume that all our readers are from the United States. Although we cannot provide URLs for every country, we do want to emphasize that these services are available everywhere, not just in the United States. Further, the Internet truly provides worldwide access, and there is no reason to assume that clients will necessarily come from the United States simply because the counselor is located in the United States.

Client Waiver

Counselors are directed by the ACA code to have clients execute a waiver of understanding related to the inherent limits on ensuring confidentiality when information is transmitted over computer networks. As well, the waiver should be worded as to hold the counselor harmless should a breach of confidentiality occur, if reasonable precautions have been taken by the counselor. As noted earlier, oftentimes information presented on a Web page may be skimmed or entirely skipped as individuals navigate to a specific page. Placing a waiver of this type online and allowing clients to verify that they have understood its content by clicking a button is the most common approach to meeting this directive. A more direct approach may be better. By creating written agreements that contain all of the disclosure information that is appropriate and requiring clients to sign the agreements and then return them to the counselor either via snail mail (i.e., by post) or via fax, the counselor can be confident that the material was presented directly, and that the client had sufficient opportunity to review it. Of course, some clients will choose to sign such documents without reading them. Even asking clients directly if they have read these documents will not always result in an honest response. If at any time a counselor is unsure about whether a client understands the limits and inherent problems with online work, the counselor should strive to engage in a direct conversation, re-presenting the appropriate information to the client and working to assure understanding. Remember that just because services are primarily provided via technology, face-to-face meetings can still be scheduled in some cases, and telephone contact is almost always available.

Records of Electronic Communications

This section of the standards addresses several important issues in addition to security concerns presented earlier. One issue presented is where e-mail communications are saved. In most cases, individuals will save their e-mail files either on their server or on their own hard drive. From a security standpoint, saving e-mail to the hard drive is preferable, particularly if appropriate security precautions have been taken to protect your desktop computer. Most e-mail clients (i.e., the software used to read your e-mail) will allow you to choose where files are saved via a "Preferences" or "Option" submenu. Check to be sure that files are stored to your hard drive, generally called the "C:\" drive. If available, use the built-in encryption feature to further protect the data. In addition, many e-mail clients occasionally archive unused messages. The archive process looks for messages that have not been opened in a specified period of time and then compresses these messages and places them in a specific folder. By default, this folder will generally be on the user's hard drive. However, it is a good idea to check. Otherwise, all of your old e-mail may be placed in a file on your school or agency network.

The process of saving e-mail to a local drive is particularly important if you use a public e-mail account such as Yahoo Mail, Hotmail, or mail provided by your ISP. Such accounts generally maintain all of your e-mail on their server, only downloading the mail to your computer if you have specifically requested this file transfer. This means that your e-mail is susceptible to hackers if they target the servers of these providers. In most cases, security measures are in place to stop these attacks, but they do occur and caution should be used. The easiest way to transfer messages from an Internet-based e-mail account to your hard drive is to set your e-mail client (e.g., Eudora, Outlook) to perform this task for you. When you configure your client to check your account, choose the option to "delete messages from server" or "save to local drive." Such an option will not be available in all cases or with all e-mail accounts. For instance, users of Yahoo Mail who pay for a premium account have the capacity to use these clients to check and download their e-mail. However, individuals who maintain free accounts with Yahoo no longer have this option. You will need to work with your e-mail account provider to determine what options are available for you.

Creating backup material is always appropriate when using technology. Backups can be created in several ways. Generally, backing up specific files is difficult because there is a risk that important files will be overlooked. One method for resolving this issue is to keep all client materials in a single folder on your hard drive, a folder that may contain dozens of subfolders. This single folder can then be backed up on a regular basis. Word processors, e-mail clients, treatment planning programs, and most other software can be configured to save all your files to this folder. Additionally, by saving all client information to a single folder, this folder can be encrypted, ensuring further security.

Common security practice suggests that backups of this type of data be performed on a weekly basis. Using a CD-R, a zip disk, or some other large capacity removable media, most users can create a backup of their data on a single disk.

• Technology Tip 11.9 •

If using media that can be rewritten, consider rotating through four disks. Each week, copy your data onto the oldest of the disks. In this manner, you will always have data from at least the previous 4 weeks.

Occasionally, users will find that a file has become corrupt or overwritten, but they may not realize this has occurred for several weeks. By keeping multiple backups, you are more likely to always be able to find the data you need. Some users maintain a more conservative approach by creating monthly backups that are kept for a period of time, perhaps 6 months. It would be a rare file that has become corrupted, gone unnoticed for 6 months, and results in the loss of critical data. Keeping backup copies of data that also exist on your hard drive beyond this time frame is generally unnecessary. Note that this is a separate issue than keeping copies of client files. Those files should be kept for a number of years, consistent with state law and agency practice.

When hard copies of communication are created, they should immediately be entered in the client file and maintained as a portion of the permanent record. In this respect, e-mail should be treated in the same manner as any other written communication. Once a part of the client file, this communication should be maintained for whatever period of time the client record is kept. When sporadic e-mail contact is made between a client and counselor, adding one or two pages to the client record will be easy. However, if services are being provided via online chat, and the session is archived so it can be printed, then the client record will quickly become bloated with numerous pages of these chats. It is our understanding that the ACA guidelines require the creation of archived materials, and that if this archive is in the format of printed copies of communication, then all electronic communication should be printed. However, material may also be appropriately stored in electronic format providing that all material is maintained and secure. If material is maintained electronically, then the client's record must clearly indicate that this material is available. Further, all electronic material should be maintained for the length of time that other records are maintained, and clients should be aware of these procedures. Office supply companies market disk protectors that can be added to the client file similar to a piece of paper. Then a computer disk can be placed in the disk protector containing archival material. This will ensure that the electronic files are always kept with the client file. This change in filing procedures may require other changes, however, to ensure that media is not exposed to magnets or excessive heat or damaged by being bent.

Electronic Transfer of Client Information

As counselors become increasingly comfortable with the Internet, and their offices become well connected, electronic transfer of documents over the Internet may become as common as fax transmissions or copies mailed. This change may serve clients well. Using the security procedures discussed in this book, the transfer of documents over the Internet provides less potential for a breach than standard fax transmissions. When documents are faxed, they often sit on the receiving tray of a fax machine for a long period of time before they are removed. As they sit unattended, numerous individuals may wander past the fax machine and pick up the material to see whether it is for them. Eventually, in most instances, someone will remove the pages and place them in the receiver's mailbox, where they may lay exposed for hours or even days until retrieved. This is tolerated on the assumption that everyone in a school or agency is bound by confidentiality rules and professional ethics. Unfortunately, not everyone manages to live up to these obligations. In many settings, cultural norms have developed wherein discussion of clients or students among employees is quite common. Documents transmitted over secure Web connections, which are carefully encrypted, are delivered directly to the receiver's inbox. Without a password, others will be unable to view the document. In some cases, a fax transmission may be the best option, particularly when the sender or receiver does not have the skills to ensure encryption, and the receiver can be available to immediately retrieve the transmitted document. In cases where documents are transmitted frequently between users, the development of procedures to transfer documents online securely will improve confidentiality.

Intake Procedures

At this point in time, the exact benefits and risks of online counseling remain unclear. As is noted in chapter 12, a number of proposed benefits and potential risks have been addressed in the literature, but the use of the Internet as a means to provide counseling services remains in its infancy, and research has yet to demonstrate the parameters of these services. It is clear, however, that online counseling services are not appropriate for every client. Anyone engaged in providing online services must carefully evaluate each client to determine whether his or her needs can be met in this environment.

Best practice in any environment mandates that clients are assessed at intake to determine whether they are in crisis, in danger from self or others, or present a risk of danger. These same assessments need to be made for clients who receive services online. As in traditional settings, counselors must make a decision at the point of intake whether they are an appropriate source of service for every individual client. This does not change because services are offered online. The only distinction that needs to be made is a recognition that the services offered are different and that clients need to be assessed on the basis of these new services. For instance, in traditional settings, counselors must look at their caseloads to determine whether they have time and energy to take on a new client; whether they have the expertise to help a particular individual; and whether their style, approach, and areas of expertise meet the individual's specific needs. The individual providing online counseling services needs to ask these same questions, with the distinction that the online client will be provided with different services than the face-to-face client. Although we endorse the general agreement in the literature that clients in crisis or those who are suicidal are not appropriate for online services, not everyone agrees with this position, and some Web sites appear to be willing to take on such clients (Tyler & Guth, in press).

In addition to the standard information collected at intake, those working online need to collect additional information. In particular, a determination needs to be made not only about an individual's needs and the appropriateness of addressing those needs with online services, but a determination must also be made about the individual's skills and online services. Clients need to be carefully assessed to determine whether they have the skills to interact in an online environment. This process is more fully discussed in chapter 9. Our experience as educators suggests that many students enroll in online courses because of the perceived flexibility, regardless of the student's technological skills or desire. It is likely that many clients may approach online work in the same manner. In these cases, counselors who agree to work with individuals without appropriate skills are creating a situation where the client is not likely to succeed. In every such instance, the counselor is responsible for not ensuring that their client had the skills and support for success.

To the extent that the intake process is seen as a time to collect data, the online environment is well-suited to the task. Intake questionnaires, as well as most traditional self-administered paper tests, can be adapted to this medium. With a well-constructed Web site on a secure server, data can be collected and immediately entered into a database that becomes the start of a client record. The strength of the Internet as a medium is readily apparent in the ability of the Intake process to build on itself. Clients who complete a questionnaire about presenting concerns such as the Behavior Problems Checklist Revised (Quay, n.d.) or the Counselor Problem Checklist (Mozee, 1978) can immediately be provided with more specific assessment instruments based on their response to these initial questionnaires. Instruments can be immediately scored and computer programs created that ask additional questions based on a client's score. In this fashion, an "expert system" can be created that tailors the intake process directly to the needs of the individual client. Such a system is superior to the more typical mass screening approach because it does not require clients to invest time in completing unnecessary instruments.

One of the clear drawbacks to working online is the loss of certain information that is obtained by working with clients as they complete various assessment instruments. Counselors who work online will need to find suitable approaches to supplement this information. As an example, when administering achievement instruments such as the Wide Range Achievement Test (WRAT), it is common practice to assess the effort that a client exerts. At times, a counselor may decide that test results are invalid because a client has not been motivated to complete the instrument in a manner that provides an accurate view of ability. In such a case, the counselor may discount the results, readminister the test at a later time, or choose an alternate measure. However, when an instrument such as this is completed online, the counselor will have no direct knowledge of the client's efforts. Therefore, supporting data such as school records, other achievement test results, and accomplishments in a variety of settings become more important in fully understanding the client.

Further, the assessment process of determining a client's suitability for online services should not be considered finished after an initial determination is made. Rather, this is a determination that needs to be continually revisited throughout the counseling process. In traditional settings, counselors are continually collecting data, modifying their approach, and altering the client's treatment plan to stay responsive to the client's needs as well as change and growth across time. This same process needs to occur in the online environment, with a recognition that across time new information may become available signaling that a client is not, and perhaps never was, an appropriate candidate for online services. Individual clients may determine that they want a more traditional approach, or changes in their life may allow them more opportunities than they believed they had at the start of counseling. Indeed, the process of online counseling may well produce growth that empowers clients to seek additional counseling opportunities that are more traditional. Counselors need to be prepared for such changes, and will best serve clients by helping to provide referral information and assisting in the transition process.

When clients demonstrate that they are not appropriate for online services, counselors have an obligation to end the current online process; if they cannot provide appropriate face-to-face service, then they have a responsibility to assist the client in finding services. In addition to online phone books, counselors may also seek referral information from other professionals who participate in listservs or through various professional associations. The seeking of referral information of this type is quite common and is appropriate providing that no information is shared that may create a potential breach of confidentiality.

• Technology Tip 11.10 •

As counseling unfolds, clients need to be continually reassessed to ensure that online counseling remains a viable option for the individual. If alternate services become more appropriate or viable for any reason, the counselor has an obligation to help the client transition to these new services.

Providing Backup Coverage

Clients who choose to work in an online environment, and have been supported in this decision by a counselor who has agreed to provide these services, have unique needs that must be overcome. In addition to the times when counselors are traditionally not available—days off, weekends, evenings, vacation—online clients must find a way to receive support when technology fails or when they are in crisis. Counselors who provide service via e-mail need to inform clients of how long the client can expect to wait to receive a response to any e-mail sent. With certain clients, there will be times when the client cannot wait through the agreed-on period. Technology failures on either the counselor's or the client's end may interfere with communication. Emergencies may keep the counselor from responding at all. In each of these cases, clients need to have backup plans to meet their needs. In traditional settings, clients are usually instructed to contact the counseling office or agency where the counselor is employed, and on-call counselors are available to intervene. Online services provided by an individual may mean that there is no alternate counselor to contact. Providing clients with the number of an agency in their community may not work in all situations because the individual will not be a client of the agency, and immediate services may not be available. Additionally, if the client has sought online services because he or she is geographically disconnected from services, then the client needs a way to receive assistance online. Counselors can respond to these needs by providing clients with a variety of contact information. In addition to Web site and e-mail addresses, clients need to be provided with a phone number and, if appropriate, a beeper number. Counselors in individual practice should make arrangements with others in similar settings or with local agencies to provide emergency services to their online clients if they are unavailable. By creating these partnerships in advance, clients can be informed at intake of the procedures in place and the circumstances under which they will be instituted.

Licensure and Client Location

As noted earlier, the Internet provides worldwide access, and there is no reason to believe that clients will seek out counselors in their geographic location. At the current time, it is unclear how the law will treat counselors who provide services to clients from areas where the counselor is not credentialed or licensed.

Whereas an individual may carry a license to practice in the state of Florida, no one would suggest that he or she cannot maintain phone contact with clients while on a trip to California. In this case, is the counselor in California or Florida? Historically it has been assumed that the license in Florida is valid because this is where the counselor's office exists, and where the client is located. In the case of work performed via e-mail, is the office where the counselor is located or where the server is located? The distinction may appear ridiculous, but imagine a counselor who lives in Michigan but winters in Florida, and provides services via a business registered in Ohio (where the server is also located) where the counselor lived prior to moving to Michigan. In such a situation it is unclear what legal jurisdiction applies. Because the counselor has chosen to maintain a business address and license in Ohio, it would appear that the laws of this state would apply, even though the counselor is working primarily from Michigan. Because some states do not require counselors to be licensed, it is possible that counselors may choose to create office addresses in these locales and provide services from these unregulated environments, regardless of where they are physically located. Counselors may even find that their best business opportunities lie in markets overseas. We know of one individual who worked online with a counselor from Italy for a period of time while living in the United States. Unlicensed and unconcerned, she provided her services as long as he was willing to pay the bill.

The ACA standards direct counselors not to provide services to clients in states where the counselor is not licensed. Guidelines from the International Society for Mental Health Online take a different view by acknowledging that there may be a legal requirement to meet licensure requirements in the jurisdiction where the client is located as well as where the counselor is located. This approach is certainly the safest and will ensure that the counselor is compliant with applicable law. In all cases, counselors need to seek legal advice from qualified counsel to understand local laws and stay current on this topic. As more services are provided online, the courts will undoubtedly clarify legal jurisdiction. In the meantime, this issue is another reason that national credentials will become increasingly important in the future.

• Technology Tip 11.11 •

By providing services only to clients in a jurisdiction where the counselor is appropriately credentialed, the professional counselor can protect him- or herself from legal claims for practicing without a license.

Client Competence

Counselors in most settings address issues of client competence regularly. Obtaining consent for minors prior to providing services and working with guardians when clients are impaired and unable to consent are common practices. As geographic boundaries become less important, understanding competence will increasingly become a problem. As an example, in many states, age differentiations are made between minors seeking substance abuse services and those seeking mental health services. In some locales, distinctions are made between completing an assessment with a minor and providing ongoing services. As noted above, it may be difficult to know at times under what laws a counselor is operating. By restricting one's online practice to the state in which one lives and where one's clients reside, there will be less potential for laws to be misunderstood. Particularly in the case of corporations that are attempting to provide services online on a national basis, it can be anticipated that at times counselors will provide services across state boundaries. In these cases, if the client is younger than 18 or for other reasons unable to offer consent, extreme care should be taken. Understanding the law in both the state where the counselor is located as well as local law where the client is located will help to provide direction. Increasingly, state Web sites contain state law in full-text files. By using a good search engine, counselors will be able to locate these files.

Counselors are advised to seek consent in writing anytime it is required. Whenever possible, it is best to have clients print from their computer whatever forms need to be signed and have the originals returned by mail to the counselor. These documents, with original signatures, may be the best protection the counselor has to demonstrate that consent was obtained. Some counselors may want to require certain forms, such as consent for treatment of a minor, to include a notarized signature from a parent or guardian. Because the counselor does not have the opportunity to meet a parent or guardian, and because verifying identities is difficult, notarized documents provide some assurance that the signatures are genuine. Obviously, the process of obtaining notarized signatures and mailing documents takes time, delaying the start of counseling. If a client is unable to wait the several days this process requires, then it is likely the client would be better served by seeking immediate services in their community.

Liability Insurance

The provision of online services is new, and everyone involved in counseling and mental health is still trying to understand its impact. Insurance companies are simply one more player in the market that need to respond to this evolving field. Many individuals will find that their insurance policies do not address services provided online. As a result, some may assume that they are covered because the service is not expressly excluded, whereas others will assume they are not covered because the service is not expressly included.

Counselors should obtain from their professional insurance provider a written statement detailing what online services are covered. The statement should include any limitations including clients who live out of state or out of country, groups of clients who would be excluded, or specific contact that will be excluded from coverage. One way to ensure that coverage will be provided is to file with the insurance carrier a detailed letter describing the services to be offered, how they will be offered, and the precautions that will be taken to protect clients. Then, request that the insurance company provide a letter that explicitly mentions this description of services and acknowledges that coverage is provided for the services described in the letter. This process will help to protect the counselor and client from miscommunication with the counselor's insurer. If the insurer will not provide a letter explicitly stating that the online services provided are covered, counselors should be aware that they may not be covered and should seek coverage from an alternate provider.

• Technology Tip 11.12 •

Prior to providing any online services, counselors should obtain from their insurance provider a written statement detailing what online services are covered.

Accessibility

When clients seek services online, it is impossible to know what limitations they may have that will create difficulty for them. For many individuals with vision problems, computers have provided access to a wealth of information that was previously difficult to access. However, many Web site developers fail to incorporate elements necessary to accommodate the special needs of some individuals. As an example, programs that "read" the Internet are often confused by the failure of a Web site builder to include alternate tags with their graphics. An alternate tag is simply a title that the reader finds, and speaks, in place of any graphics that would normally be displayed.

Increasingly, Web site development programs are addressing this issue. This is particularly true with high-end programs such as Macromedia's DreamWeaver MX (http://www.macromedia.com/software/dreamweaver/). This program provides a variety of support to help builders create sites that are fully accessible. If you are building your own site, you should become knowledgeable about the needs of individuals with disabilities and the tools that are available to make your site accessible. If you are not responsible for building your own site, then you maintain the responsibility to ensure that the site builder has considered and responded to these needs (see NBCC, 2002). Additional information on this topic can be obtained by visiting the Web sites found at the end of this chapter.

Summary

To help address the emerging ethical concerns related to the use of technology in counseling, a number of professional organizations have attempted to develop standards, codes of practice, or other guiding principles. This includes the NBCC, the International Society for Mental Health Online, the Psychiatric Society for Infomatics, and the ACA. Although these codes provide excellent resources for counselors to help guide practice, they can only be properly implemented by counselors with the technological skills necessary to enact the principles that are endorsed.

Primary among these skills is the ability to protect client information as it is being obtained, stored, transferred, or modified. It is also apparent that counselors have an obligation to help clients become informed about ethical issues when using these new technologies. Whereas counselors have a responsibility to become educated about these issues, clients generally will not even have opportunities to become educated, so the professional counselor must help the client to become more aware so that clients have the knowledge necessary to make appropriate decisions about their own needs. By ensuring that both counselors and clients are prepared in the event of emergencies, technology failures, security breaches or other mishaps, everyone involved will be better able to respond, and client needs will be better protected.

Fortunately, the needs of counselors for security and private communication are sufficiently similar to the needs of others for whom these issues have been addressed. As a result, a variety of software solutions are already available to help meet these needs. More importantly, except in very rare instances, alternatives to computer-mediated communication and interaction exist. Therefore, when a client needs more direct intervention, we can almost always resort to known and trusted modes of interacting, including telephones and face-to-face meetings! Finally, it should be remembered that any discussion of ethics and technology is intended to supplement what we already know to be best ethical practices.

Internet Sites for Additional Information

- http://www.nbcc.org/ethics/webethics.htm. The NBCC standards for the practice of Internet counseling site is a must-review for all counselors.
- http://www.ismho.org/suggestions.html. These standards from the International Society for Mental Health Online (ISMHO) and the Psychiatric Society for Informatics will help shape what is considered appropriate professional practice.
- http://www.counseling.org/resources/internet.htm. This site presents the ACA Standards for Online Counseling Services
- http://www.rbs2.com/email.htm. This site looks at some laws that apply to e-mail and e-mail privacy. It concludes with links to a few sites providing encryption software.
- http://email.about.com/cs/pgp/. This Web page provides a guide to PGP security including tutorials, downloads, and FAQs.
- http://www.darkstonedata.com/business/security5.html. This article provides an explanation of how disks store information and what it takes to really delete a file permanently.
- http://www.geocities.com/SiliconValley/1947/Links.htm. A long list of links related to security, something for everyone appears on this list.
- http://www.complaw.com/. The Computer Law Resource Center contains a variety of information on computer law, privacy, intellectual copyright, and other issues of concern.
- http://legacy.eos.ncsu.edu/eos/info/computer_ethics/. This site covers a broad spectrum of topics related to ethics and computers.
- http://www.phillipsnizer.com/internetlibrary.htm. This unique site reviews several hundred case law examples related to computers and the Internet. Users can read synopses or entire cases.
- http://www.ericfacility.net/ericdigests/ed446326.html. This article from ERIC/CASS Digest by Rosemary S. Hughes is titled "Ethics and Regulations of Cybercounseling."
- http://cybercounsel.uncg.edu/. This site provides fast-breaking information and full-text resources on all aspects of cybercounseling and cyberlearning.

- **http://bobby.watchfire.com/bobby/html/en/index.jsp.** This free service will allow you to test Web pages and help expose and repair barriers to accessibility and encourage compliance with existing accessibility guidelines, such as Section 508 and the W3C's Web Content Accessibility Guidelines (WCAG).
- **http://www.helphorizons.com.** This application service provider connects a virtual office for the mental health professional with a Web site for the general public.
- **http://psychcentral.com/best/.** The Best Practices in e-Therapy series of articles was spurred by the need to start moving the field ahead in this area and start defining what we mean by these nebulous terms.
- **http://www.gingerich.net/etherapy.htm.** This Web page is all about e-therapy and contains a useful set of links.

12

Counseling Services
Provided Over the Internet

Competency: Be knowledgeable of the strengths and weaknesses of counseling services provided via the Internet.

The following e-mail was sent to one of the authors in the fall of 1998 (Sabella, 2003):

Hello.

I type to you tonight asking for your help. I carry a secret that I have never talked about openly to anyone before. I am a 24 year old divorced mother. Very successful and still going to college. My son and I are very active in the community we live in and to other people I am a normal person. To most I am an over-achiever and extremist. God has blessed our lives, but no matter how hard I work and push myself, I'm finding that my past is always there. My over-achieving has its reasons. I have never went to anyone for help. I am usually the person people come to for help. I am very understanding and my past has educated me enough in that I've been there. Tonight, for the first time on searching the net about child abuse, I see that I'm not alone and that I'm not strange. I feel the desire to talk to someone but, unfortunately, don't have a clue as to who to talk to. I suffered emotional and physical abuse from my family and sexual abuse from a nonfamily member as a child. This is my first asking for help like this. I came across your name on the web and thought maybe you would know of someone who could help. If not, I understand.

Signed,
[First Name Only]

Although I was keeping abreast of Web counseling at the time, I had never quite become so directly involved. I was more an outside observer looking into this fascinating and curious development. As a result of this e-mail, the reality of Web counseling became more vivid and personal for me. Suddenly, the ethical and legal considerations applied to me. What would I do with this message? Was this message real or a hoax? Is the writer really 24 years old? I decided to reply and informed the author that I was not licensed in her state and therefore would not pursue providing her with professional counseling. Next, I wrote some highly facilitative sentences with the intent of instilling hope. Finally, I suggested how she might self-refer to a therapist who could fit her needs and move her toward healing. My reply arrived at this unknown person's address, although I never received further communications from her.

When you think of conducting counseling with your clients or students, you probably envision yourself doing this in your office, in their home, in the classroom, or perhaps even on a "walk and talk." However, with increasing probability, you may also have a mental image of a counselor who sits in front of the computer and conducts counseling over the Internet. Web counseling is the attempt to provide counseling services in an Internet environment. The environment may include connecting with your client via e-mail, chat rooms, instant messenger, or Internet videoconferencing. The practice of Web counseling, also referred to as cybercounseling, cybertherapy, e-therapy, e-counseling, and online counseling, to name a few, began slowly but is rapidly finding popularity among both counselors and clients. Among counseling professionals, Web counseling has created somewhat of a debate about the utility and effectiveness of this new medium and whether cybercounseling even really exists. Moreover, those involved in ethical and legal issues for traditional counseling are wondering how such matters relate to the Internet environment. This chapter focuses on the nature and development of Web counseling and includes a description of the electronic tools used by cybercounselors.

What Is Web Counseling?

Meeting and interacting with each other online has become an everyday experience for many people nowadays. Activities that are traditionally conducted via face-to-face meetings, such as communication, shopping, and even learning, have acquired new parameters in the virtual world. Counseling services are another candidate with promising potentials (Wong & Law, n.d.). Although some authors have attempted to demonstrate that online counseling can be an extension of traditional face-to-face services (Tyler & Guth, in press), a common working definition of Web counseling has not yet materialized among practitioners and researchers. In fact, it seems as if a continuum of beliefs about the nature of cybercounseling exists, ranging from a belief that it does not actually exist to a belief that it is proliferating and thriving. Some counselors would say that defining the nature and practice of Web counseling is futile and misleading. Counselors and others in this camp believe that Web counseling is a term that leads people to erroneously believe that the work of professional counselors can effectively and appropriately be conducted in an electronic or "virtual" environment such as over the Internet. They argue that although noteworthy attempts are currently in progress (e.g., see Ookita & Tokuda, 2001), empirically supported counseling theories and techniques have not yet been adequately tested in the virtual environment. Thus, we cannot confidently assume current approaches have the same effect or, even worse, do not have unanticipated negative effects for online clients. This group further argues that these online services cannot be considered counseling unless and until they can be demonstrated to be effective. Similarly, an important question has remained unanswered: Is counseling in cyberspace so different from traditional face-to-face counseling that it requires special training and certification?

Many counselors wonder whether the therapeutic alliance can reliably be established without ever working with the client in person. Even if the counseling relationship could be developed in cyberspace, they wonder whether the online personality with whom you are working is the same as the real-world personality of the client. Finally, it is unknown if potential growth or progress made during online sessions will generalize to life in the real world as we would expect to happen in face-to-face counseling. Counselors who view cybercounseling as more of a potential than an existing counseling modality may be optimistic about how developing technology can help counselors do their work in alternative environments and media. However, for now they caution us that traditional or face-to-face counseling is not well understood by the general public, notwithstanding its much longer history and exposure via public relations, and that discussing Web counseling as if it exists stands to confuse the practice of counseling even more. This group wants the public to understand the difference between the special relationship a counselor and client share, as compared with the relationships established in other related helping activities such as advising, mentoring, coaching, and teaching. These counselors argue that cybercounselors who believe they are counseling in cyberspace are more accurately providing cyberadvice, cybercoaching, cybermentoring, and distance learning. Although each of these is important and valuable, none are adequate substitutes for professional counseling.

Other counselors have adopted a more "middle of the road" belief about cybercounseling. They espouse that cybercounseling is not counseling per se but an effective means to supplement live counseling sessions. They believe that technology has not yet developed tools to create an environment that can effectively substitute for a live setting, although tools do exist to help counselors (and clients) be more effective and efficient in meeting their goals. Such counselors may indeed call themselves cyber-counselors or e-therapists, for instance, but only insofar as it describes their use of computer and Internet technologies as a part of their face-to-face work with clients. These counselors affirm the role that technology plays throughout the process of counseling, including collaboration and communication, and continue to explore how such tools can enhance the probability of successful live interaction.

On the other side of the continuum are counselors and researchers who view the Web as a new delivery and management system for doing the work of professional counseling. These cybercounselors celebrate the latest tools provided by computers and networking technologies as providing the means to work with clients they would otherwise never be able to work with. With some adaptations, they posit that they can effectively use their counseling knowledge and skills to provide counseling services in cyberspace.

We suspect that where you lie on the continuum is influenced by your approach and beliefs about the counseling process, your level of technological literacy, and your comfort with the unknown. For instance, we believe that a psychodynamic therapist might view cybercounseling very differently from a solution-focused brief therapist. How does the emphasis on a client's past relationships as guided by your approach affect your perception of the conduciveness of the Internet to appropriately conduct counseling? How important are the dynamics of transference and countertransference in your work, and how might this play a part in the usefulness of the Internet in conducting counseling? Once a counselor determines that his or her style of counseling can be supported by electronic media, how does the counselor's (and the client's) competency in using these tools help or hinder the process? A counselor's perception concerning the level of risk introduced by conducting counseling in cyberspace would probably also influence his or her belief about the utility of cybercounseling. Indeed, no matter where on the continuum of beliefs you are, research and training about the nature and practice of conducting cybercounseling promises to continue to change how we approach and engage in cybercounseling.

How Prevalent Is Web Counseling?

Sanders and Rosenfield (1998) noted that the world of social sciences in general, and counseling and psychotherapy in particular, have always had an uneasy relationship with telecommunications technology. Social scientists predicted the collapse of normal social relations after the invention of the telegraph, and even though the telephone has been with us for around 100 years, it still has difficulty being accepted into the everyday world of counseling and psychotherapy as a valid communications medium. Counseling by telephone has generally been considered a less-than-desirable alternative to face-to-face counseling in terms of professional recognition and perceived efficacy. Since the advent of the Internet and the interest in the computer as the new technology mediating communications, we might be forgiven for thinking that the telephone is dead.

In an attempt to determine the pervasiveness of counseling-related activity on the Internet, Sampson et al. (1997) conducted an analysis in April 1996 using the WebCrawler search engine. Results of the analysis revealed that two thirds of the counseling-related home pages examined were group home pages, and fully 50% were groups advertising some type of counseling-related service. Only 15% were home pages placed by individuals. Particularly noteworthy were online services offered by groups or individuals for a fee, either as a reply to questions posed via e-mail or for interactive chat sessions. The credentials for practitioners involved a wide range, including MD, PhD, MA, and LPC. Many "counselors" identified no professional credentials at all. In fact, most home pages provided little information about the nature of qualifications of those providing services other than degree-level designation. For example, an individual with "MA" listed after his or her name frequently did not disclose the subject area of the degree. In a separate nonrandom analysis of 401 sites from the same 3,764 home pages, 15 home pages were identified that offered direct online services. Offerings ranged from $15 charged for answering a question via e-mail to $65 for a 60-minute chat session. These online offerings ranged from single-treatment interventions to an individual offering services in 35 different specialty areas.

The authors concluded that the results of their search can be used to encourage debate about counseling over the Internet. On the basis of the percentage of home pages offering direct online services, the authors estimated that at least 275 practitioners were offering direct counseling services via the Internet in 1996. More recently, Tyler and Guth (in press) noted that whereas an Internet search for "online counseling" may identify thousands of Web pages, most of these do not represent sites that attempt to offer online counseling. However, there clearly are a large number of sites that do provide these services, and their approach and organization appears to be growing in sophistication in recent years. As noted in Table 12.1, the manner in which these services are provided varies widely.

Instead of being a "potential" future event, counseling and counseling-related activities in cyberspace are a "present" reality. Although the number of service providers remains relatively small in comparison with the tens of thousands of counselors currently offering services through more traditional means, the annualized growth rate of people having access to the Internet indicates that increases in cybercounseling will occur. Future enhancements in technology are likely only to accelerate the availability of counseling services via networking electronic media.

Table 12.1

Types of Service Offered by Online Counseling Sites

Service Modality	Percent	Number
E-mail	78	65
Text-chat	57	47
Telephone	47	39
Videoconferencing	12	10
Group text-chat	8	7
Online assessment materials	8	7
Snail mail services	6	5
Bulletin boards	5	4
Online audioconferencing	2	2
Online journaling	1	1

Note: Percentages and number of sites in table do not equal number of sites reviewed because most sites offered more than 1 type of service. From "Understanding Online Counseling Services Through a Review of Definitions and Elements Necessary for Change," by J. M. Tyler and L. J. Guth, 2004, in J. Bloom and G. Walz (Eds.), *Cybercounseling and cyberlearning: An encore*, Greensboro, NC, CAPS Publications and the American Counseling Association Foundation. Reprinted with permission.

Online Support Groups

As explained by Delmonico et al. (2000), traditional support groups have been used to encourage and motivate individuals toward change and self-improvement (Yalom, 1995). Studies suggest that support groups may be one way of helping individuals achieve certain aspirations and goals for personal growth and development (Jacobs, Masson, & Harvill, 1998). As technology advances, the idea of what constitutes a support group setting expands, and the use of computer-based self-help groups is being examined as a viable adjunct to current therapies (Finn, 1995). The theoretical constructs behind face-to-face group counseling are being researched for their relevance to the online group setting. Weinberg, Uken, Schmale, and Adamek (1995) found that Yalom's (1995) Therapeutic Factors were perceived as present and essential in an online group's effectiveness.

• Technology Tip 12.1 •

You may want to join an online support group for the experience. Put the words "online support group" in a search engine and choose one of most interest.

Since the 1990s, people have been discussing their distress and coping skills with others in anonymous cyber group settings through online support groups, a relatively new and growing phenomenon. People participate in thematic topics such as coping with family violence, HIV, or trauma and death caused by natural disasters or war. Online support groups can be attractive to a group of new users who may previously have resisted peer support because they possessed culturally ingrained traditions of nondisclosure of "family secrets," avoided family shame or dishonor, or evaded cultural or familial isolation and stigmatization (Gary, 2001).

The global medium of the Internet can bring people together in a shared environment to exchange ideas, learn, and engage in collaborative decision making. Shared environments on the Internet range from two people connecting over a chat room to an online community (also known as virtual community, virtual village, or invisible city; Sabella & Halverson, in press). Virtual communities have already been developed for a sundry of interests, such as in colleges to foster closer relationships among their graduates (Leibowitz, 1999); among media companies to unite fans of their shows (Gross, 1999; Lucas, 1999); for individuals with disabilities so that they may more easily overcome barriers to daily living (Kahn, 2000); with people interested in weight loss (Zetlin & Pfleging, 2001); for linking seriously ill children to play together from their respective hospital beds in a three-dimensional interactive virtual community (Holden, Bearison, Rode, Rosenberg, & Fishman, 1999); to foster mentorship and support among mothers who are practicing physicians or medical students (Greenwood, 2000); to provide online support for people who share a terrible fear of the dentist (Greenwood, 2000); or for teenagers to provide feedback for each other's writing works (Kehus, 2000), to name but a few.

The true value of virtual communities for conducting counseling came to light in the wake of the terrorist attacks of September 11, 2001. After this time, it is estimated that 33% of American Internet users read or posted material in chat rooms, bulletin boards, or other online forums. Although many early posts reflected outrage at the events, online discussions soon migrated to grieving, discussion and debate on how to respond, and information queries about the suspects and those who sponsored them (Horrigan, 2001). More than ever before, the Internet became a meeting place where people could gain solace more readily and easily than before. Group cybercounseling potentially enjoys all the advantages and suffers from the disadvantages of individual cybercounseling described later in this chapter.

The potential for meeting with others online for group counseling is tempered by several specific challenges that go beyond those already known regarding individual cybercounseling. In particular, electronic tools that bring groups of people together also allow any member of a group to have private conversations with one or more others, unrecognized by other members or the cybercounselor. Such conversations may be counterproductive and even hurtful. Another possible problem in conducting online group counseling is that group members may find it much easier to communicate with each other outside of the group if they discover other members' e-mail addresses. Like individual cybercounseling, online group counseling must be pursued with optimistic caution.

The Web Counselor's Tools

Both for individual counseling and for online group counseling, cybercounselors use a range of tools to foster communication as part of the counseling process. These tools are reviewed in more detail throughout this book. Following is a brief description of each one, including specific uses for conducting cybercounseling. Some Web sites are designed to provide many or all these tools in one place (e.g., www.horizonlive.com; www.helphorizons.com, www.videoshrink.com, and www.mytherapynet. com; see http://directory.google.com/Top/Health/Mental_Health/ Counseling_Services/Online/?tc=1 for a directory of such sites).

E-mail

Tyler and Guth (in press) reported that the most popular tool for conducting counseling online is e-mail, with 78% of their sample of online services using this mode of communication. Secure and encrypted online e-mail systems allow counselors and clients to correspond with relative ease and a high level of security. Typically, a client will complete an intake form, which includes the presenting problem. The counselor then responds with questions, comments, and other facilitative responses. After contemplating the counselor's e-mail, the client can then write back, sometimes directly from the counselor's Web site. Fees are calculated on the basis of the number of e-mail exchanges, the time required for the e-mail exchanges, or sometimes as a flat fee for a given problem as mutually agreed on by the counselor and client. An example of how this works can be seen by visiting http://www.netcounselors.com.

Instant Messaging (IM)

Attempting to re-create the traditional face-to-face counseling exchange without the wait of e-mail, over 50% of online counseling services rely on some form of online chat or instant messaging (IM; Tyler & Guth, in press). IM allows people to conduct real-time chats and more after checking to see whether others are online. According to the How Stuff Works Web site (Tyson, 1998–2002), instant messaging allows you to maintain a list of people (clients or students) that you wish to interact with. You can send messages to any of the people on your list, often called a buddy list or contact list, as long as that person is online. Sending a message opens up a small window where you and the other person can type in messages that both of you can see. Most of the popular instant-messaging programs provide a variety of features:

- Instant Messages—Send notes back and forth with a friend who is online.
- Chat—Create your own custom chat room with friends or coworker.s
- Web Links—Share links to your favorite Web sites.
- Images—Look at an image stored on your friend's computer.
- Sounds—Play sounds for your friends.
- Files—Share files by sending them directly to your friends.
- Talk—Use the Internet instead of a phone to actually talk with friends.
- Streaming Content—Real-time or near-real-time stock quotes and news.

• Technology Tip 12.2 •

If you maintain a Web site, you can include a free chat room from online services such as http://chat-forum.com/freechat.

Several popular IM utilities exist, not all of which can effectively work with each other (e.g., visit http://www.instantmessagingplanet.com for listings and reviews of each). The Internet Engineering Task Force (IETF) is developing a standard protocol for IM, called the Instant Messaging Presence Protocol to help solve this problem. In the meantime, a variety of IM software has been developed to solve this compatibility problem. These IMs include Trillian (http://www.trillian.cc), Odigo (http://www.odigo.org), and Imici (http://www.odigo.org). It is important to know that IM is not a secure way to communicate. Messages and connection information are maintained on servers controlled by the provider of the IM software that you use. Most providers do provide a certain level of encryption, but they are not sufficiently secure that you should send any confidential information through the system. There have been reported cases of IM user information being stolen and used by ill-meaning others.

Videoconferencing

Advancing technology in video compression has made videoconferencing affordable and usable. This has resulted in video interaction over high-speed connections that is fairly smooth and reliable. Such exchanges will allow counselors and clients to easily view each other and recognize large motor movements such as a wave or hearty laugh. However, small details may be missed, such as a client's eye movements or slight facial expression. One counselor reported that he was unaware a client was crying softly because the video was not clear enough to reveal tears. Clarity and resolution will continue to improve rapidly, however. Web cameras, or Web cams, are inexpensive and easy to install on any home or office computer. Some cybercounselors use free videoconferencing software such as provided by Yahoo! (www.yahoo.com) or make videoconferencing a seamless part of their Web site. The counselor may hold virtual office hours in which a client need only click a button to connect with the counselor after checking to see whether he or she is available. Other times, the cybercounselor and client may schedule an appointment via e-mail collaboration or via an online calendar. Some calendar software such as Microsoft Outlook can schedule such videoconferences and automatically connect 5 or 10 minutes before the appointment.

> • Technology Tip 12.3 •
>
> Instead of purchasing a Web cam to videoconference over the Web, you may instead be able simply to hook up your digital camera or digital video recorder.

Chat Room

Chat room sessions are very similar to videoconferencing in terms of how they are scheduled and used. The primary difference is that instead of both video and audio, counselors and clients use the keyboard or voice recognition software to type out their exchange. Private chat rooms are available for free (e.g., http://chat.msn.com) or as part of the tools available on the cybercounselor's Web site (e.g., http://www.thera-chat.com). Although limited because of a lack of visual and audio information, the distinct advantages (and sometimes disadvantages) of chat room sessions are that they provide a level of anonymity that could enhance the exchange, can help both the client and counselor reflect on what is happening as words are typed, and can provide both parties with a transcript of the session to further review and prepare for future sessions.

Web-Based Data Collection and Assessments

The seamless integration of Web design, database applications, and some computer programming have allowed counselors to collect and use data over the Internet in new and exciting ways, particularly in the area of career development (e.g., visit the Center for the Study of Technology in Counseling and Career Development at http://www.career.fsu.edu/techcenter). Whether collecting simple demographic information only or conducting a comprehensive biopsychosocial intake, Web-based data collection as part of cybercounseling can save time and decrease errors because of the way that technology can automate the process. Some cybercounselors also use the Web to administer various assessments, inventories, and surveys (see chapter 5 for further discussion of this issue.) Once the client completes an online instrument and submits the data, the counselor can instantly access the results, interpret them, and either manually or automatically generate a report to use with the client in further sessions. Some sites give clients instant results and interpretations after they submit their answers. Because most cybercounselors do not have the technological expertise to create these online instruments themselves, they often rely on test publishers and others who allow competent counselors to purchase their services. Such providers include Career Key (www.careerkey.org), Support4Learning (www.support4learning.org.uk/jobsearch/assess.htm), the Self Directed Search (http://www.self-directed-search.com/), and the JobHuntersBible (http://www.JobHuntersBible.com). Directories of online assessments may be accessed by visiting http://psychology.about.com/cs/test, http://www.socialpsychology.org/person.htm#online, and http://psychology.about.com/msub_testonline.htm.

• Technology Tip 12.4 •

Online instruments such as surveys can also be created using the database feature of your Web site authoring program (e.g., Dreamweaver or FrontPage). Once the data is collected, it can be exported to a spreadsheet such as Microsoft Excel and further analyzed. Finally, the data can be merged to a word processing template to create reports.

Listserv

You may remember that a listserv allows messages to be communicated quickly and efficiently from one individual to a complete distribution list made up of hundreds or millions. As part of their practice, some cybercounselors provide educational materials and helpful resources in the form of a periodic newsletter that clients may wish to receive. In some cases, cybercounselors may create or locate already existing listservs focusing on particular counseling issues that their clients may also elect to join. This should always be done only after the client has been fully informed about how joining such a list may compromise confidentiality.

High Speed Connections (Broadband)

The rich multimedia content offered by many Web sites can have counselors spending a great deal of time waiting for content to download, especially by using common telephone connections via modem. Cybercounselors who spend a significant amount of time conducting Web counseling may elect to connect using other quicker methods. Bandwidth, or capacity, refers to the amount of data a given technology or infrastructure can transmit over time. It is usually expressed in kilobits per second (Kbps) or megabits per second (Mbps). One kilobit is equal to about 1,000 bits, which means a 28.8 modem can transmit 28.8 kilobits, or 28,800 bits, per second. A 1-megabit modem can handle 1 million bits, or 1,000 kilobits, per second (e.g., see http://www.library.on.ca/helpdesk/Internet/connect.html). The following describes each connection type and average download speeds (in order of increasing speed and, very often, expense):

- **Telephone modem or dial-up (2400 bps to 56 Kbps).** The most common connection, the modem is a device that enables a computer to transmit data over telephone lines. 56K modems are the most common. Because of restrictions imposed by the FCC, and because of other limiting factors, download speeds never reach the modem's declared capability of 56 kbps.
- **ISDN (64–144 Kbps).** ISDN is an international communications standard for sending voice, video, and data over digital telephone lines or normal telephone wires. Most ISDN lines offered by telephone companies give you two lines at once, called B channels. You can use one line for voice and the other for data, or you can use both lines for data (http://webopedia.com).
- **Satellite (400 Kbps).** A satellite Internet connection is an arrangement in which the upstream (outgoing) and the downstream (incoming) data are sent from and arrive at a computer through a satellite. Each subscriber's hardware includes a satellite dish antenna and a transceiver (transmitter–receiver) that operates in the microwave portion of the radio spectrum (http://whatis.techtarget.com).
- **DSL (512 Kbps to 8 Mbps).** DSL (Digital Subscriber Line) is a technology for bringing high-bandwidth information to homes and small businesses over ordinary copper telephone lines. DSL technologies use sophisticated modulation schemes to pack data onto copper wires.
- **Cable modem (512 Kbps to 10 Mbps).** Cable modems are modems designed to operate over cable TV lines. Cable modem subscribers are typically charged for service on their television cable bill, rather than paying an ISP directly.
- **Wireless (2 Mbps or more).** Access is gained by connection to a high-speed cellular-like local multipoint communications system (LMCS) network via wireless transmitter–receiver. Such connections are currently seen mostly in educational institutions such as universities,

libraries, and airports. Some businesses are providing wireless connections to the Internet as a way to attract more customers and keep them in the establishment after they arrive (while drinking more coffee or eating more fries, no doubt).

- **Ethernet (10 Mbps).** Because of its expense, ethernet connections are most often a part of a local area network in agencies, schools, and middle to larger size businesses.
- **Fast Ethernet (1 gigabyte or 1,000 million bytes per second).** Also known as 100Base-T, this is the latest broadband technology being introduced as part of local area networks (LANs).

Potential and Possible Pitfalls

According to Sabella (2003; also see Sussman, 2002), the continued evolution of the Internet into the information highway offers many future possibilities and potential problems in the delivery of counseling services. Following is an overview of each:

Possibilities

- **Delivery of services:** Walz (1996) noted that the information highway "allows counselors to overcome problems of distance and time to offer opportunities for networking and interacting not otherwise available" (p. 417). In addition, counseling over the Internet may be a useful medium for those with physical disabilities who may find traveling even a short distance to be a significant obstacle. For others who are reticent in meeting with a counselor and/or self-disclosing, the Internet may prove to be an interactive lubricant that may very well foster the counseling process. Similarly, the Internet is a convenient and quick way to deliver important information. In cybercounseling, information might be in the form of bibliocounseling or a homework assignment between sessions. Also, electronic file transfer of client records, including intake data, case notes (Casey, Bloom, & Moan, 1994), assessment reports, and selected key audio and video recordings of client sessions, could be used as preparation for individual supervision, group supervision, case conferences, and research (Coursol & Lewis, n.d.; Sampson et al., 1997).
- **Assessment and evaluation:** Access to a wide variety of assessment, instructional, and information resources, in formats appropriate in a wide variety of ethnic, gender, and age contexts (Sampson, 1990; Sampson & Krumboltz, 1991), could be accomplished via the World Wide Web.
- **Communications:** Especially via e-mail, counselors and clients can exchange messages throughout the counseling process. Messages may inform both counselor and client of pertinent changes or progress. E-mail can provide an excellent forum for answering simple questions, providing social support, or to schedule actual or virtual meeting times.

Some personal information managers (PIMs) such as Microsoft Outlook allow you to schedule online meetings complete with associated Web sites and documents that automatically open right before the meeting time.

- **Marriage and family counseling:** If face-to-face interaction is not possible on a regular basis, marriage counseling might be delivered via videoconferencing, in which each couple and the counselor (or counselors) are in different geographic locations. After independent use of multimedia-based computer-assisted instruction on communication skills, spouses might use videoconferencing to complete assigned homework (e.g., communication exercises; Sampson et al., 1997).
- **Supervision:** Anecdotal evidence has shown that e-mail is an enhancing tool in the process of counselor supervision and consultation. It provides an immediate and ongoing channel of communication between and among as many people as chosen (Christie, n.d.; Myrick & Sabella, 1995).
- **Credentials:** Because cybercounseling can occur anytime and anywhere, it may very well pressure the profession and governance to formulate a national, or perhaps international, counseling licensure or certification. Definitely an enormous undertaking, this measure will facilitate uniform standards of training and practice while expediting reciprocity among states and countries. Cybercounseling may very well become the impetus for the ultimate in counselor credential portability.

Potential Pitfalls

- **Confidentiality:** Although encryption and security methods have become highly sophisticated, unauthorized access to online communications remains a possibility without special attention to security measures. Counselors who practice online must ethically and legally protect their clients, their profession, and themselves by using all known and reasonable security measures.
- **Computer competency:** Both the counselor and client must be adequately computer literate for the computer–network environment to be a viable interactive medium. From typing skills to electronic data transfer, both the counselor and client must be able to effectively harness the power and function of both hardware and software. Similar to face-to-face counseling, cybercounselors must not attempt to perform services outside the limitations of their technological competence.
- **Location-specific factors:** A potential lack of appreciation on the part of geographically remote counselors of location-specific conditions, events, and cultural issues that affect clients may limit counselor cred-

ibility or lead to inappropriate counseling interventions. For example, a geographically remote counselor may be unaware of recent traumatic events at the local level that are exacerbating a client's reaction to work and family stressors. It may also be possible that differences in local or regional cultural norms between the client's and counselor's community could lead a counselor to misinterpret the thoughts, feelings, or behavior of the client. Counselors need to prepare for counseling a client in a remote location by becoming familiar with recent local events and local cultural norms. If a counselor encounters an unanticipated reaction on the part of the client, the counselor needs to proceed slowly, clarifying client perceptions of his or her thoughts, feelings, and behavior (Sampson et al., 1997).

- **Equity:** Web counseling has the potential to exacerbate equity issues already confronting live counseling. If counseling online is a viable alternative, steps need to be taken to ensure that costs do not create another obstacle for some clients. As well, if some service providers view cybercounseling as an inexpensive alternative, then it may inappropriately become the tool for those who cannot afford more traditional approaches. Alternatively, if cost issues are addressed and access is available equally for everyone, cybercounseling may further alienate potential clients who have less technological expertise, creating a different type of equity gap.

- **High tech versus high touch:** How can counselors foster the development of trusting, caring, and genuine working relationships in cyberspace? Until virtual reality is realized for individuals and small institutions, cybercounseling relies on a process limited in nonverbal or extraverbal behavior. Similarly, questions remain about whether counseling can be effectively conducted without an actual human presence—a presence that includes a holistic experience greater than the sum of its parts.

- **Impersonation:** A famous cartoon circulated over the Internet depicts a dog sitting in front of a computer. The caption says, "The nice thing about the Internet is that nobody knows you're a dog." Experienced Internet users can relate to the humor in this cartoon because they know that there are many people who hide behind the Internet's veil of anonymity to communicate messages they ordinarily would not communicate in real life—messages that convey unpopular sentiments and would ordinarily be met with castigation. Others rely on the anonymity provided by the Internet to play out fantasies or practical jokes. The reality is that it is almost impossible to know who a cyberclient really is. A minor client may depict him- or herself as an adult. Other clients may disguise their gender, race, or other personal distinctions in a manner that threatens the validity or integrity of your efforts.

- **Credentials:** One of the counseling profession's main concerns will be of those who are unlicensed persons promoting themselves as competent Internet counselors. When a counselor is unlicensed, a state has no regulatory authority unless there is a law in that state that will allow prosecution as a criminal act for practicing counseling without a license or that gives the board regulatory authority. Unlicensed cybercounselors are almost legally untouchable, especially when a disclaimer statement is displayed stating what they are doing is not therapy (Hughes, 2000). More than ever before, cybercounseling may have created a need for the profession to educate consumers about choosing an appropriately trained and credentialed counselor (e.g., Ainsworth, n.d.). Many questions regarding cybercounseling and credentials need to be answered: How will insurance companies handle requests from cybercounselors interested in purchasing professional liability insurance specifically to conduct cybercounseling? How will certification and licensure laws apply to the Internet as state and national borders are crossed electronically? Will cybercounselors be forced to maintain licensure or certification in the states in which their clients reside, or must counselors only obtain licensure or certification in the state from which they practice? Similarly, who will monitor service complaints out-of-state or internationally?

- **Ethics:** How do current ethical statements for counselors apply or adapt to situations encountered online? For the most part, counselors can make the leap into cyberspace and use current ethical guidelines to conduct themselves in an ethical fashion. However, problems exist. The future will inevitably see a change in what it means to be ethical as we learn the exact nature of counseling online.

The Future of Web Counseling

Although predictions concerning the future of cybercounseling are likely to be rapidly out of date, it is certain that cybercounseling will continue to expand, diversify, and change, in terms of both its technology and its use. Counselors and psychotherapists, like other professionals, are likely to have an increasing degree of involvement with this new mode of communication. Some may use it only to maintain contact and manage administration with existing face-to-face clients. Some may shift the base of their practice to online work. Videocounseling via the Internet is likely to expand sharply over the next decade as the technology develops and personal communicators with video-links replace the conventional telephone and remove the need for computers and keyboards to a great extent (Goss, Robson , Pelling, & Renard, 1999). Some counseling professionals tend to be conservative, even technophobic, and they may be slower than most to accept this new way of working. Nevertheless, increasing numbers of clients are likely to seek online help with their problems, and counselors are advised to adapt to meet this growing demand; otherwise unqualified personnel may well take advantage of an obvious gap in the market (British Association for Counselling, 1999).

Even those counselors who do not integrate the Internet into their practice will need to be technologically literate to assist clients in processing problems occurring on or exacerbated by this very growing medium. Examples include issues of infidelity; online addictions to gambling, pornography, or the Internet; online access to drugs; access to sites that support hate and violence; online sexual harassment, bullying, and stalking; technology-induced depression and stress; and, increasingly, cyberchondria (i.e., clients who use the Internet to find out more about their issues and who often misdiagnose symptoms or stumble across quack cures).

The technological tools that cybercounselors use will become smaller, faster, and more portable. Handheld computers and other small appliances are increasingly processing large amounts of data and connecting to the Internet via wireless access. Desktop and laptop computers as we know them today will not exist. Instead, counselors will use appliances to access any needed software over their workplace network or the Internet. Software will increasingly be used by purchasing a renewable license or on a per-use basis. The counselor's own data will be stored not only on a desktop computer but also on a network so that he or she can access the data from other appliances throughout the world. If desired, the counselor can store the data on a storage device no larger than a stick of gum and carry it with him or her anywhere. Computer components (e.g., memory, processing, storage, retrieval, and output) will be integrated into other materials such as paper, fabric, and glass. Consequently, for example, clients will wear smart clothing that will respond to increased heart rate, temperature, muscular tension, and other physical changes and collect this data for further analysis. Perhaps the data collected by smart clothing will be wirelessly "beamed" to the counselor for continued (automated) monitoring or provide an alert that summons a specific response from the client and/or counselor.

Online environments are quickly approximating real environments by becoming more three-dimensional. Counseling in cyberspace is sure to incorporate other tools that will replace video and audio interactions with dynamic virtual learning experiences. That is, instead of talk counseling, high powered computers that can "understand" natural language programming will help the counselor and client construct a quite realistic environment to learn and practice important knowledge and skills. Once the environment is created, the counselor and/or client can enter the environment to virtually "live" an experience, with programmed representations of significant others, to gain insights and practice new behaviors. Similarly, counseling of the future may incorporate virtual environments in which the client can "relive" past experiences to gain better insight. The most powerful systems of the future may very well be just like the Holodeck in the popular television and movie series Star Trek. The Holodeck allows one or more others to live an experience in a dynamically programmed environment. The Holodeck introduces characters and plots based on a massive database of either fiction or nonfiction knowledge. Each character in this environment has a personality and responds to real participants accordingly. No two Holodeck experiences are ever the same. Even midway, a Holodeck participant may change the way the characters and plot ensues. And the Holodeck system monitors every real participant's vital signs and will stop the experience if any one is at risk. Such environments may even see the advent of on-demand counseling as clients could theoretically work with a virtual representation of their counselor. At the very least, the client can use technology to conduct important work between live sessions with his or her client (even the Star Trek series included a professional counselor, Counselor Troy, among its officers). All in all, the potential for creative drama in counseling of the future given today's technology trends is very exciting.

Whether we embrace or detest the emergence of cybercounseling, we would probably all agree that we have an emerging generation for whom interaction via the computer is a common, natural, and fully accepted means of communication. This generation of potential clients is accustomed to less actual personal contact and greater interaction in cyberspace in many aspects of their lives than previous generations. To think that clients in the new century will not expect to access Internet counseling services would probably be foolish and short-sighted on our part (Lee, 1998). If technology really does herald a new age of user-friendly computer-mediated communication for the masses, will the world of counseling and psychotherapy be left behind? E-mail, originally developed to help desk-bound students and workers in commercial organizations, was modeled on the office memorandum. If computer communications are to mediate properly and effectively in therapeutic relationships, we need to strive continually to identify the salient interpersonal processes unique to therapeutic relationships, not borrow second-hand technology designed for business organizations by computer scientists. There needs to be collaboration between counselors, social scientists, and computer scientists who together would identify therapy-salient processes, model them in terms of psychosocial communications theories, and finally design them into therapy-dedicated, computer-mediated communications systems. If we fail in this endeavor, we could find therapists in 10 years' time still using technologies designed for corporate business communications or computer-banking as the means by which they conduct therapy with their clients at a distance (Sanders & Rosenfield, 1998).

Summary

The Internet, like any tool, is either helpful or harmful depending on the user's purpose, capability, and actions. Focusing on the parts that are helpful and controlling those that are not can be a difficult task because of the vastness and morphological nature of the Internet. Issues of psychological health and overall well-being while using the Internet for commendable ventures is enhanced by knowledge and skills that promote robust discovery. As members of the counseling profession, we must take an active role in guiding the evolution of this new method of service delivery. It is important to take a farsighted approach by conceptualizing online interaction, not only in the manner that it normally occurs today, but also in terms of how technology and services will evolve over the next several years. The path toward protecting the public interest while preserving individual choice appears to be best paved not with legislation, but with certification. Clearly, it is important that adequate research be done in the area before certification guidelines are enacted. When research provides us with the necessary information to understand how counseling over the Internet can be most beneficial, then it will be important to establish international certification guidelines with the input of professional counselors, other mental health providers, and managed care (Sussman, 2002).

Internet Sites for Additional Information

- http://www.cable-modem.net/index.html. This is the Web site for the cable modem information network.
- http://www.metanoia.org/imhs/. Compiled by consumers, for consumers, this site presents an independent consumer guide to therapists and counselors who provide help over the Internet.
- http://www.online-counseling.org. This is the home page of the Japan Online Counseling Association.
- http://www.marriagematters.com/. Online counseling at Marriage Matters is an interactive process that occurs via e-mail or telephone.
- http://www.onlinecounselingalternatives.com/. This site provides online counseling alternatives specializing in counseling for the lesbian, gay, bisexual, and transsexual community.
- http://www.barnabus.com/. This site offers two types of online counseling: (a) conferences—a one-on-one or group method conducted in a private chat room environment on the site (after finding a counselor, you can sign up for an online session with that counselor); and (b) journals—a one-on-one method completed through the site with a counselor of your choice.
- http://www.ismho.org/. This is the Web site for the International Society for Mental Health Online.
- http://www.library.on.ca/helpdesk/Internet/connect.html. This site provides an Internet connection speed comparison chart and is presented by the Southern Ontario Library Service Helpdesk.

13

New Technologies Mean New Challenges

We acknowledge that there is a cost for advancing technological literacy similar to other educational endeavors. The most obvious cost is financial, although we are also aware of challenges involving human and other resources (see Table 13.1).

Part of technological literacy is being able to critically determine the types of technologies that will best serve you or help you to gain a positive return on your investments (ROI). Some use technology because it is the "latest and greatest" without careful consideration for the technology's utility. Such people usually want to achieve new levels of power, efficiency, and perhaps the ability to mesmerize or excite others when demonstrating their newfound capabilities. However, just because a new technology application promises to do more or perform a task more quickly does not mean we should all go out and purchase it. New technologies arrive on store shelves every day, and although many are alluring, only a few will truly result in great benefits to a counselor's professional and personal productivity. Every technology must be carefully evaluated for its merit. As smart consumers of technology, counselors must ask questions such as the following (Sabella, 2003):

- How much are the initial costs for purchasing the software or hardware?
- Will my computer run the software or will I need to upgrade (e.g., add more memory or purchase a new peripheral, therefore adding to the overall cost of the new application)?

Table 13.1
A Few Challenges Posed by Changing Technology

1. Finding time to maintain currency with ever-evolving hardware, software, and language.
2. Maintaining/obtaining financial resources sufficient to stay current as mandated by changing environments, alterations in stakeholder expectations, and personal needs and abilities.
3. Helping others to understand a vision of technology use in professional and personal settings.
4. Managing technology so that it improves our lives, rather than allowing negative impacts from technology infringement.
5. Responding to changes in the pace of business fostered by technology.
6. Avoiding depersonalization and isolation brought on by the increase in technology-mediated communication.
7. Protecting ourselves and others from the negative side of the Internet and Internet use.
8. Appropriately supervising the use of technology by minors in our care.

- If I choose to purchase new software or hardware, what will it cost to maintain it in the form of upgrades and especially in the form of human resources, specifically paying someone for upkeep, training, or consultation?
- How user-friendly is the technology? How much time might it require to adequately learn and apply the new technology? Can I do this on my own or will I need to spend even more money for training?
- Is the company that provides the technology reputable and stable? Or, will the technology lose long-term support because of a fleeting company?
- How well will the new technology work with other already adopted computer applications?
- How compatible is the new technology to already existing technologies? That is, will others be able to share and collaborate with someone who uses the new technology?
- Is the new technology convenient and enjoyable to use?

Ultimately, the main question is "Will this technology provide me with a significant ROI?" That is, will an initial and anticipated investment of financial and human resources provide me with a long-term and desired level of benefit to my work?

If the ROI for a technology is significant, then one might more easily make the decision to learn and use it. If the ROI is poor, then one might only spend the time to understand the technology to better make informed decisions about its use. For example, we (the authors) differ on our opinions of certain applications. Russell Sabella mostly avoids instant messaging, file sharing, and project management applications. Through careful consideration, he has determined these applications to be inefficient and too time consuming for his work style and needs. On the other hand, Mike Tyler has found file sharing and management tools to be indispensable in managing work flow and maintaining organization. For our children, chatware and instant messaging are an integral part of daily communication. Following are other challenges to consider as you continue to make technological literacy an integral part of your professional (and personal) development.

Finding the Resources and Time to Learn

One of the first challenges that we all face in relation to advancing our technological literacy is simply finding the time to learn the skills necessary to keep up. In almost every profession where a certificate or license is required for professional practice, the right to practice comes with an obligation to maintain currency in the field. In mental health fields, we have accepted this need for continuing education not only as a legal responsibility but also as an ethical responsibility (e.g., ACA, 1995; APA, 2002a; ASCA, 1998; NASW, 1999).

To meet our professional need to maintain currency, organizations and agencies, training programs, universities, and professional groups and associations all offer support for continuing education. In some cases, employers will provide opportunities for continuing education in-house, whereas others supplement their employees' needs through tuition reimbursement programs or by directly paying for continuing education. Historically, these opportunities have primarily focused on updating knowledge and skills directly related to interaction with clients.

However, today new challenges face the counseling professional that require different types of training opportunities. Professionals cannot simply go to a conference or training program to learn how to apply technology without first gaining the basic technology skills necessary for success. In the past, professionals relied heavily on support staff in offices to type reports, handle charting issues, and maintain correspondence. Today, support services are more limited by constraints in funding than at any time in the past, and the use of technology is seen as one way to respond to this shortage of support. Therefore, professionals are increasingly expected to maintain their own (and student–client) records on computers, create billing statements, and file insurance claims electronically. In the past we needed to have the knowledge to communicate what needed to go on such reports. Today, in addition to the content knowledge, we must also possess the process knowledge: the keyboard skills to create these documents, the computer literacy to save them in a protected fashion, and the network knowledge to transfer them to colleagues, oversight departments, or outside agencies.

Where will this new skill set come from? It is typical in many states to require mental health, school, and other counselors to receive 20 hours or more of continuing education units per year (Distance Learning Center for Addiction Studies, 2002). Counselors certified by the NBCC are required to have 100 hours of education in every 5-year certification period (NBCC, 2001). These numbers are based on an assumption that this amount of training is adequate to keep the professional informed of changes in the field, new techniques, alterations in our understanding of client needs, and so forth. Changes in technology demand that in addition to staying current in these discipline-specific topics, we also maintain currency in issues related to technology. However, there are currently no provisions written in national credentialing guidelines that focus on technology skills. In fact, counselors certified with NBCC are required to receive their continuing education in 1 of 10 approved content areas (NBCC, 2001); technology is not among them. As a result, we believe that counselors will need to go beyond the minimum continuing education requirements demanded by most state and national credentialing boards. Meeting the minimum requirements may allow us to stay current in specific discipline knowledge, but it will not provide the skills necessary to succeed technologically.

The good news is that the number and level of resources for counseling technology training is steadily increasing. Books, journal articles, conference workshops, and online tutorials abound for learning general technology competencies (see, for instance, the reference section and Web sites throughout this book). With some effort, counselors can adapt general technology resources to acquire the specific skills and knowledge they need in their work. Also growing in number, however, are such resources developed especially for the counselor. For instance, many school districts have recognized that providing technology training tailored especially to school counselors (as contrasted with training for teachers, administrators, and others) is needed because of how school counselors must apply technology tools to unique problems. These districts employ trainers who are typically school counselors who have both counseling experience and insights, high levels of technological competency, and the skill to teach other counselors in a way that is meaningful and easy to understand. Such trainers can be viewed as the bridge between two disciplines: counseling and educational technology. Training is increasingly being offered as an important part of professional development opportunities offered by employers and conducted as part of the counselor's regular day. It will probably not be very long from now when the counselor education profession begins to discuss the need and development of a new master's degree or certification in counseling technology. We are confident that these trends will only become amplified as the need for counseling technology training increases and as the availability of trainers who are expert in both counseling and technology increases as well.

• Technology Tip 13.1 •

Make a personal commitment to engage in continuing technology training. Whenever you attend a state or national conference, include at least one technology-focused session in your list of sessions to attend. Even if you choose not to use new skills learned, you will be better informed about the state of the field.

Finding the Money to Succeed

The second technology challenge for all professionals to address relates to the financial impact of rapidly changing technology. A quick understanding of this need can be seen by looking at the hardware changes that have occurred in personal computing in the 25 years between 1975 and 2000. In 1975, a company called Micro Instrumentation and Telemetry Systems Inc. began selling a kit to build a computer known as the MITS Altair 8800. This computer had no keyboard, no monitor, no printer, and could not store data. Its capabilities were so limited, many hobbyists who purchased the kit were at a loss as to what to do with it. Some early users have related the excitement generated at a computer club meeting when one member figured out how to program the machine in such a way that the beeps it made when working would play a simple melody (Cringely, 1996).

This was followed by another computer kit, the Apple I in 1976, which was replaced in 1977 by the fully assembled Apple II. This change moved the personal computer from a hobbyist's project to a toy. Over the final 3 years in that decade, a large number of computers were introduced, including the Sinclair ZX-80, the Commodore PET, and Radio Shack's TR-80. Then in 1980, Commodore introduced the Vic-20, a computer that had a color monitor (or could be attached to a television like any current game console) and became the first computer to sell over 1 million units. By the mid-1980s, Apple Computer had introduced and stopped producing no fewer than three new computer models while Microsoft was busy creating a new user interface known as Windows. Software titles by the mid-1980s reached over 16,000 for the Apple computer line, and the software industry for IBM PCs was growing just as rapidly. With over 100 manufacturers marketing computers, the revolution was on. Within this fast-growing and competitive market, the groundwork for our second challenge was laid.

Purchasing a computer and learning to use it was and remains a short-term investment. For most users, by the time a computer is purchased, set-up, and operated for several months, it has been replaced in stores by newer hardware and software with improved features. In the computer industry there is a rule referred to as Moore's Law (named after Intel Corporation Founder Gordon Moore) that states the power of integrated circuitry doubles every 18 months (Webopedia, 2002a). This suggests that even if a user purchases the very best (and most expensive) computer available, within 18 months the system is only half as powerful as the newest systems. Therefore, organizations that rely on computers, as well as the professionals within these organizations, can expect that they will be required to continuously update their hardware and software at a very rapid pace. The financial impact of this change alone will affect all other aspects of our professional lives. In the current economy, a new computer and related support may cost 8%–10% of a starting counselor's annual wage. If this computer needs to be replaced every 2 years, then the cost of supporting that counselor is 4%–5% higher than it was just a few short years ago. That 4%–5% is equivalent to a very nice annual raise. For a small agency with 15–20 employees, this cost may signify the difference between another full-time counselor to help clients, or keeping updated technology on the desks of employees to allow them to function most effectively. In larger organizations with hundreds of employees, the cost is quite high indeed. Our second challenge then is finding ways to fund the needed technology without reducing services to clients. As individuals, we will be challenged to find ways to fund our own technology needs at home or in our private offices so that we can meet the obligations we have accepted that occur outside of an agency or school-supported site.

This challenge may be tempered in several ways. For one, the assumption that the counselor should—or worse, *must*—have the latest technology may not be correct. Counselors may not, especially at the beginning level, need to have screaming computers with all the bells and whistles. Investing in updates and upgrades should be done as a function of need, not as a function of availability. Second, many technology stores, especially online (e.g., put the words "software discount" into a search engine and view the results) offer educational and institutional discounts for both software and hardware. Third, the advent and proliferation of online auctions (e.g., http://www.ebay.com) have made purchasing gently used and new technology convenient and reasonably affordable. Fourth, in the case of software, counselors may take advantage of shareware and freeware versions of the upscale commercial software that oftentimes perform at least adequately and at a significantly reduced price (e.g., such as those found at www.hotfiles.com). Shareware is inexpensive because it is typically produced by a single programmer and is offered directly to customers. Thus, there are practically no packaging or advertising expenses. Fifth, many counselors have forged collaborative partnerships with others, including universities and businesses that have a great deal of technology hardware and software and that have expertise in using them. Finally, schools and institutions may develop grants that include technology (e.g., U.S. Department of Education, 2002) that can be used by not only the grant participants but by others throughout the workplace. The importance of technology tools has seemingly spurred a flurry of grants that seek to help others acquire and demonstrate how various technologies can help people achieve their goals.

• Technology Tip 13.2 •

Before purchasing new hardware, understand your needs. Most office applications such as word processing or spreadsheet manipulation do not require a great deal of computing power. If this is the bulk of your computer work, settle for a relatively inexpensive model with less power. Individuals focused on high-end video games are the ones who require the most powerful equipment.

Developing the Support to Achieve Goals

As those early hobbyists sat crowded around their blinking and beeping MITS Altair 8800 computers, most observers brushed them off as outside the mainstream, engaged in behavior that was inconsequential and of little real value. We are aware that some counseling professionals who have embraced technology have been similarly marginalized over the past several years. Counselors who have tried to use the Internet in their work have been told that the effort is too great, the payoff too small, and the risks too high. Yet, millions of individuals daily access the Internet seeking information on specific concerns they have in their lives. Counselors who don't recognize their own clients among these users are clearly unaware of one aspect of many clients' lives. Other counselors have sought to use personal computers as a tool to engage clients or to support their work in many interesting and innovative ways. Often these innovators and early adopters have a vision or dream that is so different from what others are doing that they are dismissed without an adequate attempt to understand. The dismissive party may be a colleague, a supervisor, or someone from outside the agency. In my own work (J. Michael Tyler) in the 1980s, a review team for an accreditation organization visiting the psychiatric hospital where I was in charge of staff development refused to accept computerized records showing that staff trainings had been held and who attended! Today, computers are a common tool used to maintain databases showing such information.

This brings us to our third challenge: finding ways to create the enthusiasm among others to support our use of technology. Consistent with much of what we do as professionals, creating this enthusiasm is often a matter of educating those with whom we interact. Such an idea is essential because our most powerful technologies are by nature interactive and require two or more, sometimes many more, people to become useful. The high-tech tools that help us to find, develop, and share resources; make collaborative decisions without limitations of space or time; and efficiently communicate at the touch of a button all rely on multiple users of technology. In some ways, helping others use technology is self-promoting because it gives us more people to work with via various electronic media.

To obtain support for our work from administrators, we need to understand the language they use and the goals they have for themselves and the units they oversee. In times of budget crisis, professionals who can speak with a supervisor about fiscal management and conserving money through the use of technology will be listened to and supported. During times of service retrenchment, the best approach may be to focus on ways in which technology can help to provide more service to greater numbers of clients on the basis of increased efficiency, better use of time, or increased access.

• Technology Tip 13.3 •

Whenever implementing new technology in a work setting, after the implementation of the technology has stabilized it is good practice to engage in a time study. Without collecting data, it is impossible to accurately determine whether a technology provides the ROI expected. Such a study will also provide the data necessary for future technology implementation or upgrade decisions.

As with administrators, colleagues may not always understand the benefits to be gained from technology. Many individuals choose not to even consider using technology any more than mandated simply because they lack skills or believe that learning and implementing new systems and procedures will be too time-consuming. In many environments, individuals have seen so many changes occur over time that they believe technology, like many other initiatives, will simply go away if it is ignored long enough. In seeking support from colleagues, we need to remember that comfort and knowledge levels vary widely. Not everyone in an organization will ever want or need to have a high level of technology skills. However, those who are interested in using technology will find that gaining the support of those who are less interested remains a critical step. Often this support is best earned through a course of patience and support for the technology-disinclined. Answering questions simply, offering brief periods of education as appropriate, and never criticizing or demeaning others will serve you and your clients well.

For many, using technology directly with clients is the ultimate goal. Although we believe that at some point in the future all clients will seek some services that are technology-based, that time has not arrived. However, it is true that many of our clients (and others such as parents or family members) are technologically savvy and willing to use technology to support their own growth. This is the group of clients to target in your current use of technology. Individuals who use e-mail regularly, who have mastered chat room etiquette, or use the Internet to seek information will readily use these same tools to support learning and change in personal aspects of their lives. Clients who do not have these skills need to be assessed carefully before technology is introduced into their lives.

For some, there is a strong desire to learn technology skills, but for many reasons opportunities have been unavailable. In such a case, the professional counselor must consider the reasons that the individual has not obtained the skills or had the opportunity to learn these competencies. Significant financial barriers may exist for many clients which would keep them from successfully accomplishing tasks in an online environment. For other clients, lack of academic skills, including an inability to read, will make technology use difficult. Other clients may have the capacity and will use the counseling process as their motivation to make the time available or commit the resources to gain the skills.

In cases where clients want to use technology and have the skills, using technology to mediate communication or provide access to information should be considered. However, if a client is reluctant, does not have the skills required for success, or becomes anxious or unsure, then technology should not be seen as a viable tool at that time. It is important to remember that technology should never be an end in itself. At best, it is a tool that provides us another way to help clients; at worst, it distracts clients from achieving the personal growth they otherwise would achieve.

Getting Away From Work

In the past, during training and early work experiences, counselors were warned not to "take their work home." A healthy level of professional detachment or strong boundaries was advocated to allow personal space. This was seen as a necessary component of the caregiver taking care of the self. Technology is making that task more difficult. Because technology can help us transcend the barriers of space, place, and time, we may easily find ourselves working at home and playing at work.

Today, clients can visit an organization's Web site, find a counselor's e-mail address, and begin a conversation with the counselor that follows him or her everywhere. As individuals we can choose not to answer the telephone or respond to a message from a client, but e-mail is somewhat more invasive. E-mail messages can be sent any time of the day or night and are placed directly into our inbox. Although we can choose not to open the message, we cannot as easily ignore its existence. Just the knowledge that the e-mail exists, or that many e-mail messages are waiting, may increase our stress and impinge on our attempts to relax. This is further complicated because some clients may expect responses to their e-mails in a short period of time. Still other messages, communicating information about an emergency, may demand a response.

If a client sends a professional counselor an e-mail message indicating that the client may be in crisis, the counselor may have more obligation to respond than in the past. Previously, if clients were in crisis, they were expected to work through appropriate channels, perhaps a specific on-call counselor or a crisis-line. However, e-mail may allow the client to bypass these structures to reach directly into the life of the counselor. Once contacted and knowledgeable, the counselor has both an ethical and legal obligation to respond. The response may be as simple as providing the client with a phone number of an appropriate contact. Such a response, while quick, still represents an invasion into the private life of the clinician, and has the potential to increase our stress. This example provides the basis of our fourth challenge: finding a way to appropriately disconnect from professional obligations to allow for personal growth and renewal. There are ways that the professional can respond that may assist in this process.

• Technology Tip 13.4 •

Set and maintain appropriate boundaries to keep technology from allowing your professional life to interfere with your personal life. Maintain separate e-mail accounts, do not provide clients with the address of chat rooms or your chat room nickname, and keep private your nickname if you use IM software for fun.

Policy for E-mail Limitations

One step that can assist the counselor in "unplugging" is to take active measures to draw appropriate boundaries. If your agency or school uses e-mail, work with the administration to develop appropriate policies to respond to client e-mails. Such a policy may include written clarification that organizational e-mail will not be accessed outside of normal business hours and will never be accessed on holidays or weekends. Also consider a policy that offers a specific time frame, perhaps 24 or 48 hours, in which staff will have to respond to e-mail. Once policies are established within the organization, make sure the information is available to clients. This can be done by providing clients with written copies of agency policy as part of an intake packet, similar to information that clients already receive concerning methods or payment, confidentiality, and policies on missed appointments. Parents, teachers, and other stake holders should also be informed about the limitations for school counselors of e-mail communications and requests via newsletters, posted policies on the Web site, and other appropriate communication media.

Automatic Responses

Some e-mail programs allow users to set up "automatic responses" to incoming e-mail. In your e-mail Help menu, search for "auto-reply" or "out-of-office-assistant" to see whether your software supports this feature. Follow the instructions to set up an automatic reply. If your e-mail system uses Microsoft Exchange, then you can use the "Out of Office Assistant" in Microsoft Outlook or Outlook Express. Access your out-of-office assistant by choosing Tools and then Out of Office Assistant. Then check the box marked "I am out of the office." Then you may create a message that will automatically be sent to everyone who sends you a message. This reply may contain similar information to what is often provided in voice mail messages. The message may explain that you are out of your office and unavailable to respond to e-mail immediately. Then, consider including appropriate phone numbers or contact points for clients who may wish more immediate assistance. These numbers would be the same as those provided to a client calling your office and receiving an answering service or voice mail. By using this auto response feature, clients are reminded that you will not respond immediately, and if they are in crisis they will need to make additional contacts. This can be particularly useful when you will be out of your office for extended periods such as long weekends, holidays, and vacations. Many e-mail clients allow you to chose to send an auto-reply only once to every incoming email address. If you are gone for several days, this means your colleagues will only get your auto-reply once. In most cases, once is enough. If your e-mail client provides this option, computer etiquette requires you to use it.

Time and Place Boundaries

It is not enough, however, to simply set up such a system. It must be used. Set appropriate boundaries for your own behavior as you would for a client. If evenings and weekends are your time away from the office, then avoid checking your work e-mail account. Increasingly, we can all access our e-mail from anywhere in the world over the Internet, but this does not mean that we have to access it. Setting appropriate boundaries to separate work from leisure is an important and healthy task in which we should all engage. Likewise, nowhere is it written that you must check your e-mail first thing every morning. What if you were to complete other important tasks and save e-mail processing for later? This strategy may help you to prioritize and gain better balance among your tasks. Finally, every now and then, about once every couple of weeks or less, on a Friday, we like to take what we call an e-mail vacation. The vacation begins on Friday morning and ends on Monday afternoon. During this time, even though we may work on the computer, we do not even open our e-mail software.

Personal Versus Professional

Another important step in this process is to separate our personal online activities from our professional activities. One way to do this is to maintain at least two e-mail accounts, one professional and one personal. There are two strong reasons for this. First, an account provided and maintained by an employer is designed for professional use. Employers have a right to expect that these accounts will be used for professional purposes and will not be clogged with extraneous personal e-mail. Just as agencies expect their phones to be used only for business purposes, they maintain the same expectation for their computer equipment. In some cases, employers monitor e-mail and are aware of the amount of personal traffic that is being sent through their machines. Even in settings where it is not policy to monitor e-mail, certain computer system personnel have access to e-mail servers, allowing them to read all incoming and outgoing messages. The second reason for a personal e-mail account is that it allows you to maintain personal contacts without having to look at business e-mail. Thus, a second account allows you to correspond in the evenings and weekends with friends or family while blissfully ignoring whatever e-mail is arriving in your school or agency inbox. While we are all aware that there will be mail waiting when we return to the office, life remains less stressful when we remain unaware of whom the messages are from and what their content may be. Setting up a personal account is easy, and as noted in chapter 7, many free options are available.

Dealing With Spam

Spam (also known as unsolicited commercial e-mail, or UCE) is the equivalent of junk mail or more simply, unwanted e-mail. It is the Internet's version of telemarketing calls during dinner, crank phone calls, and leaflets passed around town, all rolled up into a single annoying electronic bundle (Schwartz, Garfinkel, & Russell, 1998). However, spam is quite different from other forms of bulk advertisement or information delivery. For one, it's easy to send—anyone with basic computer skills can send an e-mail. Second, it is highly cost-efficient—with a $15 Internet account and $10 for an e-mail list containing a million e-mail addresses you can send hundreds of thousands of e-mails.

According to the Webopedia (2003), "there is some debate about the source of the term, but the generally accepted version is that it comes from the Monty Python song, "Spam spam spam spam, spam spam spam spam, lovely spam, wonderful spam…" Like the song, spam is an endless repetition of worthless text. Another school of thought maintains that it comes from the computer group lab at the University of Southern California, which gave it the name because it has many of the same characteristics as the lunch meat Spam™:

- Nobody wants it or ever asks for it.
- No one ever eats it; it is the first item to be pushed to the side when eating the entree.
- Sometimes it is actually tasty, like 1% of junk mail that is really useful to some people.

The problem with spam is that it takes up valuable time to detect and delete, it clogs up precious bandwidth and computer network resources, and it is increasing at an alarming rate. Unfortunately, there is not any guaranteed way to completely stop spam. Some well-known Internet service providers (e.g., AOL, MSN) have already incorporated into their systems software that filters out spam. There are also other methods for reducing the number of spam messages you receive:

- When you receive an unsolicited message, do not respond to it even to request your removal from the list. Responding to an unwanted message often has the opposite intended effect—it confirms for the spammer that your e-mail is valid and should be used again.
- Use the filtering and rules function of your e-mail software to automatically delete spam before it arrives in your inbox.
- Use third-party software that integrates with your e-mail system to identify, block, and/or delete spam. Several such programs exist, including Cloudmark Spamnet (http://www.cloudmark.com), iHateSpam (http://www.sunbeltsoftware.com), Matador (http://www.mailfrontier.com), SpamCatcher (http://www.mailshell.com), Choicemail One (http://www.digiportal.com), MailWasher (http://www.mailwasher.net/), and Qurb (http://www.qurb.com).
- Report spam to the culprit's ISP if possible. This may be difficult because spammers have become quite clever in concealing both their identity and the source of their unwanted e-mail. However, if you can detect the origin of the e-mail, write an administrator at the source. Sometimes, the spammer's account can be frozen or even eliminated (although they know this and often set up a new one).
- If you suspect that the spam is promoting a fraudulent service or product, report them to the Federal Trade Commission (FTC) by visiting http://rn.ftc.gov/dod/wsolcq$.startup?Z_ORG_CODE=PU01. Or you can forward the spam directly to the FTC at http://UCE@FTC.GOV.
- Keep a special e-mail account, perhaps a free account from providers such as Yahoo! or Hotmail, that you use when asked for an e-mail address over the Internet. Often, before downloading a file or entering a sweepstakes, companies will ask for your e-mail address which they will include in a list that may very well be sold to spammers.
- If your e-mail address is available on a Web site, there is a good chance that you will increase the volume of spam you receive.

Spammers use software that automatically combs the Internet for such addresses and includes them in huge e-mail databases. Some software can even develop targeted lists based on the keywords it finds on the Web site where the e-mail address is located (e.g., see http://www.lencom.com/FEE.html). In response, many Web designers are moving toward using e-mail forms that can forward messages to you without revealing your address.

• Technology Tip 13.5 •

Spam is a huge business, and the procedures used to keep it flowing change constantly. You can learn more online at http://spam.abuse.net/userhelp/. You might even consider using anti-spam software such as SpamCatcher Universal (http://www.mailshell.com/mail/client/fd.html), MailWasher (http://www.mailwasher.net/), or Spam Inspector (http://www.giantcompany.com/).

Increased Immediacy of Business

While technology has a tendency to allow professional activities to creep into our personal lives, it also can creep into our professional lives in a way that creates an increased pace of business. This increase in pace may rob us of opportunities to reflect, relax, and prepare for future tasks. The metaphor of the worker as machine seems more applicable today than ever before.

In years past, when counselors sat down at their desk, they were confronted with a small stack of pink phone messages, the daily mail, and a paper calendar with numerous appointments listed and notes scribbled in the margins. Although they all required attention, they were all somehow impersonal and distant. Expectations were created, but there was distance between the message and writer or caller. Phone messages may be hours old, and mail was days old by the time it reached our desk. Immediate responses were required, but immediacy could easily be conceived of as within hours or even days. After all, no one really knew when you received their request in the mail! Those days have passed and we have truly entered into an era of immediacy.

Phone messages are likely not taken by a receptionist or secretary but are left by a human, with a real voice, on our voice mail for us to hear. We cannot ignore the message because lights flash, soft tones beep, or the dial tone wavers whenever we pick up the phone and a message is waiting. Voice mail distribution allows us to proliferate messages simultaneously to many colleagues, perhaps everyone in the organization. And if someone in the office down the hall chooses not to address a particular message, they can forward it directly to your phone in its entirety, along with their own voice, making you suddenly responsible. These messages, coming immediately to our desk, demand attention in a more direct fashion than the pink message slip of yesterday.

E-mail is an even more immediate attention grabber. Depending on how your computer is configured, your e-mail system may even notify you every time a message arrives by flashing an icon on the screen or making some small noise. Stamped with a date and time, we are aware that the sender is sitting at their computer, at this very moment, waiting for a reply. Down the hall or across the country makes little difference. E-mails can arrive within seconds of being sent. Some e-mail programs even allow the user to track when the message was received and when it was opened.

• Technology Tip 13.6 •

You can request receipts of e-mail you send. When writing a message in Outlook, choose View, then Options, and check the box for a return receipt or read receipt. When the addressee receives or reads the message, a receipt is automatically returned to your machine with a date and time. AOL users can automatically receive a return receipt from other AOL users by setting the message priority to "high" or choosing AOL2Pop Configuration, then SMTP Service, then Request Return Receipt. Most e-mail programs have similar settings.

It is much more difficult today to procrastinate and pretend a piece of mail did not arrive when it did. E-mail messages can declare to the user exactly when you opened the message to read it. Receiving messages in this more direct and immediate fashion creates a psychological pressure to respond just as quickly, leading to an increase in overall pace of doing business. Whether it is to try to keep our Inbox as clean as our desktop, or to demonstrate our efficiency, many people feel pressured to respond as quickly as possible to e-mail. The pressure may also exist for other forms of communication including fax and electronic document transfer.

• Technology Tip 13.7 •

Are others watching when you read their e-mail message? Many programs allow you to refuse to send the requested return receipt. In Eudora, edit the X-Eudora options (learn more at http://email.about.com/cs/eudoratips/a/et050303.htm). In Outlook, choose Tools, then Options, then E-mail Options, then Tracking Options. Choose the receipt option that is best for your needs.

This immediacy leads us to our next challenge: Finding ways to respond to the increased pace of professional life. A healthy focus and sense of balance is critical to the longevity and long-term success of the counselor in today's high-tech world. Especially important is to keep a steady course of comprehensive (i.e., physical, mental, emotional, spiritual, etc.) creative relaxation and needs fulfillment. Take periodic breaks to rejuvenate and celebrate achievements. This is especially true when one acknowledges that time spent online or on the computer seems to pass more rapidly than in other situations. In cybertime, distinctions between past, present, and future fade, and our sense of time passage becomes distorted. (e.g., see Strate, 1995).

Technology as a Double-Edged Sword

The very same technology that gives us time-saving shortcuts and expanded human potential can also present barriers to basic human needs of love, belongingness, and even safety. The Internet for some is a swamp of human frailties including compulsive behaviors of spending, gambling, online trading, obsessive or compulsive surfing the Web, indulging in pornography, or breaking the vows of marriage by having "cyberaffairs." Surfing the Web for information, playing games, shopping, and online chatting can easily become solitary activities that shelter individuals from journeying with their loved ones in person. Isaacs and Sabella (2002, p. 10) wrote that "the influence of technology can sharpen and strengthen family ties, for instance, by assisting with family leisure planning, entertainment, shopping for needed items the world over, conducting genealogy research, sharing family photos and events, staying in touch with e-mail, fostering new interests, managing finances, and helping us to focus on family-centered learning." Effective families have learned to adapt technology over the years to provide them with shared activities such as with watching videos or playing games together. However, there are times when the cutting edge of technology does not sharpen family ties; it severs them or at least substitutes or interferes with healthy family functioning. These range from the less serious—allowing e-mail contact to substitute for more human contact through phone calls or visits—to the more serious—Internet affairs or addictions (e.g., Mitchell, 2000; Pratarelli & Browne, 1999; Suler, 2002) leading to marital separation, divorce, and a great deal of family strife. Research in this area is growing as the intrusion of the Internet on family life increasingly becomes a major topic for investigation. Preliminary indications are that there may be some problems ahead. For instance, recent surveys by the Pew Internet Interest Group (Kommers & Rainie, 2002) suggest that although the vast majority of people do not see Internet use as creating any problems, one-third of the small number who did perceive problems identified that family members were spending too much time online.

Cyberaddictions

One problem in particular—cyberaddictions—has gained a great deal of attention among professional helpers and the media (Howard & Hall, 2000). One study that focused on the impact of Internet addictions on marriages and families (Young, Pistner, O'Mara, & Buchanan, 1999) described various forms of cyberaddictions:

- Cybersexual Addiction—compulsive use of adult Web sites for cybersex and cyberporn.
- Cyber-Relationship Addiction—overinvolvement in online relationships.
- Net Compulsions—obsessive online gambling, shopping, or trading.
- Information Overload—compulsive Web surfing or database searches.

- Computer Addiction—obsessive interaction with computer applications, especially game playing (e.g., Doom, Myst, or Solitaire).

Also, consider these Internet addiction briefs:

- Counterculturalist Timothy Leary was one of the first to liken computers to LSD, noting the mind-expanding, mesmerizing, and ritualistic similarities between the two.
- In April, 1998, police in a Milwaukee suburb reported one of the first known cases of an Internet-induced spat turning to physical violence. When a woman decided she'd had enough with her husband's obsession with the Internet (and with an Australian woman he met in a chat room), she took to the phone wires outside her house with a pair of scissors. The incident escalated into a shoving and punching match, and the couple wound up in separate jail cells for the night on charges of battery and criminal damage to property (Grumman, 1996).
- In another case, a Maryland woman destroyed her marriage and neglected her children because she was online as much as 21 hours a day. She wasn't taking (her children) to the doctor, they were running out of heating oil in the winter and not having enough food because she was spending all her time on the Net (Grumman, 1996).
- Dr. Young's Center for Online Addiction (http://netaddiction.com/) offers training for psychologists, educators, and human resources managers on how to identify and deal with individuals who spend excessive amounts of time on the Internet. As part of a 3-year study that she conducted, results indicated that nearly 6% of 17,251 respondents met the criteria for compulsive Internet use and over 30% report using the Net to escape from negative feelings. The vast majority admitted to feelings of time distortion, accelerated intimacy, and feeling uninhibited when online (Young, 1998)
- An 18-year old from Portland, Oregon, signed onto the Internet every day and spent hours telling people he had never met about his life and his dreams. He told them things he wouldn't dare tell his high school buddies. Eventually, his grades suffered; he didn't visit his grandparents as often as he used to; and he started feeling restless if he went more than a day without connecting to the World Wide Web. In an interview, he stated, "I once went two days without being online. I didn't like it. I was bored. Talking to real people just wasn't as exciting." (Grumman, 1996).
- In 2001, Serena Williams, a famous tennis player, admitted to being treated for a compulsive online shopping habit. "Every day I was in my room and I was online," she said. "I wasn't able to stop and I bought, bought, bought. I was just out of control" (Pacienza, 2002).
- What does it feel like to be addicted to the Internet? ABCNEWS.com readers who completed a comprehensive survey on Internet addiction answered that question, and the responses may shock you. One woman writes that she had to smash her fiancé's monitor with a wrench to get

him off the Net. Another reader tells of staying up all night waiting to get on a bulletin board to chat. (Visit http://abcnews.go.com/sections/living/DailyNews/netaddictletters032699.html to read more.)

These cyberaddictions are likely to occur in places where people can use computers and access the Internet in isolation or disguised as an appropriate behavior such as conducting research. High-speed connection to the Internet, also known as broadband, is now readily available in K–12 and postsecondary institutions, agencies, and community libraries. Colleges and universities in particular are now likely to include broadband connections throughout their campus—in libraries, computer labs, and increasingly in every campus residence hall room. It has been suggested that one reason for an increasing college drop-out rate is that some students frequently choose to be on the computer instead of attending class (Fox & Straw, 1998). Moreover, some estimate that these cyberaddictions now account for between 5% and 10% of those in recovery programs. As the availability of broadband connections for residential neighborhoods continues to steadily grow, families will have to contend with technology that will present opportunities for becoming stronger as well as weaker.

Spouses and partners are beginning to report patterns of behavior in which they find evidence of cyberaddiction, cyberaffairs, or cybersex while visiting pornography sites (e.g., see Oravec, 2000). These patterns include the following behaviors:

- Intimate e-mails or chats with a new romantic partner.
- Meetings for cybersex in the middle of the night.
- Increased secretiveness or need for privacy while on the Internet.
- Personality changes.
- Family or work chores going undone as the compulsion to be online draws their partners away from normal life activities.

John Suler, PhD, a professor of psychology at Rider University and a practicing clinical psychologist, wrote that "with the explosion of excitement about the Internet, some people seem to be a bit too excited. Some people spend way too much time there." (Suler, 1999). He asks "Is this yet another type of addiction that has invaded the human psyche?" Addiction specialists are not even sure yet what to call this phenomenon. Some label it an "Internet Addiction Disorder." Some cyberspace addictions are game- and competition-oriented, some fulfill more social needs, some simply may be an extension of workaholicism. Nevertheless, some people are definitely hurting themselves by their addiction to computers and cyberspace. When people lose their jobs, or flunk out of school, or are divorced by their spouses because they cannot resist devoting all of their time to virtual lands, they are pathologically addicted. These extreme cases are clearcut. But as in all addictions, the problem is where to draw the line between "normal" enthusiasm and "abnormal" preoccupation. Addictions—defined very loosely—can be healthy, unhealthy, or a mixture of both. If you are fascinated by a hobby, feel devoted to it, would like to spend as much time as possible pursuing it, then this could be an outlet for learning, creativity, and self-expression. Even in some unhealthy addictions you can find these positive features embedded within (and thus maintaining) the problem. But in truly pathological addictions, the scale has tipped. The bad outweighs the good, resulting in serious disturbances in one's ability to function in the real world (Suler, 1999).

Psychiatrist Nathan Shapira of the University of Cincinnati College of Medicine conducted a study that provided evidence suggesting that people who seem addicted to the Internet often show a bumper crop of psychiatric disorders like manic-depressive disorder, and treating those other conditions might help them control their urge to be online. He and colleagues studied 14 people who spent so much time online that they were facing problems like broken relationships, job loss, and dropping out of school. One 31-year-old man was online more than 100 hours a week, ignoring family and friends and stopping only to sleep. A 21-year-old man flunked out of college after he stopped going to class. When he disappeared for a week, campus police found him in the university computer lab, where he'd spent seven days straight online. The study participants, whose average age was 35, were interviewed for 3 to 5 hours with standard questions to look for psychiatric disorders. Being hooked on the Internet is not a recognized disorder. Shapira writes that it is unclear whether the Internet problem should be considered a disorder or just a symptom of something else, or whether certain disorders promote excessive online use (Associated Press, 1998).

What makes the Internet addictive? According to Young (1998), the Internet itself is a term that represents different types of functions that are accessible online. Generally speaking, Internet addicts tend to form an emotional attachment to the online friends and activities they create inside their computer screens. They enjoy those aspects of the Internet that allowed them to meet, socialize, and exchange ideas with new people through highly interactive Internet applications (such as chatting, playing online games, or being involved with several news groups).

These virtual communities create a vehicle to escape from reality and seek out a means to fulfill an unmet emotional and psychological need. On the Internet, you can conceal your real name, age, occupation, appearance, and your physical responses to anyone or anything you encounter online. Internet users, especially those who are lonely and insecure in real-life situations, take that freedom and quickly pour out their strongest feelings, darkest secrets, and deepest desires. This leads to the illusion of intimacy, but when reality underscores the severe limitations of relying on a faceless community for the love and caring that can only come from actual people, Internet addicts experience very real disappointment and pain. Online personas may be created whereby they are able to alter their identities and pretend to be someone other than who they are in real life. People who use such online personas help build their confidence, express repressed feelings, and cultivate a certain type of fantasy world inside their computer screens. Those with the highest risk for creating a secret online life are those who suffer from low self-esteem, feelings of inadequacy, and fear of disapproval from others. Such negative self-concepts lead to clinical problems of depression and anxiety, which also may be intertwined with excessive Net use and manipulated self-presentations.

A special type of Internet addict is the user who hurts him- or herself and others by engaging in cyberporn and/or cybersex, especially with children. The abundance and accessibility of such material makes it effortless to fall into compulsive patterns of use for sexual gratification or exploitation. This creates special problems for those who suffer from sexual addiction or deviance only to use the Internet as another vehicle to fulfill their needs. For others, cybersexual addiction is a unique problem in their lives. Sexual feelings are awakened through the anonymity of private chat rooms and other eager participants.

What are the warning signs for the development of cybersexual addiction? According to Young (1998), several include:

- Methodically spending significant amounts of time in chat rooms and private messaging with the sole purpose of finding cybersex.
- Feeling preoccupied with using the Internet to find online sexual partners.
- Frequently using anonymous communication to engage in sexual fantasies not typically carried out in real-life.
- Anticipating your next online session with the expectation that you will find sexual arousal or gratification.
- Finding that you frequently move from cybersex to phone sex (or even real-life meetings).
- Hiding your online interactions from your significant other.
- Feeling guilt or shame from your online use.
- Accidentally being aroused by cybersex at first, and then finding that you actively seek it out when you go online.
- Masturbating while online and engaged in erotic chat.
- Less investment with your real-life sexual partner only to prefer cybersex as a primary form of sexual gratification.

The following are tips to consider for preventing Internet addictions, especially for those that believe they may be susceptible to an online addiction (Sabella, 2003):

- Allow yourself a set period of time, perhaps 1 hour, to stay online. If you need to, set a timer with an alarm (perhaps a computer program) that reminds you to log off. When you hear the alarm, remind yourself that there is always another site of interest that can be discovered later. Also, remind yourself that there exists no Web site or e-mail communication that will make or break your career or professional effectiveness if you were to disregard it.

- Install software that keeps track of the time you spend online and report it to someone else who can help you monitor your online usage.
- Let others surf the Internet for you to find Web nuggets. That is, subscribe to one or more of the many available listservs that provide annotated descriptions of Web sites of particular interest. After you receive the posting, visit the sites of particular interest and create a bookmark for those sites so that you can visit them during your next scheduled surf session.
- If appropriate, only maintain Internet access from your work rather than also obtaining access from your home. This will help to foster clear parameters for work, family, and leisure.
- Use a debit card rather than a credit card when signing up with your ISP so that you will not accrue any outstanding debt. With a debit card, if you do not have funds in your checking account to cover the expense, you will lose your Internet access.
- When surfing for leisure, consider it an activity you might share with your significant other. This way, it will be more difficult for you to submit to adult Web sites which can easily strain a relationship.
- Prioritize your tasks. For example, if a task is pressing, postpone checking your e-mail until tomorrow.

Pornography on the Web

On September 2, 1998, an event made news headlines in every major newspaper in the world. About 100 people in 14 countries were arrested in what police said was the biggest ever worldwide sweep of alleged pedophiles using the Internet. Dozens of addresses were raided, including 32 in the United States alone. The raids were based on an investigation of a pedophilia ring known as the "Wonderland Club," which used sophisticated encryption codes originally developed by the KGB.

The Internet, from the very beginning, has been a tool for distributing a wide variety of information to large numbers of people, and until recently it was not a place frequented by young children. With the introduction of user-friendly online systems and the World Wide Web, and the introduction of the Internet to the classroom, more and more children are taking advantage of the power of the Internet. Its potential for education, communication, and a sense of global community is practically limitless. However, the Internet remains largely an adult forum, and so it carries with it adult subjects. This raises the question: What happens when the adult themes and a child's naive explorations meet?

Amid the material available on the Internet that is of enormous educational and clinical potential, there is also material that even the hardiest civil libertarian would probably agree is not appropriate, especially for youngsters—for example, graphical depiction of child pornography, vicious racism from bigots of various stripes, and detailed instructions on how to build bombs from some highly destructive people. The analogy might be walking into a video store where the Disney movies are mixed in with the adult videos. Further, the titles may only differ in a few letters; for instance, www.whitehouse.gov (a government site from the White House) versus www.whitehouse.com (a graphic adult-oriented site). In some cases this material can raise questions that go beyond those of appropriateness and taste: Its distribution and ownership may also be illegal, particularly within certain jurisdictions. For example, possession of child pornography is illegal as well as reprehensible. In most cases, pornography is also readily available from non-Internet sources (your local adult bookstore, for example), but its availability on the Net is a particularly sensitive issue because it is harder to monitor the age of persons accessing material on the Net than to check the age of patrons at the adult bookstore.

Sex and pornography occur in every part of the Internet. This includes the World Wide Web, Virtual Communities, online simulation games, chat rooms, and newsgroups. The presentation of sexually explicit materials differs from platform to platform, as does the degree of obscenity or indecency. While some are more visible than others, sexually explicit material can easily be found on all of them. The Web is the most visible aspect of the Internet, and the way that most people explore it. The nature of the Web itself—a multimedia carnival of pictures, movies, sounds, and colors—makes it much more popular with the general public than the other platforms. The multimedia aspect of the Web also makes it a place where all kinds of sexual material can be displayed, and many people have taken advantage of this whether for profit or for fun. One example of a type of pornography that is specific to the Web is live "videoconferencing" in which the "caller" interacts with one or more individuals who perform sexual activities at the prompting of the user. These live shows vary from the tame to the lewd and can include any number of users all typing or speaking commands simultaneously.

A simple search for any one of a number of sexually explicit words, especially slang terms for genitalia or sexual intercourse, on any search engine will yield a list of countless pornographic sites. Some of these are more of a soft-core nature, displaying "simple nudes"—Playboy and Penthouse are prime examples. These sites tend to make available material much like that displayed in their paper publications. On the opposite end of the spectrum, there are a large number of hardcore sites—far more numerous than their softer cousins. These sites display blatant indecency such as penetration of the vaginal, anal, and oral orifices of men and women by penises, hands, and various devices. They show hetero- and homosexual intercourse, bestiality, bondage, and fetishes. Since all of these sites have a common goal—profit—they tend to have a built-in security device. Namely, they only display a sampling for free, and further access is limited to credit card holders who are willing to pay a fee. This certainly helps to keep younger children from having full access to such sites, but even without ever gaining full access to any service, the amount of pornographic pictures, movies, and sounds that someone can compile for free and without ever encountering any age verification roadblocks is enough to fill a hard drive.

One other type of page on which pornography can be found is a personal home page. The number of personal home pages—pages maintained for individuals, by individuals, and for no profit—is tremendous, and the content of these pages are as varied as the people who maintain them. Any level of sexual material can be found on personal home pages, from softcore to hardcore. Whereas many sexual home pages follow the design of a shrine to a celebrity, others display their owners engaged in sexual activities, and still others display movies, sounds, or pictures from their favorite X-rated movies. Finally, although most ISPs do not allow pornographic advertising on space not designated to contain it, some individuals use their home pages to advertise and sell their own homemade sex tapes, or various sundries such as sex toys or used undergarments. These personal pages present even a tougher challenge for regulation for at least two reasons. First, unlike commercial sites, they are not as widely recognized. Second, there are no measures taken to regulate these pages and prevent minors from accessing them, not even semieffective measures such as credit card authorization.

The power of computers and the vast power of the Internet has provided counselors and families with unprecedented tools for communicating, learning, and having fun. With this power comes the responsibility of maintaining technological literacy to best supervise and make decisions for how these tools are used, especially to enhance ethical and legal practice and a set of core family values. Currently, and increasingly in the future, counselors need to recognize how technology influences individuals and society to support their clients in living healthy and successful lives.

Technological Implementation

Just because one has a high level of technological literacy does not mean that he or she actually applies technology in his or her work. Literacy is necessary but not sufficient. What is also necessary is using one's literacy to actually put one's tools to work in real life. The question "What can you do with computers?" is not enough. One must also ask "What *do* you do with computers?" The Level of Technology Implementation (LoTi; http://www.learning-quest.com/LoTi/), a popular framework conceptualized by Dr. Christopher Moersch in 1994, is one way of providing educators with a hierarchical approach for quantifying technology use in the classroom (LoTi, n.d.) and can serve as a model for us. In the LoTi framework, Moersch (1995) proposed seven discrete implementation levels teachers can demonstrate, ranging from Nonuse (Level 0) to Refinement (Level 6). As a teacher progresses from one level to the next, a series of changes to the instructional curriculum is observed. The instructional focus shifts from being teacher-centered to being learner-centered. Computer technology is employed as a tool that supports and extends students' understanding of the pertinent concepts, processes, and themes involved when using databases, telecommunications, multimedia, spreadsheets, and graphing applications. Traditional verbal activities are gradually replaced by authentic hands-on inquiry related to a problem, issue, or theme. Heavy reliance on textbook and sequential instructional materials is replaced by use of extensive and diversified resources determined by the problem areas under study. Traditional evaluation practices are supplanted by multiple assessment strategies that use portfolios, open-ended questions, self-analysis, and peer review.

As such, much work lies ahead in how we measure and enhance the use of counselor levels of technology integration: how we move counselors from nonuse to refinement to become even more client- or person-centered and how we help counselors to use more "extensive and diversified resources" and "multiple assessment strategies" as in the example with teachers. In summary, counselor LoTi means that computer technology is used as a tool that supports and extends clients' understanding of the pertinent concepts, processes, and themes that are known to facilitate mental health and life success. Advances in counseling technology implementation will stem from those creative counselors who dare to innovate and share their findings.

Summary

Technology provides tools to help us accomplish our work more effectively and efficiently beyond what we can do without it. Counselors now have high-tech methods for better managing, supporting, conducting, delivering, and describing their work as never before imagined. Such power, however, comes with great responsibility and sometimes at a premium price. Counselors must work diligently to make certain that technological literacy and implementation is an important part of their ongoing professional development. They must identify and plan for overcoming barriers that technology can pose, such as intrusions into our personal lives. Finally, counselors must recognize how the very same technology that helps can also hurt them and their clients. Thus, an important part of counselor technological literacy and implementation is to understand potentials and opportunities that technology affords us, evaluate how technology is used, and consider the impact that technology has on our lives.

Internet Sites for Additional Information

- **http://www.securitysoft.com.** Cyber Sentinel allows user to block inappropriate material (Web pages, e-mail, pictures, and word processing documents) no matter what format it is in or what it is. It also allows the owner to configure the program to run in stealth mode (so the end-user doesn't know it is running). The owner can then run

Cyber Sentinel later and see screen shots of any inappropriate material the user was viewing.

- **http://www.cauce.org/.** The Coalition Against Unsolicited Commercial E-mail Web site is designed to provide information about the problems of junk e-mail along with some proposed solutions, and to provide resources for the Internet community to make informed choices about the issues surrounding junk e-mail.
- **http://www.howtofightspam.com.** This site provides highly useful tips on how to fight spam and increases awareness of the nature of spam.
- **http://www.ftc.gov/ogc/coppa1.htm.** This page contains the Children's Online Privacy Protection Act of 1998 (COPPA).
- **http://www.n2h2.com/products/bess_home.php.** Bess filtering software works with a wide variety of implementations to meet the needs of schools and libraries. Whichever device you prefer, every Bess product uses the categorized filtering database recognized as the most effective available.
- **http://www.cyberpatrol.com.** Cyber Patrol is used to manage Internet access, limit the total time spent online, and restrict access to Internet sites that you deem inappropriate.
- **http://www.vci.net/spamwatch/spamprimer.php.** This page is titled "A Primer on Spam: A Brief Guide on How to Control Your E-mail."
- **http://www.cybersitter.com.** CyberSitter is an award-winning filtering software.
- **http://www.netnanny.com.** Net Nanny allows you to monitor, screen, and block access to anything residing on or running in your PC, whether you are connected to the Internet or not, and in real-time.
- **http://www.career.fsu.edu/techcenter.** This is the Web site for the Center for the Study of Technology in Counseling and Career Development.
- **http://www.cybercrime.gov.** This is the home page of the Computer Crime and Intellectual Property Section (CCIPS) of the Criminal Division of the U.S. Department of Justice.
- **http://www.cyber-hood-watch.org/.** CyberHood Watch provides Internet Safety awareness and privacy protection information to the Internet community.
- **http://www.theguardianangel.com.** Resources for Internet safety and privacy protection for kids and adults.

References

Ainsworth, M. (n.d.). *How to choose a competent counselor.* Retrieved June 21, 2002, from http://www.metanoia.org/

Albion.com. (1994–1999). *Netiquette home page.* Retrieved December 5, 2002, from http://www.albion.com/netiquette/

American Association of University Women. (1998). *Gender gaps: Where schools still fail our children.* Retrieved July 17, 2003 from http://www.aauw.org/2000/gg.html

American Counseling Association. (1995). *Code of ethics and standards of practice.* Retrieved August 15, 2002, from http://www.counseling.org/resources/ethics.htm

American Counseling Association. (1999). *Ethical standards for Internet online counseling.* Retrieved August 17, 2003, from http://www.counseling.org/site/PageServer?pagename=resources_ethics

American Mental Health Counselors Association. (2000). *Code of ethics of the American Mental Health Counselors Association* (2000 revision). Retrieved February 15, 2003, from http://www.amhca.org/ethics.html

American Psychological Association. (2002a). *Ethical principles of psychologists and code of conduct.* Retrieved November 27, 2002, from http://www.apa.org/ethics/code1992.html

American Psychological Association. (2002b). *Testing governance in APA.* Retrieved November 27, 2002, from http://www.apa.org/science/testgov.html

American School Counselor Association. (1998). *Ethical standards for school counselors.* Retrieved on November 15, 2002, from http://www.schoolcounselor.org/library/ethics.pdf

Association for Counselor Education and Supervision Technology Interest Network. (1999). *Technical competencies for counselor education students: Recommended guidelines for program development.* Retrieved January 15, 2002, from http://filebox.vt.edu/users/thohen/competencies.htm

Association for Specialists in Group Work. (1998). *Association for Specialists in Group Work best practice guidelines.* Retrieved February 15, 2003, from http://asgw.educ.kent.edu/best.htm

Barlow, D. H., & Durand, V. M. (1999). *Abnormal psychology* (2nd ed.). Pacific Grove, CA: Brooks/Cole.

Bleuer, J. C., & Walz, G. R. (1983). *Counselors and computers.* Ann Arbor: ERIC/CAPS.

Bloom, J. W. (1997, November). NBCC Webcounseling standards. Alexandria, VA: *Counseling Today.*

Bolles, R. N. (2003). *What color is your parachute 2003: A practical manual for job-hunters and career.* Berkeley, CA: Ten Speed Press.

Brent, E. E., & Anderson, R. E. (1990). *Computer applications in the social sciences.* Philadelphia: Temple University Press.

British Association for Counselling. (1999, September). *Counselling online … Opportunities and risks in counselling clients via the Internet: A BAC special report for purchasers and providers.* Warwickshire, England: Author.

Browne, M. N., & Keeley, S. M. (2003). *A Prentice Hall guide to evaluating online resources.* Upper Saddle River, NJ: Prentice Hall.

Cabaniss, K. (2002). Computer-related technology use by counselors in the new millennium: A delphi study. *Journal of Technology in Counseling, 2*(2). Retrieved August 15, 2003, from http://jtc.colstate.edu/vol2_2/cabaniss/cabaniss.htm

Campbell, T. (1998, March/April). The first email message. *Pretext Magazine.* Retrieved February 4, 1999, from http://www.pretext.com/mar98/

Casey, J. A., Bloom, J. W., & Moan, E. R. (1994). Use of technology in counselor supervision. In L. D. Borders (Ed.), *Counseling supervision.* Greensboro: University of North Carolina, ERIC Clearinghouse on Counseling and Student Services. (ERIC Document Reproduction Service No. ED372357)

CBS News. (2002). *New treatment for depression.* Retrieved December 5, 2002, from http://www.cbsnews.com/stories/2002/01/31/health/main326736.shtml

Children of divorce. (n.d.). Retrieved December 5, 2002, from http://www.angelfire.com/rant/chilrenofdivorce1/

Christie, B. S. (n.d.). *Counseling supervisees experiences of distance clinical supervision.* Retrieved June 21, 2002, from http://cybercounsel.uncg.edu/book/manuscripts/tenets.htm

CNN. (1998, May 31). *Study: Internet 'addicts' often show other disorders.* Retrieved from http://www.cnn.com/HEALTH/9805/31/internet.addiction

Cockburn, A., & McKenzie, B. (2001). What do Web users do? An empirical analysis of Web use. *International Journal of Human–Computer Studies, 54,* 903–922.

Code of Fair Testing Practices in Education. (2002). Washington, DC: Joint Committee on Testing Practices.

Commision on Rehabilitation Counselor Certification. (2003). *Draft CRCC code of professional ethics for rehabilitation counselors.* Retrieved February 15, 2003, from http://www.nchrtm.okstate.edu/NRCA_files/code.html

Corel Corporation. (1999). *Online WordPerfect 9.0 Help.* [Computer software]. Ottawa, Ontario, Canada: Author.

Coursol, D., & Lewis, J. (n.d.). *Cybersupervison: Close encounters in the new millennium.* Retrieved June 21, 2002, from http://cybercounsel.uncg.edu/book/manuscripts/cybersupervision.htm

Cringely, R. X. (Director). (1996). *Triumph of the nerds* [Television series]. New York: RM Associates.

Croft, V. (1991, March). *Technological literacy: Refined for the profession, applications for the classroom.* Paper presented at the 1991 annual conference of the International Technology Education Association, Salt Lake City, UT.

Currall, J. (1991). *Choosing a statistical analysis package.* Retrieved June 2002 from http://www.gla.ac.uk/services/computing/documentarchive/general/un11.html

D'Andrea, M. (1995). Using computer technology to promote multicultural awareness among elementary school-age students. *Elementary School Guidance & Counseling, 30*(1), 45–54.

Delmonico, D. L., Daninhirsch, C., Page, B., Walsh, J., L'Amoreaux, N. A., & Thompson, R. S. (2000). The Palace: Participant responses to a virtual support group. *Journal of Technology in Counseling, 1*(2). Retrieved from http://jtc.colstate.edu/vol1_2/palace.htm

Depression Central. (2002). *Vagus nerve stimulation in depression.* Retrieved December 5, 2002, from http://www.psycom.net/depression.central.vagus.html

Diederich, T. (1999). *45% of big firms monitor workers.* Retrieved December 6, 2002, from http://www.cnn.com/TECH/computing/9904/21/spy.idg/index.html

Digital Divide. (2003). Retrieved July 17, 2003, from http://www.finance-project.org/digdividehome.htm

Distance Learning Center for Addiction Studies. (2002). *State by state & other credentialing body approvals for distance learning.* Retrieved November 28, 2002, from http://www.dlcas.com/states.html

Doctor's Guide Publishing. (1999). *Vagus nerve stimulation successful for depression.* Retrieved December 5, 2002, from http://www.pslgroup.com/dg/15131a.htm

Donna, R. (2002). *Handheld computers: Helping community volunteers conduct rapid and accurate surveys.* Digital Opportunity Channel. Retrieved from http://www.digitalopportunity.org

DyslexiaMyLife.org. (n.d.). *What is dyslexia?* Retrieved December 5, 2002, from http://www.dyslexiamylife.org/wb_dyslexia.htm

EmailReplies.com. (2001). Retrieved December 5, 2002, from http://www.emailreplies.com/

Fanning, J. M. (1994). Integrating academics and technology: Uncovering staff development needs. In J. Willis, B. Robin, & D. A. Willis (Eds.), *Technology and teacher education annual, 1994* (pp. 331–334). Washington, DC: Association for the Advancement of Computing in Education.

Family-connection.org. (n.d.). *Social skills therapy.* Retrieved December 5, 2002, from http://www.family-connection.org/social_skills_training.htm

Finn, J. (1995). Computer-based self-help groups: A new resource to supplement support groups. *Social Work With Groups, 18*(1), 109–117.

Florida Department of Health. (n.d.). *491 board approved CE providers.* Retrieved June 10, 2002, from http://www.doh.state.fl.us/mqa/491/1st_CEproviders.pdf

Fox, R., & Straw, J. (1998). Student cyberaddiction. *Communications of the ACM, 41*(3), 11–14.

The Fun Place. (1998). *Consumers should question Internet health information.* Retrieved December 6, 2002, from http://www.thefunplace.com/guild/aap/98-06june.html

Gagne, R. M. (1985). *The conditions of learning and theory of instruction.* New York: Holt, Rinehart & Winston.

Garcia, R. A. (2002, April 2) *Writing email about problems can improve health.* Texas A&M University. Retrieved from http://www.newswise.com/articles/2002/4/EXPRESS.TXM.html

Gary, J. M. (2001). *Impact of cultural and global issues on online support groups.* ERIC Digest CG-01-01. Retrieved from http://ericcass.uncg.edu/digest/2001-01.html

Getting America's students ready for the 21st century: Meeting the technology literacy challenge. (1996, June). Retrieved February 15, 2003, from http://www.ed.gov/Technology/Plan/NatTechPlan/priority.html

Giedd, J. N. (n.d.). *Brain development study.* Retrieved on June 15, 2002, from http://intramural.nimh.nih.gov/research/chp/brainimaging/

Gladding, S. T. (2000). *Counseling: A comprehensive profession* (4th ed.). Upper Saddle River, NJ: Merrill.

Google.com. (2002). *Benefits of a Google search.* Retrieved December 6, 2002, from http://www.google.com/technology/whyuse.html

Goss, S., Robson, D., Pelling, N. J., & Renard, D. E. (1999). The challenge of the Internet. *Counselling, 10,* 37–43.

Greenwood, A. (2000). How the net can make a difference. *New Statesman, 129,* 24–26.

Gross, N. (1999, March 22). Building global communities. *Business Week, 3621,* EB42.

Grumman, C. (1996, June 26). HTTP: www.help logged on, tuned in and hooked on the Internet: There are those who just can't stop surfing. *Chicago Tribune,* 1.

Hayden, M. (1989). What is technological literacy? *Bulletin of Science, Technology and Society, 119,* 220–233.

Helwig, A. L., Lovelle, B. S., Guse, M. S., & Gottlieb, M. S. (1999). An office-based patient Internet education system. *Journal of Family Practice, 2,* 123–127.

Holden, G., Bearison, D. J., Rode, D. C., Rosenberg, G., & Fishman, M. (1999). Evaluating the effects of a virtual environment (STARBRIGHT World) with hospitalized children. *Research on Social Work Practice, 9,* 365–382.

Horrigan, J. B. (2001). *Online communities: Networks that nurture long-distance relationships and local ties.* Washington, DC: Pew Internet & American Life Project. Retrieved October 12, 2002, from http://www.pewinternet.org/reports/pdfs/PIP_Communities_Report.pdf

Howard, S., & Hall, M. N. (2000). Computer addiction: A critical consideration. *American Journal of Orthopsychiatry, 70*(2), 162–168.

Hughes, R. S. (2000). *Ethics and regulations of cybercounseling*. ERIC digest EDO-CG-00-3. Retrieved September 22, 2002, from http://ericcass.uncg.edu/digest/2000-03.html

Hughes, D. K., & James, S. H. (2001). Using accountability data to protect a school counseling program: One counselor's experience. *Professional School Counseling, 4*, 306–309.

ICD. (2001, September 20). *36 million emails per day by 2005*. Retrieved June 6, 2002, from http://www.e-gateway.net/infoarea/news/news.cfm?nid=1876

Indiana Health Professions Bureau. (2002). *Continuing education requirements*. Retrieved June 10, 2002, from http://www.in.gov/hpb/boards/mhcb/ceinfo.htm

International Technology Education Association. (2000). *Standards for technological literacy: Content for the study of technology*. Retrieved October 3, 2002, from http://www.iteawww.org/TAA/PDF/xstnd.pdf

Internet2. (1997–2002). *About Internet2*. Retrieved June 11, 2002, from http://www.internet2.edu/html/about.html

Isaacs, M., & Sabella, R. A. (2002, September/October). For better or for worse: Technology and the family. *ASCA School Counselor*, 10–11.

Jacobs, E. E., Masson, R. L., & Harvill, R. L. (1998). *Group counseling: Strategies and skills*. New York: Brooks/Cole.

Kahn, J. (2000, February 7). Creating an online community—and a market—for the disabled. *Fortune, 141*(3), 188–190.

Kehus, M. J. (2000). Opportunities for teenagers to share their writing online. *Journal of Adolescent & Adult Literacy, 44*(2), 130–137.

Kim, P., Eng, T., Deering, M. J., & Maxfield, A. (1999). Published criteria for evaluating health related web sites: Review. *British Medical Journal, 318*, 647–649.

Kommers, N., & Rainie, L. (2002). *Use of the Internet at major life moments*. Washington, DC: Pew Internet & American Life Project. Retrieved July 17, 2002, from http://www.pewinternet.org/reports/pdfs/PIP_Major_Moments_Report.pdf

Koufman-Frederick, A., Lillie, M., Pattison-Gordon, L., Watt, D. L., & Carter, R. (1999). *Electronic collaboration: A practical guide for educators*. Providence, RI: The LAB at Brown University. Retrieved May 26, 2001, from http://www.alliance.brown.edu/pubs/collab/elec-collab.pdf

Lee, C. (1998, April). Counseling and the challenges of cyberspace. *Counseling Today*. Alexandria, VA: American Counseling Association. Retrieved July 11, 1999, from http://www.counseling.org/ctonline/sr598/lee498.htm

Leibowitz, W. R. (1999). Alumni offices use electronic media to forge closer ties with graduates. *Chronicle of Higher Education, 46*(8), A45.

Lindsay, G. (1988). Techniques and technology—Strengthening the counseling profession via computer use: Responding to the issues. *The School Counselor, 35*, 325–330.

Lope, M., & Edelbaum, J. (1999). *I'm popular! Do I need social skills training?* Retrieved December 5, 2002, from http://www.personal.psu.edu/faculty/j/g/jgp4/teach/497/socialskillstrainingframe.htm

LoTi (Level of Technology Implementation). (n.d.). Retrieved August 2, 2002, from http://www.learning-quest.com/LoTi/

Lucas, S. (1999, October 18). CBS builds interactive web communities. *Brandweek, 40*(39), 61–64.

Lundberg, D. J. (2001). The evolution of standards and policies in counseling technology: Emphasis on the Internet [Electronic version]. *Association for Assessment in Counseling NewsNotes.* Retrieved from http://aac.ncat.edu/newsnotes/y98spr1.html

Lundberg, D. J., & Cobitz, C. I. (1999). Use of technology in counseling assessment: A survey of practices, views, and outlook. *Journal of Technology in Counseling, 1*(1). Retrieved November 2, 1999, from http://jtc.colstate.edu/vol1_1/assessment.htm

Lyon, G. R. (1995). *Toward a definition of dyslexia.* Retrieved December 5, 2002, from http://www.greenwoodinstitute.org/resources/reslyon.html

Marshall University Libraries. (2001). *Psychology and counseling materials.* Retrieved December 5, 2002, from http://www.marshall.edu/library/psylist.htm

Massy, W. F., & Zemsky, R. (1995). *Using information technology to enhance academic productivity.* EDUCOM: Wingspread Enhancing Academic Productivity Conference. Retrieved November 11, 1995, from http://www.educause.edu/nlii/keydocs/massy.html

McClung, H. J., Murray, R., & Heitlinger, L. (1998). The Internet as a source for current patient information [Electronic version]. *Pediatrics, 101*(6). Retrieved February 9, 1999, from http://www.pediatrics.org/cgi/content/full/101/6/e2

McFadden, J. (2000). Computer-mediated technology and transcultural counselor education [Electronic version]. *Journal of Technology in Counseling, 1*(2). Retrieved December 5, 2002, from http://jtc.colstate.edu/vol1_2/transcult.html.

McLean Hospital. (2000). *Researchers locate key area of the brain impacted by ADHD.* Retrieved December 5, 2002, from http://www.mcleanhospital.org/PublicAffairs/20000328_adhdnews.htm

Merriam-Webster Online. (2002). Retrieved July 19, 2002, from http://www.m-w.com/

Microsoft Corporation. (1995–2001). Microsoft Outlook 2002 [Computer Software]. Redmond, WA: Microsoft Corporation.

Mitchell, P. (2000). Internet addiction: Genuine diagnosis or not? *Lancet, 355,* 632–633.

Moersch, C. (1995). Levels of technology implementation (LoTi): *A framework for measuring classroom technology use.* Retrieved from http://www.learning-quest.com/software/LoTiFrameworkNov95. pdf

Morrissey, M. (1998). ACES technology interest network drafts technology competencies for students. *CTOnline*. Retrieved July 27, 2002, from http://www.counseling.org/ctonline/archives/ct0598/aces.htm

Mozee, E. (1978). Counselor problem checklist. *Journal of College Student Personnel, 19,* 73–74.

Murphy, L. J., & Mitchell, D. L. (1998). When writing helps to heal: E-mail as therapy. *British Journal of Guidance & Counselling, 26*(1), 21–32.

Myrick, R. D. (1990). Retrospective measurement: An accountability tool. *Elementary School Guidance & Counseling, 25*(1), 21–29.

Myrick, R. D., & Sabella, R. A. (1995). Cyberspace: New place for counselor supervision. *Elementary School Guidance & Counseling, 30*(1), 35–44.

National Alliance for the Mentally Ill. (2001). *Child and adolescent action center.* Retrieved December 5, 2002, from http://www.nami.org/youth/adhdgirlsbrains.html

National Association of Social Workers. (1999). *Code of ethics of the National Association of Social Workers.* Retrieved November 15, 2002, from http://www.socialworkers.org/pubs/code/code.asp

National Board of Certified Counselors. (2001). *Guidelines for maintaining your credentials.* Retrieved November 28, 2002, from http://www.nbcc.org/recert/guidelines.htm

National Board of Certified Counselors. (2002). *Code of ethics.* Retrieved August 20, 2003, from http://www.nbcc.org/depts/ethicsmain.htm

National Board of Certified Counselors. (n.d.). *NBCC approved providers of continuing education.* Retrieved December 6, 2002, from http://www.nbcc.org/providerlists/all/ceproviders_all.pdf

National Career Development Association. (1997). *NCDA guidelines for the use of the Internet for provision of career information and planning services.* Retrieved June 9, 2002, from http://www.ncda.org/about/polnet.html

National Center for Education Statistics. (2003). *Internet access in U.S. public schools and classrooms: 1994–2000.* Retrieved July 17, 2003, from http://nces.ed.gov/pubs2001/InternetAccess/figs.asp

National Institute of Mental Health. (1996). *Subtle brain circuit abnormalities confirmed in ADHD.* Retrieved on December 5, 2002, from http://www.nimh.nih.gov/events/pradhd.htm

National Institute of Mental Health. (2000). *Depression in children and adolescents* [Electronic version]. NIH Publication No. 00-4744. Retrieved December 5, 2002, from http://www.nimh.nih.gov/publicat/depchildresfact.cfm

National Telecommunications & Information Administration. (2000). *Falling through the Net: Toward digital inclusion.* Retrieved July 17, 2003, from http://www.ntia.doc.gov/ntiahome/digitaldivide/

National Telecommunications & Information Administration. (2003a). *Americans in the information age: Falling through the Net.* Retrieved July 17, 2003, from http://www.ntia.doc.gov/ntiahome/digitaldivide/

National Telecommunications & Information Administration. (2003b). *Falling through the Net: Toward digital inclusion.* Retrieved on July 17, 2003, from http://www.ntia.doc.gov/ntiahome/fttn00/falling.htm#1

National Telecommunications & Information Administration. (2003c). *Percent of U.S. households with a computer by income.* Retrieved on July 17, 2003, from http://www.ntia.doc.gov/ntiahome/fttn00/chartI-7.htm#f7

National Telecommunications & Information Administration. (2003d). *Income and education differences account for half the gap between Blacks and Hispanics and the national average.* Retrieved on July 17, 2003, from http://www.ntia.doc.gov/ntiahome/fttn00/chartI-12.htm

Nisenholz, B. (n.d.). *Counselor education counseling links.* Retrieved December 5, 2002, from http://www.uark.edu/depts/cned/web/orglinks.html.

Nolan, R. (2000). *Children of divorce and adjustment.* Retrieved December 5, 2002, from http://www.psychpage.com/family/divorce/childrenadjust.htm

Notess, G. R. (2000). *Search engine statistics: Dead links report.* Retrieved December 6, 2002, from http://www.searchengineshowdown.com/stats/dead.shtml

Notess, G. R. (2000). *Search engine statistics: Unique hits report.* Retrieved August 19, 2003, from http://www.searchengineshowdown.com/stats/unique.shtml

Ookita, S., & Tokuda, H. (2001). Virtual therapeutic environment with user projective agents. *CyberPsychology & Behavior, 4*(1), 155–167.

Oravec, J. A. (2000). Internet and computer technology hazards: Perspectives for family counselling. *British Journal of Guidance & Counselling, 28*(3), 309–414.

Owen, S., & Heywood, J. (1988). Transition technology in Ireland. *International Journal of Research in Design and Technology Education, 1*(1), 23.

Pacienza, A. (2002, November 14). Online shoppers battle addiction: People can't control their compulsions. *The Edmonton Sun.*

PDC Profiles. (n.d.). Retrieved December 5, 2002, from http://www.pdc.co.il/articles.htm

PGPi. (n.d.). *PGP products.* Retrieved December 6, 2002, from http://www.pgpi.org/products/

Pratarelli, M. E., & Browne, B. L. (1999). The bits and bytes of computer/Internet addiction: A factor analytic approach. *Behavior Research Methods, Instruments, & Computers, 31*(2), 305-314.

Psychtests.com. (1996–2002). Retrieved June 10, 2002, from http://psychtests.com/

Quay, H. C. (n.d.). *Behavior Problems Checklist–Revised.* Unpublished manuscript, University of Miami.

Rogers, C. R. (1957). The necessary and sufficient conditions of therapeutic personality change. *Journal of Consulting Psychology, 21,* 95–103.

Rust, E. B. (1995). Applications of the International Counselor Network for elementary and middle school counseling. *Elementary School Guidance & Counseling, 30*(1), 16–25.

Sabella, R. A. (1996). School counselors and computers: Specific time-saving tips. *Elementary School Guidance & Counseling, 31*(2), 83–96.

Sabella, R. A. (1998). Practical technology applications for peer helper programs and training. *Peer Facilitator Quarterly, 15*(2), 4–13.

Sabella, R. A. (2000). School counseling and technology. In J. Wittmer (Ed.), *Managing your school counseling program: K–12 developmental strategies* (2nd ed., pp. 337–359). Minneapolis, MN: Educational Media Corporation.

Sabella, R. A. (2001, September/October). *E-learning.* Alexandria, VA: ASCA School Counselor.

Sabella, R. A. (2003). *SchoolCounselor.com: A friendly and practical guide to the World Wide Web* (2nd ed.). Minneapolis, MN: Educational Media Corporation.

Sabella, R. A., & Booker, B. L. (2003). Using technology to promote your guidance and counseling program among stake holders. *Professional School Counseling, 6,* 206–213.

Sabella, R. A., & Halverson, W. (in press). Building virtual communities in school counseling. ERIC document.

Sabella, R. A., & Isaacs, M. (2002, March/April). Navigate your way to a new (or renewed) career. *ASCA School Counselor,* 10–11.

Sabella, R. A., Thomas, D. M., & Myrick, R. D. (1995). Peer helper training evaluations: A retrospective approach. *The Peer Facilitator Quarterly, 12*(3), 22–27.

Sabella, R. A., & Tyler, J. M. (2001). School counselor technology competencies for the new millennium. In D. S. Sandhu (Ed.), *Elementary school counseling in the new millennium* (pp. 261–280). Alexandria, VA: American Counseling Association.

Sampson, J. P., Jr. (1990). Computer-assisted testing and the goals of counseling psychology. *The Counseling Psychologist, 18,* 227–239.

Sampson, J., Kolodinsky, R., & Greeno, B. (1997). Counseling on the information highway: Future possibilities and potential problems. *Journal of Counseling & Development, 75,* 203–212.

Sampson, J. P., Jr., & Krumboltz, J. D. (1991). Computer-assisted instruction: A missing link in counseling. *Journal of Counseling & Development, 69,* 395–397.

Sanders, P., & Rosenfield, M. (1998). Counselling at a distance: Challenges and new initiatives. *British Journal of Guidance & Counselling, 26*(1), 5–10.

Saskatchewan Education. (2002). *Understanding the common essential learnings: A handbook for teachers.* Regina, Saskatchewan, Canada: Saskatchewan Education.

Schwartz, A., Garfinkel, S., & Russell, D. (1998). *Stopping spam.* Sebastopol, CA: O'Reilly & Associates.

Shostrum, E. L. (Producer & Director). (1965). *Three approaches to psychotherapy* [Motion picture]. United States: Psychological Films.

Sound Behavior. (2001). *Sound behavior: Coaching, training & consulting home page.* Retrieved December 5, 2002, from http://www.soundbehavior.bigstep.com/

Steffens, H. (1986). Issues in the preparation of teachers for teaching robotics in schools. In J. Heywood & P. Matthews (Eds.), *Technology, society and the school curriculum.* Manchester, England: Roundthorn Publishing.

Stone, C. B., & Turba, R. (1999). School counselors using technology for advocacy [Electronic version]. *Journal of Technology in Counseling, 1*(1). Retrieved August 20, 2003, from http://jtc.colstate.edu/vol1_1/advocacy.htm

Strate, L. (1995). Experiencing cybertime: Computing as activity and event. *Interpersonal Computing and Technology: An Electronic Journal for the 21st Century, 3*(2), 78–91. Retrieved August 20, 2003, from http://jan.ucc.nau.edu/~ipct-j/1995/n2/strate.txt

Suler, J. R. (1999) To get what you need: Healthy and pathological Internet use. *CyberPsychology and Behavior, 2,* 385–394.

Suler, J. (2001). Assessing a person's suitability for online therapy: The ISMHO clinical case study group. *Cyberpsychology & Behavior, 4,* 675–679.

Suler, J. (2002). *The basic psychological features of cyberspace.* Retrieved from http://www.rider.edu/suler/psycyber/basicfeat.html

Sussman, R. J. (2002) *Counseling over the Internet: Benefits and challenges in the use of new technologies.* Retrieved June 21, 2002, from http://cyber-counsel.uncg.edu/book/manuscripts/internetcounseling.htm

Symptoms of Depression.Com. (2002). *Childhood depression.* Retrieved December 5, 2002, from http://www.symptoms-of-depression.com/html/children_and_teens.php3

Taglang, K. (2003). *Content and the digital divide: What do people want?* Retrieved July 17, 2003, from http://www.digitaldividenetwork.org/content/stories/index.cfm?key=14

Tyler, J. M. (2000, January). *Computer-mediated group counseling: A demonstration.* Unpublished manuscript.

Tyler, J. M., & Guth, L. J. (2004). Understanding online counseling services through a review of definitions and elements necessary for change. In J. W. Bloom and G. R. Walz (Eds.), *Cybercounseling and cyberlearning: An encore.* Greensboro, NC: CAPS Publications and the ACA Foundation.

Tyson, J. (1998–2002). *How instant messaging works.* Retrieved December 6, 2002, from http://www.howstuffworks.com/instant-messaging.htm

U.S. Department of Education. (2002). *Welcome to school support and technology programs.* Retrieved December 3, 2002, from http://www.ed.gov/offices/OESE/SST/

Vacc, N. A., & Loesch, L. C. (2000). *Professional orientation to counseling* (3rd ed.). Philadelphia: Brunner-Routledge.

Waetjen, W. B. (1993). Technological literacy reconsidered. *Journal of Technology Education, 4*(2). Retrieved August 20, 2003, from scholar.lib.vt.edu/ejournals/JTE/v4n2/waetjen.jte-v4n2.html

Walz, G. R. (1996). Using the I-Way for career development. In R. Feller & G. Walz (Eds.), *Optimizing life transitions in turbulent times: Exploring work, learning and careers* (pp. 415-427). Greensboro, NC: University of North Carolina, ERIC Clearinghouse on Counseling and Student Services.

Webopedia. (2002a). *Moore's law*. Retrieved December 3, 2002, from http://www.webopedia.com/TERM/M/Moores_Law.html

Webopedia. (2002b). *Spreadsheet*. Retrieved December 3, 2002, from http://www.webopedia.com/TERM/s/spreadsheet.html

Webopedia. (2002c). *Personal information manager*. Retrieved December 3, 2002, from http://www.webopedia.com/TERM/P/personal_information_manager.html

Webopedia. (2002d). *Emoticon*. Retrieved December 4, 2002, from http://webopedia.com/TERM/e/emoticon.html

Webopedia. (2002e). *Videoconferencing*. Retrieved December 4, 2002, from http://webopedia.com/TERM/v/videoconferencing.html

Webopedia. (2003). *Spam*. Retrieved August 20, 2003, from http://webopedia.com/TERM/S/spam.html

Weinberg, N., Uken, J. S., Schmale, J., & Adamek, M. (1995). Therapeutic factors: Their presence in a computer-mediated support group. *Social Work With Groups, 18*(4), 57–69.

What is Usenet? (2002). Retrieved December 3, 2002, from http://www.faqs.org/faqs/usenet/what-is/part1/

Whitehead, N. E. (2002). *The importance of twin studies*. Retrieved December 5, 2002, from http://www.narth.com/docs/whitehead2.html

Williams, M. (2001). *Wired appliances add surfing to kitchen duty*. Retrieved July 17, 2003, from http://www.pcworld.com/news/article/0,aid,51584,00.asp

Wong, Y., & Law, C. (n.d.). *Online counseling for the youth in Hong Kong: A synchronized approach*. Retrieved June 21, 2002, http://www2.uta.edu/cussn/husita/proposals/wong.htm.

Yahoo.com. (n.d.). Retrieved December 5, 2002, from http://promo.yahoo.com/videomail/

Yalom, I. D. (1995). *The theory and practice of group psychotherapy* (4th ed.). New York: Basic Books.

Young, K. S. (1998). *Caught in the net: How to recognize the signs of Internet addiction—and a winning strategy for recovery*. New York: Wiley.

Young, K., Pistner, M., O'Mara, J., & Buchanan, J. (1999). Cyber-disorders: The mental health concern for the new millennium. *CyberPsychology and Behavior*. Retrieved August 20, 2003, from http://www.netaddiction.com/articles/cyberdisorders.htm

Zetlin, M., & Pfleging, B. (2001). Creators of online community. *Computer World, 35*(44), 34–36.

Index

financial assistance programs, 184–85
financial impact of changing technology, 250–52
FindArticles.com, 113
firewalls, 92–93, 137–38
fixed width files, 73
flame wars, 133
floating cells, in word processing tables, 52–53
Florida Department of Health, 189, 200
folders
 deleted files, 207
 e-mail, 127, 128
 temp and cache, 206
Fong, Margaret, 6
Forms Data Format (FDF) file, 77
formulas, in spreadsheet applications, 53, 70
Frequently Asked Questions (FAQs), listserv, 132–33, 197

gender gap, Internet access and the, 172
getting away from work, 254–55
 automatic responses, 256
 dealing with spam, 257–59
 personal vs. professional, 257
 policy for e-mail limitations, 255–56
 time and place boundaries, 256–57
Gladding, S. T., 159
Gnutella, 114
Google, 12, 62, 135, 172, 173–76, 177, 178, 193, 198, 201
graphics editor, 63–64
Greeno, B., 1–2, 17, 232
Greenwood Institute, 155
group supervision meetings, 212
Guidelines for the Use of the Internet for Provision of Career Information and Planning Services (NCDA), 85–86
Guth, L. J., 118, 233, 235

hackers, 92, 93, 204, 209
handheld computers, 74–75, 244
Hayden, M., 4
Heitlinger, L., 150
helping clients use the Internet, 161, 186
 addressing the digital divide, 169–72
 Internet sites for additional information, 186–87
 searching for information on the Internet, 172–80

what kinds of information are clients seeking?, 180–86
when is it appropriate to help clients seek information on the Internet?, 162–68
Hertzog, J. B. M., 117
Heywood, J., 4
high speed connections (broadband), 239–40, 263
Hispanic households, computer and Internet use in, 169, 170
Hohenshil, Thomas, 6
HotJobs, 183
Hotmail, 217, 258
How Stuff Works Web site, 236
Hughes, D. K., 68
hyperlinks, 61
Hyperstudio program, 14
hypertext markup language (HTML), 9, 60–61, 77
 HTML-based e-mail, 124
 HTML editors, 59–60
Hypnosoft (software program), 21

IClean (software program), 206
iLISTEN (software program), 44
Imici (IM program), 236
immediacy of business, increased, 259–60
impersonation and anonymity, in Web counseling, 242
income and computer ownership, relationship between, 169
increased access, technology and, 14–15
Individual Educational Programs (IEPs), 21
Infomine, 178–79
information and resources, using the Web for, 7–9
information overload, 261
information technologies, computers and, 1
inLARGE (software program), 44
instant messaging (IM) programs, 11–12, 39, 40, 138, 208, 236–37
Instant Messaging Presence Protocol, 236
intake procedures, 219–21
Intel Corporation, 251
interactive tools, Web-based programming and, 7
International Counselor Network (ICN), 131
International Society for Mental Health Online (ISMHO), 203, 223

school counselors, software for, 22
SchoolCounselor.com: A Friendly and Practical Guide to the World Wide Web (Sabella), 58–60
SchoolCounselor.com Newsletter, 112
scoring programs, computerized, 102
search, database, performing a, 106–7
search engines, 172–78, 232
Secure Delete, 208
secured Web sites, 209
security
  confidentiality and file, 204–10
  and confidentiality in computer-based assessment, 88–94
security statements, 211–12
Self-Directed Search Form R, 21
Self-Directed Search (SDS), 15, 238
September 11, 2001, events of, 235
sex and pornography, on the Web, 167, 175, 266–68
sexual addiction, cyber-, 261, 265
Shapira, Nathan, 264
shareware, 252
sharing documents, through electronic collaboration, 10
Sierra's Print Artist, 22
signatures, e-mail, 124–26
SilverPlatter interface, 105
slide presentations, 55
smiley, 128
SMPT (server name), 122
social-personal information sites, 185–86
software tools, 20–22
sound-filtering technology, 29
spam, 133, 257–59
SpamCatcher, 258
spreadsheets and databases, 53–55, 69, 70
  templates, 79–80
Spy Cop, 213
spyware, 137, 213
SQL (Structured Query Language), 54
state credentialing boards, Web sites for, 200
State Trait Anxiety Index (STAI), 88
Statistical Analysis Software (SAS), 69–70
Statistical Package for the Social Sciences (SPSS), 69–70
statistical software, 67–68, 81–82
  choosing, 77–78
  data alphabet soup, 72–73
  having others enter the data, 80–81
  how do counselors use data processing software, 68–69

Internet sites for additional information, 82–83
  other methods for collecting data, 73–77
  planning ahead, 78–79
  tips and recommendations, 77–81
  types of data processing software, 69–72
  using data processing across other applications, 81
  using online tutorials, 81
  using relevant existing data, 79
  using templates and plug-ins, 79–80
  working with your local college, 78
Steffens, H., 4
streaming media technology, 25, 38–39
Students.Gov, 185
Suler, John, 263–64
sunshine laws, 205
supervision
  counselor, 241
  of online activities, 166–67
support groups, online, 234–35
Support4Learning, 238
surveys
  online, 73–74
  PDF, 77
Symptoms of Depression.com, 150
synchronous communication activities
  chat rooms, 135–36
  through electronic collaboration, 10

tab-delimited files, 72
table function in word processing, 52–53
Task Force on Psychological Testing on the Internet (APA), 86
technological literacy, 2–4, 17
  advancing, 248
  technological implementation and, 268–69
  what is, 4–6
technology and assessment, 85, 103
  assessment and evaluation in Web counseling, 240
  choosing an appropriate computerized or Internet-based test, 94–96
  computerized interpretations, 102–3
  computerized scoring programs, 102
  computerized vs. Internet-based assessment, 85–86
  confidentiality and security, 88–94
  Internet sites for additional information, 103–4
  pros and cons of computerized assessment, 96–99